D1226686

The current fascination with urban life has encouraged a growing interest in the Chicago School of sociology by students of sociological history. It is generally accepted that the field research practised by the Chicago sociologists during the 1920s – the 'Golden Age of Chicago sociology' – used methods borrowed from anthropology. However, Rolf Lindner also argues convincingly that the orientation of urban research advocated by Robert Park, the key figure in the Chicago School and himself a former reporter, is ultimately indebted to the tradition of urban reportage. *The Reportage of Urban Culture* goes beyond a thorough reconstruction of the relationship between journalism and sociology. It shows how the figure of the city reporter at the turn of the century represents a new way of looking at life, and reflects a transformation in American culture, from rejecting variety to embracing it.

IDEAS IN CONTEXT

THE REPORTAGE OF URBAN CULTURE

IDEAS IN CONTEXT

Edited by QUENTIN SKINNER (*General Editor*)
LORRAINE DASTON, WOLF LEPENIES and
J. B. SCHNEEWIND

The books in this series will discuss the emergence of intellectual traditions and of related new disciplines. The procedures, aims and vocabularies that were generated will be set in the context of the alternatives available within the contemporary frameworks of ideas and institutions. Through detailed studies of the evolution of such traditions, and their modification by different audiences, it is hoped that a new picture will form of the development of ideas in their concrete contexts. By this means, artificial distinctions between the history of philosophy, of the various sciences, of society and politics, and of literature may be seen to dissolve.

The series is published with the support of the Exxon Foundation.

A list of books in the series will be found at the end of the volume.

THE REPORTAGE OF URBAN CULTURE

Robert Park and the Chicago School

ROLF LINDNER

Professor of European Ethnology, Humboldt-Universität zu Berlin

translated by

ADRIAN MORRIS

Fellow of the Institute of Linguists

with Jeremy Gaines and
Martin Chalmers

CAMBRIDGE
UNIVERSITY PRESS

Published by the Press Syndicate of the University of Cambridge
The Pitt Building, Trumpington Street, Cambridge CB2 IRP
40 West 20th Street, New York, NY 10011–4211, USA
10 Stamford Road, Oakleigh, Melbourne 3166, Australia

Originally published in German as *Die Entdeckung der Stadtkultur: Soziologie aus der Erfahrung der Reportage*
by Suhrkamp Verlag 1990
and © Suhrkamp Verlag Frankfurt am Main
First published in English by Cambridge University Press 1996 as
The Reportage of Urban Culture: Robert Park and the Chicago School
English translation © Cambridge University Press 1996

Printed in Great Britain at the University Press, Cambridge

Library of Congress cataloguing in publication data
Lindner, Rolf, 1945–
[Entdeckung der Stadtkultur. English]
The reportage of urban culture: Robert Park and the Chicago
school / Rolf Lindner; translated by Adrian Morris.
p.   cm. – (Ideas in context ; 43)
Includes bibliographical references and index.
ISBN 0 521 44052 1 (hc)
1. Park, Robert Ezra, 1864–1944.   2. Chicago school of sociology –
History.   3. Sociology, Urban – United States – Study and teaching –
History – 20th century.   I. Title.   II. Series.
HM22.L6P344413   1996
301′.072′077311–dc20   95-40693   CIP

ISBN 0 521 44052 1 hardback

To Gudrun and Sarah

His favorite professor at the University of Chicago, Robert Park, had told Allan that he was an intelligent young man with closed eyes. Allan was working at getting them open, but it was hard to satisfy Mr. Park. Around the seminar table, whenever Allan or some of the other graduate students ventured an opinion, they risked having Mr. Park look at them owl-eyed and inquire, 'Vas you dere, Cholly?'

Nicholas von Hoffman, *Organized Crimes*

Contents

Illustrations

Acknowledgements

This book would not have been written without the continued encouragement and support of Wolf Lepenies.

My thanks go to him. My thanks also to Hermann Bausinger, Hans Peter Dreitzel, Hans Joas and Joachim Moebus for their help and advice. Martin Bulmer, Paul M. Hirsch, Edward Shils and above all Donald N. Levine gave up their time to talk with me; I hope they don't regret it. Elizabeth Clemens, Wendy Espeland and Bruce Carruthers made sure that I was able to feel myself among friends during my time in Chicago. The Special Collections Department in the Joseph Regenstein Library, University of Chicago was an inexhaustible source; the library of the John F. Kennedy Institute for North American Studies in the Free University of Berlin made my work much easier. The generous and non-bureaucratic assistance given by the Fritz Thyssen Foundation in Cologne enabled the book to be completed successfully. Last but not least, I am grateful to Gudrun, who read through the manuscript with a critical eye, and to Sarah, who treated it kindly.

Abbreviations

EWB   Ernest W. Burgess Papers
JTC   James T. Carey Interviews
REP   Robert E. Park Papers
REPA   Robert E. Park Addenda
SNF   Samuel N. Fuller Papers
SNH   Samuel N. Harper Papers
UCP   University of Chicago Press Collections

All are in the Joseph Regenstein Library, Special Collections Department, University of Chicago; the first number after the abbreviation refers to the box, the second to the folder.

Introduction

The first thing they gave me to look at on the campus of the University of Chicago, while I was in Chicago to carry out my research, was the weekly 'crime map', published in the student newspaper *The Chicago Maroon*.

The 'crime map' is a plan of the university grounds and the adjoining residential area between 47th Street and 60th Street, on which the crimes which have taken place during the week are recorded by means of pictograms. These crimes vary from assault to sexual harassment, from burglary to mugging. Burgess and Park would have enjoyed looking at this map, even if with mixed feelings, because the technique which they made into a trademark of Chicago urban sociology – 'mapping' – is here being used in its own 'natural area', even if not in a particularly happy context. A case of 'The Savage Hits Back'?

The whole thing, including the white emergency telephones on the campus which connect passers-by with the nearest police station, which promise security but have the effect of making the newcomer more worried than might otherwise be the case, may be in the interest of prevention, may even be put down to that enjoyment of anxiety which Raeithel described as being typical of the American mentality; the fact is, however, that the campus today is not just an island of academia – it is also one of prosperity, in the midst of areas inhabited by the poorer black population. The ecological processes that the Chicago sociologists of the 1920s described in such detail have not spared their working and living environment, even if they are defiantly halted at the gates of the campus.

I could not help asking myself what Robert Park, who so much enjoyed 'nosing around', and who developed it into an empirical art form, would have done in the face of the well-meaning advice not to venture beyond Cottage Grove when going west. 'You must imagine Park as a tireless pedestrian, roaming through Chicago in every direction, this way and that, noting down his observations as he goes', wrote

I

René König in his essay on the pioneers of social ecology in Chicago (1978). This reminds me of Riehl's 'Wanderstudium' [Itinerant studies] and the figure of the flâneur as drawn by Walter Benjamin.

'Nosing around' is what this book is about. Within the present renaissance of Chicago sociology in Europe, which is not least a response to the new longing for urbanity, there is a link-up with that tradition of naturalistic observation which is seen as the methodological legacy of the Chicago sociologists. Of course, what irritates their re-discoverers, particularly in our method-conscious age, is the fact that Park, considered to be the inspiration behind naturalistic observation in the Chicago style, very rarely took up a position on questions of research methods.

Instead of lamenting this state of affairs, it may be an appropriate time to ask ourselves whether this 'abstinence' should not be understood as an indication of a particular understanding of procedure. What Park might say about present-day discussions on methods can naturally only be a subject for speculation; however, there is more than a grain of truth in René König's remark that Park's particular talent, in contrast to later sociologists with their much more elaborate research techniques, '*was that he still knew how to "see" with his own eyes*' (René König 1984, p. 28; emphasis in the original). What Park was obviously concerned about in his teaching was to convey to his students the art of 'seeing'; and that meant, above all, getting rid of the blinkers with which they were going through life. 'Go into the district', 'get the feeling', 'become acquainted with people': the fundamental premise of Chicago sociology is contained in these instructions, banal as they seem to us today, to leave the study rooms and go out on to the uncertain terrain of 'real life'.

René König is at the same time one of those sociologists who advocate what I would like to call the 'adoption hypothesis', i.e., the assertion that it is ethnology/anthropology, with its paradigm of field research, which acted as the model for sociological ethnography. Robert Park himself made a not insignificant contribution to this 'adoption hypothesis'. In one of the few passages in his work where he explicitly addresses the question of method, in the essay 'The City: Suggestions for the Investigation of Human Behavior in the Urban Environment' (1925a), he compares the approach of urban sociologists with that of the patient observation methods used by anthropologists to investigate primitive cultures.

In this context, it is not unimportant to note the date the essay was published: 1925. The major monographs by Malinowski and Radcliffe-Brown based on field research had already made their appearance; the famous introduction by Malinowski which gave him the reputation of being the founder of participant observation was available; and last but not least, sociologists and anthropologists in the Department of Sociology and Anthropology in Chicago were (still) working under one roof. Reason enough therefore to agree with the supposition that sociology was inspired by ethnology/anthropology in the principles which guided its investigations. But even Park's favourite expression to characterise his way of working, 'nosing around', should make us stop and think: it does not sound very serious when measured by the standards of the scientific community. No doubt even ethnologists and anthropologists poked their noses into things which did not necessarily concern them, but they did at least manage to conceal this by the use of terminological retouching. The somewhat coarser expression has its sources elsewhere: 'nosing around' is an expression from the jargon of reporters.

This book sets out to show that the orientation of urban research represented by Park ultimately owes its origins to the reporting tradition. This is not surprising when we consider that Park himself, after acquiring his BA, worked as a reporter and editor in New York, Chicago, Detroit and other big cities from 1887 to 1898. This influence is directly reflected both in the areas he investigated and the techniques he used in his research. Park's recourse to anthropology, in the revised version of the essay which originally appeared in 1915, appears in this context as a form of justification, which serves to conceal the considerably less prestigious relationship with journalistic reporting.

The particular significance of Park's years as a journalist and newspaper correspondent (not forgetting his work for Booker T. Washington) would not be understood, however, without taking into account the habitual or attitude component. In research and teaching, the character of his *habitus* (Bourdieu), understood as a system of durable dispositions and schemata, is clearly stamped by his experience in the world of journalism. Park's image of himself as a 'captain of inquiry', leading a team of investigators, corresponds to the rôle of city editor in America. One of the features of this self-image (of the rôle of editor, as well) is the conveying of a view of reality which is unclouded by moral assumptions. That this is not just a question of how knowledge is imparted is revealed by Park's distinct anti-reformer attitude, which to me is the most significant indication of his legacy from journalism. Park certainly does combine his sociological activity with an interest in social reform; what he vehemently objects to, however, is the variety of improvement prevalent up until the First World War. This particular mixture of social reform and moral education can scarcely be better (or more grotesquely) illustrated than by the cover of the American edition of William Booth's *In Darkest England and the Way Out* (1890), on the back of which there is an advertisement placed by Enoch Morgan & Sons Co., that publicises their brand of soap Sapolio with the motto, 'Dirt and Despair Are Close of Kin'. In Park's opinion, in order to turn sociology into a science with an empirical basis, it is essential to abandon that particular perspective of social reality, which, inspired and guided by a civilising mission, perceives reality only from a biased point of view; this perspective was certainly still present in the American colleges of the 1920s. In contrast to this, Park insists that we can only allow ourselves to consider how people might possibly live (together) when we know how people do actually live (together).

This change in perspective, exemplified by replacing the phrase 'life as it ought to be lived' by 'life as it is lived',[1] leads on to considerations which go beyond the confines of a reconstruction, focused on one particular person, of the relationship between journalism and sociology.

Embedded in a cultural transformation, bidding farewell to the genteel tradition of 'New England exclusiveness' (Randolph Bourne), with its emphasis on appearances and its social complacency, the figure of the turn-of-the-century reporter, in whom there is at the same time a cultural dissident, now becomes the archetype of an approach to social reality where what counts is reporting and not improvement. Such an attitude of disinterested interest is very much closer to the modern idea of scientific objectivity, which attempts to uncouple the process of finding the truth from any link with a moral point of view, than to a practical sociology influenced by the perspective of reform. Ultimately, this shift illustrates the transition from a perspective of prevention to a perspective of understanding.

---

[1] This expression becomes a sort of trademark of the new sociological literature. Frances R. Donovan's *The Saleslady* (1929), for example, is announced in advertisements with the slogan 'Life as it is lived behind the counter . . .'

PART I

CHAPTER I

'News': the reporter and the new

Ours, it seems, is an age of news, and one of the most important
events in American civilisation has been the rise of the reporter.
Robert Ezra Park

NEWS: THE SYMBIOSIS OF BIG CITY AND PRESS

'So entirely absorbed do these urchins become in their vocation', wrote
Leslie's Illustrated Weekly Newspaper about newspaper boys on 2 August
1856, 'that they keep up their cries along an entire block of buildings in
which every house is closed and not a possible purchaser in sight.'

It is true to say that the occupation of newspaper boy offers the street
urchin a most favourable constellation of two different circumstances:
here, he can conveniently combine the need to earn his daily bread with
a pleasure in making noise. The indignant tone of the subscription newspaper is not so much directed at the street urchins, who were themselves
scarcely a new phenomenon. What is meant is rather the object which
requires this kind of praise, an object for which the street urchins are
sympathetic mediators. Just as the noisy newspaper boys stand out as
different, so does the article which they are offering for sale. The news
whose essence they proclaim so loudly is striking because it breaks
through people's expectations of the normal course of affairs, drawing
their attention to unusual facts and abnormal events. This understanding of news as something aiming at the atypical, the unexpected
and the abnormal, is at the heart of the New Journalism which, in the
1830s, began to change fundamentally the nature of the press. It was not
by chance that Park, in the context of the rise of New Journalism, spoke
of the secularisation of the press. The partisan press, from which New
Journalism breaks away, is a pulpit from which the publisher who holds
the office of pontiff proclaims the political gospel to his readers. In consequence, as Park's student Helen MacGill Hughes (1940) puts it, news

turns into a sermon. Financed as a rule by political parties or party factions, the newspaper is the mouthpiece of these bodies; it is a sounding-board for factional views which are in democratic conflict with each other.

Right from the start, the rising mass-circulation press understands itself to be democratic in a quite different sense. Now it is no longer public discourse itself which is democratic, but the fact that everyone is potentially in a position to purchase and to understand the appropriate organ, the coincidence of what Habermas (1975) characterised as the economic and psychological facilitation of access. The slogan of the *New York Sun* in 1833, the first paper of the penny press to personify the New Journalism, summarises this perception: 'It shines for ALL!'

That the promise to be a newspaper for all was heralded in New York points to one of the necessary preconditions for the mass-circulation press, the existence of conurbations. However, it would be short-sighted to connect the existence of the mass-circulation press exclusively to the existence of the big city as its market; the big city is at the same time the place which continuously generates news. The feeling of mutual estrangement, which is regarded as a central characteristic of life in big cities, provides the material and also promotes sales. It is not surprising, therefore, that the first mass-circulation newspapers come into being at the historical moment when New York is emerging as a big cosmopolitan city.

With the penny press, which takes its name from its price, there now appears the sort of commercially run form of press that in the famous remark of Karl Bücher 'produces advertising space as a commodity which can only be sold through an editorial section'. As a commercially run press, the penny press necessarily disregards factional party views: in the beginning it does this quite aggressively, out of an understanding of democracy which links it to the market economy. Itself tied to this market economy, the mass-circulation press turns conventional wisdom on its head: the customer no longer finds his way as subscriber to the newspaper; the newspaper goes to look for its customers. The idea of a newspaper printing news merely because it is interesting to buyers (and not because it serves a political purpose) shocked contemporaries. Just how shocking this was is shown by the abuse heaped on the *Herald* by its rivals from the partisan press: 'obscene vagabond', 'profligate adventurer', 'unprincipled conductor' (Hapgood and Maurice 1902, p. 578). What, above all, separates the news policy of the early 'penny papers' from that of the political papers is the local type of news. The penny press discovers the near-at-hand, but at the same time the abnormal and curious, as newsworthy material. This is where the symbiotic relationship, as Barth characterises it, between the modern press and the modern big city begins: the biggest press story of the nineteenth century is life in the big city itself (Barth 1980, p. 59). While the political newspapers restrict themselves to reporting political affairs, while the trade press informs its readership about wholesale prices, stock market quotations, exchange rates and events from all over the world relevant to business, the mass-circulation press, as a genuine organ of the big city (not representing any interests) makes big city life ('stories about town') its central theme. A characteristic genre of the penny press is the report from the police-courts, short scenes from summary trials, in which curious and picturesque persons, or at all events, persons from big city life who have become 'conspicuous', are pilloried in public.

With the report from the police-courts, the press, as Park emphasises, assumes the rôle once occupied by small-town gossip. With it begins also the history of that type of article which from a European viewpoint stands for American journalism in miniature: the human interest story, 'chatty little reports of comic incidents in the lives of the people' (Helen MacGill Hughes 1940, p. 147).

The 'new news' can only be understood in terms of the double meaning of the Anglo-American concept of 'news' as both news and novelty. A piece of news which, detached from its social, political and economic context, is supposed to be of interest in itself to a particular public, tends to be reduced to the formal category of novelty, and nothing more. Its beginnings are relatively modest: they correspond to the small-town gossip of the 'Have you heard?' type. However, these chatty little reports mark the beginning of a revolutionary change in what from now on is considered to be newsworthy: reports about people, institutions and events which are unfamiliar and unheard-of, which when measured by our own experiences, expectations and ideas, are unusual.

This is precisely what gives the mass-circulation press its opportunity as the mouthpiece of the big city. For what, it might well be asked, actually is familiar, ordinary and usual in the American big city of the nineteenth century? To an inhabitant, compared with the experiences he has brought with him as a migrant from the countryside or an immigrant from the Old World, everything is unusual and novel to begin with, not least the newspaper 'for all' itself. In this respect, the notion of a symbiotic relationship between mass-circulation press and big city makes sense, since the New Press is as much a product of the process of urban-isation as it is mediator and promoter. The new type of newspaper is a central institution and an instance of the transition from the traditional to the modern, represented as a transition from country to town, from the Old World to the New World.

The symbiotic relationship between press and big city is evident not least in the interrelationship between urbanisation and change in mentality. The process of internal, as opposed to external, urbanisation is driven forward by the big city press. Headlines and slogans not only appeal to the ready wit of the big city dweller, with his talent for quick and pointed responses, they also serve as model and material for this wit, both syntactically and semantically. In the manner of its publication (morning, evening, Sunday and extra editions) just as much as in its dis-tribution (street sales), the big city press is the ideal synchronisation of urban forms of communication, perception and behaviour. Since not only does it insert itself into the unceasing succession of impressions but also, because of its understanding of news as novelty, it stimulates this succession, day after day, it is at the same time both expression and pro-moter of the 'intensification of living on your nerves' (Simmel 1957 [1903], p. 228), regarded as specific to big city life. The self-referential reporting – 'The New Reporter', 'A Night in a Metropolitan Newspaper Office', 'The Business of a Newspaper' – is evidence of the awareness of itself being 'news', i.e., being unusual and in need of explanation. Printed right next to reports about new big city institutions such as the department store, the vaudeville theatre or the big hotel, these reports are one more testimony to the symbiotic relationship between press and big city. The cries of the newspaper boys – which, as a German ency-clopaedia at the turn of the century put it, systematically heighten the craving for novelties, a craving seen as a product of urban life – are themselves just as much part of the sensations perceived as being specific to the big city as the rhythm of the rotary printing machines is one of the symbols of the tempo of the big city, and the 'boiler shop' of the metro-politan editorial office is a symbol of its hectic pace.

Thus the big city press becomes both an expression and a symbol of the modern. Just as communications and transport systems are a means of accelerating things in general, their main function being to speed up circulation, so the press (which as an advertising medium serves to shorten circulation time) is a carrier of signs, a mental accelerator, which contributes to a radical transformation in the experience of these and to an increase in the speed of social turnover. Its understanding of news, like the big city itself, is inscribed in the imperative of change, an imperative which gives its approval to change for change's sake.

In this way, the press contributes to the moulding of 'a new race of people', which, as Werner Sombart remarks, in its lack of restraint and restlessness, perceives change not as 'calamity', but on the contrary, 'wants' it. The new, as Benjamin diagnosed with respect to modernity in general – though the judgement can be applied to the news media in particular – becomes 'a quality which is independent of the use value of the commodity' (Benjamin 1983, vol. 1, p. 55). Expressed another way: the new *is* the use value.

A professional ideology of the new journalist, corresponding to this conception of news, was formed quite early on, presenting a mutation conditioned by the challenges of the big city and the demands of the job: the proverbial 'nose for news'. Having a 'nose for news' means tracking it down, being in the right place at the right time and recognising what is special about a situation. Since the deviant and abnormal is central to the way 'news' is understood, places which are full of news in this sense become advance posts of the New Journalism. The penny press, which was the first to discover the police-station and the courtroom as places which breed news, marks the beginning of the 'assignment' system.

But although the political-partisan conception of traditional journalism was undermined by the penny press, the partisan press itself did maintain its leading position at the national level until the American Civil War. Only after the Civil War, and helped along by innovations which are related to the reporting of the war – such as the introduction of a network of correspondents ('eye-witnesses') for instance – did the New Journalism achieve its breakthrough. The great era of the reporter was about to begin.

TYPES OF REPORTERS AND STYLES OF REPORTING

Like other professions which mark the beginning of a new era, the activity of the reporter at first became an object of satire. In March 1877, a comic strip appeared in the magazine *Puck* about 'The Great American Interviewer' (illustration 1), in which the reporter appears as a snooper, who literally as well as metaphorically pokes his nose into people's private affairs. In this satirical cartoon, the kinship between the reporter and the private detective (who appears on the stage of society at roughly the same time) is still openly expressed. What had undoubtedly at first

1   The drawings from *Puck* (March 1877) caricature the new 'art' of the interview

been interchangeable activities increasingly became differentiated, with
respect both to the required skills and to the social profile of the representatives of the two professions, and we see the close relationship
rapidly being forgotten. The memory of an interrogation situation
which sometimes appears in the iconography of ethnographic practice –
the seemingly forceful anthropologist/ethnographer sitting opposite the

somewhat intimidated informant – is not an unreasonable one in its
origins. The interview technique, as used by both reporter and field
researcher, is a question-and-answer method borrowed directly from the
practice of interrogation in court. The way in which the interview technique outside the courtroom was distilled from the verbatim reports of
interrogations in the context of police-court news appearing in the
penny press was demonstrated by Nilsson (1971), using the example of
James Gordon Bennett and the *Herald*.

With such a legacy, it is not surprising that the 'art of the interview',
which of course consists in drawing answers out of people, was at first
condemned as an invasion of the sphere of privacy. In view of the
novelty of the procedure, one which misled the inexperienced person
who did not yet have enough stock phrases at his disposal into giving ill-
considered answers, the periodical *The Nation* in 1873 concluded that the
interview makes fools out of great men.

As early as 1842, John Quincy Adams was writing contemptuously in
his diary that the sons of President Tyler are giving away all the cabinet
secrets to people ('named Permalee and John Howard Payne'), who were
'hired' reporters of Bennett's *Herald*. This contempt, which was
expressed in the description of the reporters as men writing for money,
was an indication both of the novelty of the profession and the low social
standing of those engaged in it. The fact that the first representatives of
this species were considered dubious types, job-hoppers who had tried
first one thing and then another, 'ne'er-do-wells' and 'braggarts', not to
mention 'boozers', all fits this image of the reporter.[1]

Regardless of how accurate this image might have been on the whole
– Harvard's President Eliot speaks as late as 1890 about reporters being
'drunkards, deadbeats and bummers' – the reason for it lies, above all, in
the lack of understanding of a new type of professional activity, a lack of
certainty as to its sense and purpose. The first journalists seem to Adams
to be hired hacks because they do for money something previously
accomplished by printers/publishers/editors combining all functions in
one person; the new species seems to him to be not worthy (and repug-
nant) because its representatives, instead of waiting for the official bulletin, go out and obtain information off their own bat. Adams obviously
does not yet grasp what the principle of 'news' is all about, any more
than do those people who ask (themselves) what on earth someone who

[1] H. L. Mencken speaks of drunken pimps, depraved clergymen and failed lawyers (Dovifat 1927, p.
236). Characteristically, Bergmann (1971), in portraying the journalistic career of Walt Whitman,
feels compelled to emphasise that Whitman was a serious editor, and not a 'ne'er-do-well'.

lounges around in the courtroom and in the police-station and pumps people for information can be up to.

The image of the journalist as a ne'er-do-well and incompetent only gradually faded; this rectification was certainly helped by the fact that in the 1870s Bachelors of Arts start to appear in editorial offices. However, a formal training was still very far from being established. While it is true that, in the 1870s, the first courses in journalism were being offered both at Washington College and Cornell University, these had a strong emphasis on printing technology, deriving from the traditional link between printer and editor. In the 1870s, the first press clubs were also founded. However, as an indication of incipient professionalism, the clubs should be treated with caution, since they tended to have been informal meeting places where (convivial) sociability played an more important rôle rather than just representing the interests of a new professional group. Nevertheless, the existence of these press clubs heralds the aspiration to professionalism to the extent that, in them, people with a common job identity, a common language and common values came together.

In 1898, the organ of the profession, *The Journalist*, founded in 1884 and itself an indication of incipient professionalism, notes, not without pride, that every one of the big New York newspapers has at least ten college graduates in its editorial offices. But an institutionalised specialised training, as one of the preconditions for raising the occupation of journalist to the status of a profession, was still lacking. To achieve this was the explicit goal of the publisher Joseph Pulitzer, who in 1908 founded a 'College of Journalism', financed by himself, in the expectation of being able 'to raise journalism to the rank of a learned profession, growing in the respect of the community as other professions far less important to the public interests have grown' (Pulitzer 1904, p. 657). Not only is the place where this historically important document (entitled 'The College of Journalism') was published of interest – the *North American Review*, a high-brow magazine and not a professional or scientific journal – but also the reason for its publication, a statement which had appeared some months previously opposing the establishment of a specialist school for journalism, whose main argument ran as follows: 'that the university has nothing to teach journalists in the special sense that it has to teach lawyers, physicians, architects and engineers' (White 1904, p. 25). In essence, Pulitzer had little to set against this argument, orientated as it was toward the ideal of the classical professions, even if – in answer to the question, 'What should be taught?' – he did unfold a palette of disciplines and subject areas, ranging from 'style' to 'ethics', from 'law' to 'statistics', from 'history' to 'physical science', the basic principles of which were to be taught to future journalists.

To justify the claim that this programme of general studies would raise the occupation of journalist to the rank of a profession, Pulitzer stressed the distinction between 'business' and 'profession': 'To sum up, the banker or the broker, the baker or the candlestick-maker is in business – in trade. But the artist, the statesman, the thinker, the writer – all who are in touch with the public taste and mind, whose thoughts reach beyond their own livelihood to some common interest – are in professions' (Pulitzer 1904, p. 658).

Amongst the disciplines whose basic elements were to be taught at the College of Journalism was sociology. What Pulitzer had to say about sociology in 1904 not only provides a better understanding of the curriculum he was aiming at, but is also very relevant to what this book is about:

Sociology, the science of the life of man in society, is the systemization of facts which it is the daily business of the journalist to collect. The chief difficulty in teaching this science is that it is so very broad – like a river in flood, without any definite channel. But a professor who knows what to leave out can frame a course, theoretical and practical, that will be one of the best possible introductions to newspaper work. (Pulitzer 1904, pp. 669ff.)

How far-sighted these statements are, and the remarkable extent to which they coincide with those of Park, will become clear later in this book. On the other hand, the limited extent to which the establishment of schools of journalism is able to guarantee professional status is shown by Mencken's caustic comments about the 'decayed editorial writers and unsuccessful reporters who teach in schools of journalism' (Mencken 1975 [1927], p. 91). Mencken writes in an article on 'Journalism in America', in 1927, that the journalist, far from having achieved the status of a doctor or a lawyer, lingers 'in the twilight zone, along with the trained nurse, the embalmer, the rev. clergy and the great majority of engineers' (see Mencken 1975 [1927], pp. 129ff.).

The police reporter

The job of the reporter is to look for, track down and hunt out pieces of news; just as the detective is seen as a 'blood hound', so the reporter is seen as a 'news hound'. The similarities between detective and reporter go even further: just as the actual investigative activity is preceded by observation, so the stage prior to journalistic investigation is termed 'nosing around'.

It is self-evident that a reporter, who has the task of tracking down items of news in the sense of the unusual and abnormal, goes to places where the probability of coming across such news is relatively high and relatively constant: places which may be termed distribution centres for news of this sort. In the language of journalism, such places, borrowing from police terminology, are termed 'runs' or 'beats'.[2] By using the assignment system, the reporters are allocated certain 'runs' or 'beats': the court, the hospital, the mortuary and, above all, the regular produc-ers of 'news', the police-station and the fire-brigade. Thus, the police reporter, who is assigned a certain 'police-beat' or 'crime-beat', is also the characteristic type of reporter of the period; again, what represented a baptism of fire for the 'cub reporter', the trainee reporter, was the daily bread of the hardened old hand.

The police reporter of that period who still remains the most famous today was Jacob A. Riis. Born in Ribe, a small Danish town, in 1849, Riis worked for more than two decades, from 1877, as a reporter for, amongst others, the *Tribune*, *World* and *Sun* in New York, as well as being a contrib-utor to magazines including *Scribner's* and *Century*. Riis' 'beat' was Mulberry Street in New York's East Side, which was a sort of social dividing line: beyond Mulberry Street began the territory of the 'other half', the immigrants and paupers. In the early 1890s, a number of people worked there as reporters who were later to become famous in other contexts: Lincoln Steffens, who later became a commentator on political affairs; Stephen Crane, the Naturalist author; and Robert Park, the future sociologist. At 300 Mulberry Street was the headquarters of the New York Police and the detective department, under the manage-ment of Thomas Byrnes, who had to leave the service in 1896 when accused of corruption. Riis, like some of his other colleagues, had a room opposite police headquarters, a sort of office, which was, for Lincoln Steffens, the ideal observation post (see Steffens 1931, pp. 202ff.). Byrnes and Riis were the most colourful and outstanding figures in their respective provinces. Whereas Byrnes was considered to be an autocratic police chief, with a tendency toward unconventional (to put it mildly) criminal investigation methods, Riis was the undisputed 'boss reporter' of Mulberry Street.

Riis, who described the raw material of the police reporter as 'murder,

---

[2] 'Beat' also means an exclusive story, similar to a 'scoop'.

fire and sudden death' (1899, p. 119), wrote the usual reports about cases of murder and suicide, conflagrations, accidents and prostitution, as well as about a variety of other standard topics covered by the police reporter. What set Riis apart from his colleagues was not only his eye for detail (for example, he wrote an article about graffiti in prison cells) but that, above all, he did not content himself with the usual sensational treatment of the raw material of journalism. Starting with the raw material – 'The remains of Harry Quill, aged fifteen, were discovered at the bottom of an air shaft in the tenement where his parents lived' – Riis researched the housing and living conditions in the tenement blocks which led to such cases of murder or suicide.

It is his reports into working, living and housing conditions in the slums of Lower East Side that made him famous beyond everyday journalism and turned him into a committed reformer. The decisive turning point in his career was the article, 'How the Other Half Lives: Studies Among the Tenements', which appeared in *Scribner's Magazine* in December 1889. This was the first time he succeeded in doing a broadly based study of social conditions in the slums of New York. Admittedly, the sensation which this article caused had less to do with the text than with the fact that the report included photographs, to some extent as evidence. Even today, Riis is known less as a reporter of social affairs than as the founder of social documentary photography.[3] In particular, the fact that Riis, as far as is known, was the first person to use flash lighting for interior photographs in asylums and tenements, cellars and gloomy backyards, has given him a place in the history of photography.

On the strength of the great success of his article, *Scribner's* offered to publish an extended version of his report as a book. In 1890, 'How the Other Half Lives: Studies Among the Tenements of New York' appeared in book form; this was undoubtedly Riis' major work, a classic of social photography which has been re-published again and again up to the present day. According to Donald N. Bigelow, Riis was 'a kind of sociologist, but without the benefit of academic training' (1957, p. x), a view which he is not the only one to hold. Indeed, Riis' 'How the Other Half Lives' can be read as a comprehensive study into living conditions

---

[3] That Riis had a nose for the marketing potential of his photographs is shown by the fact that, even before the *Scribner's* article, he secured copyright for the book title 'The Other Half, How it Lives and Dies in New York, With One Hundred Illustrations, Photographs from Real Life, of the Haunts of Poverty and Vice in a Great City' (see Lane 1974, p. 50). The formulation of the original title shows Riis still to be in the tradition of the city 'mystery' literature ('The Mysteries of Paris', etc.), a tradition which he in fact leaves behind in his work.

in the slum districts of New York, even if we cannot ignore the additive character of the study which results from the use of the journalistic material. Riis goes to great pains to draw a comprehensive picture in a systematic way.

He begins with a general account of the housing conditions in New York, especially in the tenement blocks; he then sketches the location of the various ethnic populations, in the form of a town plan of ethnic groups; he then takes the reader for a look inside a tenement block; he describes the characteristic establishments of the slum, such as the two-cent restaurant and the cheap lodging-houses, and he subsequently deals at length with individual districts (Chinatown, Jewtown), as well as portraying individual groups and types in the population, e.g., the street urchins and gangs; he describes the situation of the young women who work in factories; and, at the end of the book, he tries to summarise the current situation. Provided as it is with plans and statistics in the appendix, 'How the Other Half Lives' can certainly be read as an early contribution to urban literature, a view held by Park, who saw in Riis' book a direct precursor of the American survey (REPA 5:1). However, it must also be realised that Riis, who in the eyes of his biographers was a sentimental idealist, had close connections with the reform efforts of the Charity Organization Society, which made him an exception amongst his colleagues. It was not by chance that his colleagues gave him the nickname 'the pious Dane', reflecting the frequent pathos of his style and his moralising arguments. What is surprising, in retrospect, is that Riis managed to hold his own in a trade full of cynics.

Rôle reporting

Apart from the city beat reporter, who conventionally takes the form of the police reporter, it is the stunt reporter who most clearly embodies the New Journalism. The stunt reporter does not track down news, he makes it. He therefore corresponds in an ideal way to the self-image of the New Press as a news factory, which operates according to the motto that where nothing is happening, something must be made to happen. The term 'stunt report' sums it up: the reporter, like the later stunt man in films, puts on daring show numbers. One of the first and most famous stunt reportages, was initiated by George Bennett Jr, who coined the slogan, 'I make news'. In 1869, he commissioned the reporter Henry Morton Stanley (actually John Rowlands) to go and find the missing

British explorer David Livingstone.[4] George Bennett financed other expeditions, which – as ventures with the purpose of finding something unknown – have news value by definition and, furthermore, have the advantage of supplying a paper with reports over a fairly lengthy period of time.

In the context of this book, however, these spectacular large-scale undertakings are of secondary interest compared to the genre of exposure reporting, which forms part of stunt reporting. The interesting thing about exposure reporting, from the sociological point of view, is the use of the method of concealed participant observation, for which the term 'rôle reporting' has become standard in journalism:

> a clever adventurous writer assumes a disguise or forges documents to gain admission to a hospital, jail or asylum, and then makes the narrative of his experiences an exposé of the administration of the institution. (Mott 1950 [1948])

That defines the preferred fields of investigation of exposure reporting; it focuses on those locations in society which today are subsumed under the sociological term coined by Erving Goffman: the 'total institution'.

The most famous contemporary representative of exposure journalism – possibly the first female reporter at all – was Elizabeth Cochrane, who under the pseudonym 'Nellie Bly' became the uncrowned queen of the genre. Born in 1867 in Cochran's Mills, a small town founded by her father, a judge, Elizabeth Cochrane[5] began her career in 1885 as a journalist with the *Pittsburgh Dispatch*, whose publisher George A. Madden also suggested to her the pseudonym Nellie Bly, a character from a song of the day. Among other things, Cochrane wrote a series about the slums of Pittsburgh, in which she paid particular attention to the situation of workers' wives. Her time in Pittsburgh also includes a series on social conditions in Mexico, specifically for which she learned Spanish as well as a Mexican dialect. In 1887, Cochrane left Pittsburgh and went to New York, where she worked for Pulitzer's *New York World*. Her most spectacular reporting feat, carried out at considerable cost, was a journey round the world inspired by Jules Verne's book, which she accomplished in 72 days, beating the fictional record of 80 days.

More important in this context, however, is the fact that Cochrane developed the art of exposure reporting, based on concealed participant

---

[4] For more on the history of this reportage, see Mott 1950. For a view of Stanley as the embodiment of bourgeois hero, see Moebus 1976. As a testimony to self-glorification, see Henry M. Stanley's 'Autobiography', first published in 1909.

[5] In her first article, sent in under the name of 'E. Cochrane', she added an 'e' to her surname; she then retained this spelling of her name.

observation, to a masterly degree. She pretended to be mentally deranged (official medical diagnosis, 'dementia with persecution complex') and had herself admitted into the notorious lunatic asylum on Blackwell's Island, in order to describe the situation of the patients and the methods of treatment; she had herself arrested in order to get into a women's prison and describe the conditions inside as well as the situation of the female prisoners; pretending to be ill, she went to the general hospital for the poor, in order to examine the medical care there; she exposed herself to malaria, yellow fever and cholera; she disguised herself as a member of the Salvation Army in order to research both the movement from the inside and the reaction of the people on the street; among other things, she worked in department stores and as a housemaid, in order to portray working conditions. She was so successful with her reports and so famous and notorious that: 'The officials of public institutions began to look at every beggar woman's face with the suspicion that the deadly Bly girl might be lurking behind some disguise' (Ross 1974, p. 52).[6]

The variety of Elizabeth Cochrane's areas of investigation was exceptional, compared with those of her male and female colleagues, and was an index of her sociological imagination. Whatever she did, she soon found imitators (male as well as female), the most famous of whom was Annie Laurie (in actual fact Winifred Black), who worked for Hearst's first paper, the *San Francisco Examiner* (see Zuckerman 1984). Just how far the imitation of the Bly model went is shown by the fact that even the pseudonym 'Annie Laurie' was taken from a song of the day. For quite some time, exposure reporting was extremely fashionable, so that scarcely a prison or a mental asylum in the United States was safe from stunt reporters (see Lyons 1971, p. 80). For all the sociological inventiveness on which exposure reporting drew, this illustrates its problematic aspect in the context of a press geared toward the making of news. Each new field of investigation and every new method of access that proved successful soon became fashionable and were then dropped just as quickly when the readers' interest in the subject flagged.

Milieu reporting (urban colour)

Of all the types of reporter, the urban colour reporter comes closest to the figure of the flâneur. The flâneur carries out 'studies', and this,

---

[6] Cochrane carried secretiveness (promoting sales as well as protecting herself against discovery) so far that she only appeared in the editor's office wearing a large hat with a veil. This type of disguise also demonstrates the elegance which was attributed to her.

'studies', is also just what the urban colour reporter does, calling his impressions of metropolitan life (printed mostly in the Sunday supplements of daily newspapers and in magazines) 'sketches', 'stories' or simply 'studies'. Nevertheless, the comparison is an imperfect one: the flâneur, with his deliberateness and air of absorption in his own thoughts, is more of a European figure, similar to the philosophising walker, whereas the American reporter rather seems to be involved in a hunt. In addition, there is an important difference, one which sums up the difference between the Old World and the New: the European journalist/literary figure is historically orientated, a priest of the *genius loci*, as Benjamin expressed it, whereas the American 'hunter after the authentic' is totally engrossed in the present. The European flâneur, for whom the city is a 'mnemo-technical device' (Benjamin), must thus learn to understand the language of the stones:

The pavement on which the dead walked, the door-handles on which they laid their hand, the steps which they climbed in fear or in joy, the stone mantelpieces against which they leant, the window-ledges on which they rested their elbows: all these thousand fragments of past times, of which Paris consists, begin to speak in tongues and tell of the destinies, whose imperturbable witnesses they were. (Sieburg n.d., p. 14)

Friedrich Sieburg's *Blick durchs Fenster* [Glimpse through the window] (n.d.), just as much as Franz Hessel's *Spazieren in Berlin* [A flâneur in Berlin] (1984 [1929]), are both impressive documents of this type of approach to the city, one which contributes to a 'mythological topography'. For their American counterparts, following the threads back into the past is 'a charm in addition' (Hutchins Hapgood 1917, p. 471), but above all, it is the present which is important, 'the way the old culture meets and strives with the new ideas, the conflict between Old World and New World conceptions of literature and life, the process of adjustment to our special American conditions . . . this is a state which gives birth to a very large number of forcible, vehement, and most interesting personalities, and creates a milieu which is, in the most profound sense of the word, picturesque' (Hutchins Hapgood 1917, pp. 471ff.).

The major theme of the American flâneur (if we may even call him that) is the process of inner exoticisation which the American city of the nineteenth century experiences as a result of the immigrants coming from every conceivable country:

From all parts of the world they are pouring into New York: Greeks from Athens and realms of Sparta and Macedonia . . . Jews from Russia, Poland, Hungary, the Balkans, crowding the East Side and the inlying sections of Brooklyn . . .

Italians from Sicily and the warmer vales of the South, crowding into great sections of their own, all hungry for a taste of New York; Germans, Hungarians, French, Polish, Swedish, Armenians, all with sections of their own and all alive to the joys of the city, and how eager to live – great gold and scarlet streets throbbing with the thoughts of them. (Dreiser 1923, p. 7)

The pictures which the journalist draws are ones from the culture and the rituals of the various ethnic groups; they are sketches of the life and bustle in the ethnic quarters, in 'Little Italy', 'Chinatown' and, especially, in the Jewish ghetto.

In contrast to reform-orientated reporters such as Riis, though, the reform attitude is almost completely lacking. As far as the urban colour reporter is concerned, the way of life which unfolds before his eyes is fascinating as an expression of variety. Metaphorically speaking, he draws the eye away from sweatshops, places of work and exploitation, to the synagogues, the places of religious rites and cultural practice. The argument that it tended to be new immigrants such as Riis who developed the gaze of the reformer cannot be denied. It was not only that they themselves had been through a phase of hardship, something which helps to sharpen a person's eye for poverty and misery, but besides this, the immigrants – *plus royaliste que le roi* – inclined to a demonstrative ultra-Americanism. For New Englanders such as Hutchins Hapgood and Lincoln Steffens, the city of the end of the nineteenth century was a terrain whose population was there to be discovered. It is not surprising that, in the process, the life of the immigrants from southern and eastern Europe, which compared to the sobriety of the 'old-line Americans' seemed colourful and spirited, was often romanticised. But the reporter also had both an eye and, in conversation with his informants, an ear for the changes taking place, so that the thesis of the 'second generation', in the studies of the ethnic enclaves, was something already preconceived.

A particularly impressive example of this genre is a series of articles by Hutchins Hapgood, printed in the *Commercial Advertiser* and published in 1902 in book form under the title of *The Spirit of the Ghetto* (1967 [1902]). Although the study is primarily about the intellectual and artistic milieu, about journalists, writers and actors, about newspapers, magazines and theatres, the editor of the new edition, Moses Rischin, described Hapgood's book as the first authentic study of the inner life of an American immigrant community from the pen of an outsider (Rischin 1967, p. vii). The first chapter ('The Old and the New'), in which he describes the way of life of Orthodox Jews in Russia and Galicia and how it gradually disintegrates in America, is especially impressive because, sociologically, it is ahead of its time. It would not be an exaggeration to see in this sketch an anticipation of the theme which Thomas and Znaniecki dealt with later, in their classic *The Polish Peasant in Europe and America* (1974 [1918–20]).[7]

Particularly remarkable are the observations about the second generation, in which the special situation of the young generation is described, a generation vacillating between love for their parents and shame about their appearance, their imperfect knowledge of the language, their ignorance and their awkwardness. Hapgood attempts to understand the factors which influence and affect the second generation and which shape them in a specific way: on the one hand, the Orthodox Jewish milieu of the parental home which insists on strict adherence to the traditional way of life; on the other, the compulsory American school, which not only teaches the younger people a language of which their parents have little or no knowledge, but also exposes them to influences which remain unknown or irrelevant to their parents' generation; plus, to some extent as a synthesis or solution to this dilemma, the significance of socialist groupings.

In his introduction, Moses Rischin compares Hapgood's book both with Riis' *How the Other Half Lives* as well as with Louis Wirth's study *The Ghetto* (1956 [1928]). Riis' 'Jewtown' and Hapgood's 'Ghetto' are worlds apart, even though they are concerned with one and the same place, a difference which reflects the contrasting angles from which the authors perceive the world of the eastern European Jewish immigrants. Riis' metaphors and his moralising tone are, as Rischin stresses, still an echo of missionary endeavours, whereas Hapgood's portrayal, both in style and content, is an expression of the sober realism of the younger generation.

Comparing it with Wirth's book, Rischin considers Hapgood's journalistic study to be far superior, because Wirth's research is lacking in 'humanity of method', by which he means the capacity for empathy that makes it possible for the author to conjure up the 'spirit' of the ghetto before the eyes of the reader. Rischin's criticism certainly does not do

---

[7] It is not without interest that Hutchins Hapgood and William Thomas had an informant in common, namely Abraham Cahan, publisher of the *Jewish Daily Forward*. Thomas was stimulated, amongst other things, by the readers' letters to the *Forward* into considering letters as source material. On Cahan, see: Gollomb 1912, Poole 1911, Rischin 1953. Park noted in his travel diary of 1929, concerning Cahan: 'Abr. Cahan probably produced the best newspaper that was ever published' (REPA 4:7). The paper, which in 1917 reached a circulation of 240,000 copies, still exists today, though with a circulation of only 20,000 copies. See 'At 90, Yiddish Paper Is Still Vibrant', *New York Times*, 25 May 1987, p. 10.

justice to Wirth's study, long sections of which are historical, but it does touch upon a sore point that arises from the attitude of American Jews toward the Jewish immigrants from eastern Europe, an attitude at once patronising and defensive (see Szajkowski 1951). Wirth also follows this pattern when he defines the Orthodox way of life of the Jews in Chicago, the forms and institutions of which are described in detail, as being sectarian, outmoded and, judged by American standards, inferior. It is this conclusion which makes Wirth's study appear tendentious in Rischin's eyes. He gives a good reason for this judgement, in saying that as a Jew of German origin, Wirth is prejudiced against the eastern European Jewish immigrants.

It says a great deal for Hapgood's insight and perspicacity that, in the first chapter of his book, he addresses the differences between eastern European Jews and the Jews of German origin, who, as founding settlers, identify themselves with the American way of life. In contrast to Wirth's ghetto, which is a 'world in miniature', provincial and outmoded, Hapgood conjures up another world before the eyes of his readers, one able to hold up a mirror to the American reality.

Muckraking

At the beginning of this century, journalistic interest in the life of the big city took on a political character in the form of 'muckraking'.[8] Muckraking is understood as being the composition of socially critical articles based on facts. The great importance which is attached to facts – 'Facts, facts piled up to the point of dry certitude' (Ray Stannard Baker) – can only be understood if they are seen as the opposite of illusions, which are the result of innocent trust. The facts which the muckrakers expose are not there on the street; on the contrary, they flourish in secret places: the thing that is important to the 'exposure' journalist is the look backstage, at what is going on behind the scenes. Unlike the stunt reporter, who reveals a closed institution to the public, the exposure journalist uncovers the secret aspect of public institutions. Here, the *process* of exposure is just as important as the *fact* which is being exposed: unmasking people who in public pretend to be upright citizens as

---

[8] Theodore Roosevelt is credited with coining the term 'muckraker'; he used it in a speech he gave on 14 April 1906, when referring to Bunyan's *Pilgrim's Progress* (the speech is printed in Shapiro 1968, pp. 3ff.). Roosevelt, who owed his career in no small measure to revelations of cases of corruption, was obviously reacting to the increasingly socialist tendencies amongst exposure journalists.

hypocrites is a motive which goes far beyond the disclosure of actual irregularities – it forms the basis of the activity of exposure itself.

The new popular 'ten-cent' magazines provide the forum for exposure journalism. In contrast to the traditional high-brow magazines such as *Atlantic*, *Century* and *Scribner's*, which, still influenced by continental models, are more or less books appearing periodically, the popular magazines such as *McClure's*, *Cosmopolitan* and *Everybody's*, which take up and expose the pattern of the Sunday supplement, in particular the feature story, are considered as newspapers appearing on a monthly basis. The advantage which magazine journalism offers to authors coming from daily newspaper journalism is the vitally necessary additional time and money for research; just how immense these demands could be, in part, is shown by the example of Ida M. Tarbell, who carried out four years of research for her series 'History of the Standard Oil Company', published in *McClure's* in 1903–4, spending around $50,000. Furthermore, unlike the daily newspapers, these magazines were distributed nationally: this drew the attention of the public from all over the country not only to the state of affairs being denounced, but also to journalists like Tarbell, Gustavus Myers or Lincoln Steffens, who with a single series go down in the history of American journalism.

The beginnings of exposure reporting, precursors to the classic muckraking period between 1903 and 1906, are formed by additions to the studies about slums and the underworld. This can be readily illustrated by looking at reports done by Josiah Flynt Willard, who published series of articles such as 'True Stories from the Underworld' (jointly with Francis Walton, i.e., Alfred Hodder) (*McClure's*, vol. 15/16, 1900/1) and 'In the World of Graft' (*McClure's*, vol. 16/17, 1901). Neither the method of approach (undercover observation) nor the theme (underworld) is new; what is new is the angle, which from now on concentrates on the links between underworld and respectable society.

The reports aim primarily to disclose what Flynt, borrowing a term from underworld slang, describes as 'graft' (racketeering, corruption). The curious-seeming significance given to the borrowing of a term from the language of crooks[9] illustrates the importance muckraking had for the reading public better than any one revelation. 'Graft' signals a look behind the scenes, promises 'inside' knowledge and so constitutes a metaphor for the detective character of journalistic activity, which, as

[9] The Literary Digest (2 February 1907) headlined their obituary of Josiah Flynt with 'The Man Who Gave Us the Word Graft'.

exposure journalism, possesses news value, independent of aim and purpose. 'In the World of Graft' is based on interviews with professional criminals in New York, Chicago and Boston. Flynt not only uncovers the various specific 'business links' between crooks, on the one hand, and politicians, police and judges in these cities, on the other; what is more important is the irritation resulting from the inversion of traditional ideas of 'good' and 'evil', 'honesty' and 'dishonesty'. For the crooks, Chicago is an 'honest' city, because the police there, in contrast to those in New York, keep to their side of the bargain; ultimately, what is being exposed is the illusion that certain virtues go with certain positions.

A characteristic of muckraking is that racketeering and corruption are first of all demonstrated to exist amongst those who because of professional ethics have a duty to be honest: the police, politicians, judges. It was only afterwards that the muckraking wave spread over into the world of business. The historical sequence of themes covered by 'exposure' journalism, even though Lippman (1968, pp. 17ff.) may have over-emphasised them as ideal types, ultimately points to the moral character of this campaign of disillusionment. At first, representatives of public life are pilloried, then these standards are applied to privately owned commercial companies who administer public services (railways, insurance companies, etc.) and, finally, the practices of individual private business areas are exposed (sweatshop industry, foodstuffs industry, patent medicines).

Whether, ultimately, the muckraking movement contributed to the monopolisation of capital, as Vowe (1978, p. 264) maintains, is difficult to decide at this level of generality. What is clear, however, is that the attacks on certain areas of private enterprise and certain practices in these areas favoured the interests of big industry more than they harmed them; we only have to think of the sweatshop industry and patent medicine. Certainly, muckraking as a reform movement was not without its effects; thus it succeeded in getting child labour banned and in pushing through the Pure Food and Drug Edict. But by and large, in the end, it was not much more than a case of 'social face-washing' (Hofstadter 1968, p. 99), where long overdue changes were being accomplished.

Contrary to *McClure's* self-promoting affirmation that these investigations (meaning Flynt's 'Graft' series) had not been done merely to satisfy idle curiosity, exposure journalism did also have its own curiosity value, since it actually named names, places and dates. Cantwell's assertion that the muckraking articles were not read because they uncovered corruption in Minneapolis, but rather because they reported what was happening in Minneapolis, is not so easy to dismiss:

In doing this, they drew a new cast of characters for the drama of American society: bosses, professional politicians, reformers, racketeers, captains of industry. Everybody recognized these native types; everybody knew about them; but they had not been characterized before; their social functions had not been analyzed. At the same time, the muckrakers pictured stage settings that everybody recognized but that nobody had written about – oil refineries, slums, the red-light districts, the hotel rooms where political deals were made – the familiar, unadorned homely stages where the teeming day-to-day dramas of American life were enacted. (Cantwell 1968, pp. 22–3)

The exposure reports – which, because they were disseminated nationwide, proceed by making comparisons – are rudimentary contributions to a comparative urban sociology. The readers are given a descriptive introduction to the sociology of modern American society, to the sociology of new professional groups and institutions. For the first time, successful generalisations can be made. It turns out that certain practices are not specific to New York, Chicago or Philadelphia, but that they arise from social circumstances.

THE REPORTER AS URBAN EXPLORER

The American press at the end of the nineteenth century, both institution and authority in the transition to modern life, made a contribution to the formation of a mentality which corresponds to the conditions of the big cities. The rhythm of the big city is reflected in its mode of appearance (morning, evening, Sunday and special editions), in the manner of its distribution (street sales) and in its presentation (headlines). The front page of the daily newspaper, with its presentation of various events, is itself, as Fisher (1975) noted, a sort of 'crowd of people', representing a rapid succession of experience. By presenting the reader with a picture of the town as a theatre, in which sudden, violent events follow each other with convulsive speed (Weisberger 1961, p. 136), the 'crime-and-fire' press, to pick up a remark which Benjamin made about the feuilleton section, 'injects the poison of the sensation of experience intravenously as it were' (Benjamin 1983, vol. II, p. 966). But, however justified the criticism of the sensational press might be, it at the same time forgets that this 'poison of sensation' is itself rooted in the nature of big city experience. For those who come to the city from the countryside or from the Old World – and that is the overwhelming majority – the

American big city is indeed a sensation, a spectacle, a theatre where the show never stops. This fact contributes not only to the human interest story, but also to the early big city novel; the description of Caroline Meeber's ('Sister Carrie') arrival in Chicago may be considered as a paradigm in this respect.

Finding one's way in the big city, with its uninterrupted succession of impressions, its confusing multiplicity of signals and its fragmented spaces, is an adventure which requires an effort of cultural adaptation from the newcomer, even a 'remaking of character and nature, of mind and body' (Korff 1986, p. 145). Could this be made any clearer than in the account by the German traveller Arthur Holitscher, who, in 1912, in Chicago, 'the most dreadful city on earth', feels himself driven into such a 'whirlwind of people' on the street, that 'my ears and eyes fail me' (1916, p. 9)? The big city almost invites exploration; it suggests entry into unknown places. As a newspaper reporter, Theodore Dreiser appreciated Chicago's heterogeneity, the districts which were 'crowded with great black factories, stockyards, steel works, Pullman yards', '[t]hese raw neighbourhoods where . . . drunken and lecherous slatterns and brawlers were to be found mooning about in a hell of their own' and as a contrast, those neighbourhoods 'where liveried servants stood by doors and carriages turned in at spacious gates and under heavy porte-cochères' (Dreiser 1922). In Dreiser's eyes, the wonderful thing about the big city is its variety. The reports owe everything to this variety: with their descriptions of the city, their portrayals of city institutions and professional groups and their stories about ethnic quarters and their inhabitants, they offer their readers a substitute for seeing it for themselves; they bring strange things closer and make new things comprehensible.

In this context, the reporter functions as a scout, who reports to his readers on the glitter and the misery of the big city. On the readers' behalf, he sets out on a journey into the interior of the metropolis: it is he who reports from the inner world of the sweatshops, the slaughterhouses and the factories; he brings the reader the world of the vaudeville theatres, the great hotels and the department stores; he reconnoitres tenement blocks and roams through red-light districts, and it is he who embarks on the journey into the 'mosaic of the miniature worlds' of metropolis, on a trip 'Around the World in New York', as the title of a series of articles reviewed by Park puts it. As an explorer, the reporter develops research techniques which correspond both to the image of the adventurer and to the altered conditions in the world of the big city: observation and interview, on-the-spot investigation and undercover research. The big city gives free rein to the art of observation: only there does the rôle of observer become possible; only there does the opportunity exist for slipping into different rôles. Just like the ethnologist, the reporter has his sources, 'key persons', like the concierge, the hotel porter, the bartender and his 'native' informants in the ethnic quarters. Like the undercover participant observer, he or she takes on the rôles of an unemployed person and somebody looking for a place to live, of a worker and a salesman/woman, of a beggar and an insane person, in order to provide the readers with an insight into unfamiliar worlds and into the functioning of certain institutions.

In however fragmentary a way, the reporter conveys to his readers views from inside unfamiliar worlds. By portraying the unknown (the service in a synagogue, the festival of a patron saint in Little Italy, the social organisations of Chinatown), he helps to overcome ignorance and encourage tolerance. The details of location ('between Ninety-sixth street and One Hundred Sixteenth on the East Side of Manhattan Island') are not merely decorative but also allow the readers to open up the space of the big city for themselves.

'Around the World in New York' enables blank spaces on the reader's mental map to be erased and filled with life. In this way, the reporter makes a contribution to 'welding [the big city] into a structure of diverse worlds, ways of life and forms of culture' (Korff 1987, p. 645).

Thus the reporter fulfils the aesthetic function which George Herbert Mead talks about in his essay 'The Nature of Aesthetic Experience'. Mead sees every invention that makes it possible to put oneself in the place of others, and to participate in others' thoughts, as contributing to socialisation. Amongst these inventions he includes the press. He differentiates between the informative function, providing the public with news which is directly related to activity (the stock market report and election results are mentioned as the prototype of this kind of news), and the aesthetic function, which is reflected in 'story' journalism. As a rule, the journalist is not sent out to gather facts, but to get a 'story'. This may be of a trivial nature, it may only provide the reader with sentimental compensation for his own misery. But if the story which the reporter brings in serves 'to interpret to the reader his experience as the shared experience of the community of which he feels himself to be a part' (Mead 1925/6, p. 390), then the press fulfils an aesthetic function, i.e., it contributes toward bringing people together in such a way that they can enter into the life of the other person concerned. The aims of the 'literary journalism', which Lincoln Steffens propagated when he was chief editor of the *Commercial Advertiser* (1897–1901), completely correspond to the model of story journalism as drawn by Mead: 'it is scientifically and artistically the true ideal for an artist and for a newspaper: to get the news so completely and to report it so humanly *that the reader will see himself in the other fellow's place*' (Steffens 1931, p. 317; my emphasis).

The examples of reportage I have given are certainly amongst the best of their type, i.e., they show what it is possible to achieve, rather than being the expression of everyday journalism. Around the turn of the century, the latter is unmistakably dominated by the sensational reporting of 'yellow journalism', which with its shock effects contributes to a sort of experience which, according to Habermas, does not cumulate but regresses, providing the reader with those daydreams which Mead describes as compensating us for our defeats, our inferiority and our unconfessed failures.

That this is the case does not make my hypothetical conclusion, that big city reportage was the model for Chicago urban sociology, necessarily incorrect, rather the reverse. It is precisely because reportage, in the context of a press which aims to make a profit, has limits imposed on it that it can be taken up as an unredeemed model of investigation into the big city by a realist sociology which understands itself as a medium for communicative understanding.

In his autobiography, Steffens put this view into words, when he said that what reporters know but do not report is either sociology or literature. Because just as important, if not more important, as the value of journalism as a field of professional activity, is its significance as a space in which to gather experience.

CHAPTER 2

The sociologist as city editor: Robert Ezra Park

Why go to the North Pole or climb Everest for adventure when we have Chicago?

Robert Ezra Park

DAILY NEWS AND *THOUGHT NEWS*

Don Martindale once described the Chicago School of sociology as 'urbanism incorporated'. Although the spectrum of subjects covered by Chicago sociology is very wide-ranging,[1] as the list of completed dissertations from the classic period of 1920 and 1935 shows, it is more or less identified with field (the metropolis of Chicago) and research (ethnography) (Bulmer 1984, p. 12).

This identification is not only demonstrated by which studies have been accepted in the history of sociology as classics, but also by what is regarded, in the context of its rediscovery, as the legacy of the Chicago School: both the neo-Chicagoans within the circuit of the journal *Urban Life*, as well as the ethnologists within the orbit of the journal *Terrain* who rely on the Chicago tradition, concentrate on ethnographical research in the urban space.

When it was asserted that journalistic reportage was the major influence on big city sociological research, that statement has been a reference to the biography of a man, who, if we are to believe Everett C. Hughes, saw himself at the age of 50 as a failure: Robert Ezra Park (1864–1944). This estimation of failure may, of course, derive from a taste of drama which biographers like to indulge in whenever the career they are tracing – which after all was a successful one – allows it. For long periods Park saw himself as a seeker who had not yet found his 'calling'. Of such material are indeed failed lives made, lives which founder on the

---

[1] See Faris 1970, pp. 137ff., as well as the ranked list of MA and Ph.D subjects between 1915 and 1935 in Lofland 1983, p. 499.

discrepancy between desire and reality. The dramatic effect of the assertion is due, however, to the reversal of this principle, one which has
become proverbial in the phrase, 'like a phoenix from the ashes': in the
same year of his life in which, according to Hughes, Park regarded
himself as a failure, he arrived at the sociology department of the
University of Chicago and, for around two decades, became its central
figure.

Park, born in 1864 in Harveyville, Luzerne County, Pennsylvania and
brought up in Red Wing, a little town on the banks of the Mississippi, first
of all studied engineering for a year and then, from the autumn of 1883 to
the spring of 1887, psychology, history and philosophy at the University of
Michigan, the last under Dewey.[2] After acquiring his BA, he worked as a
reporter and editor in Minneapolis, Detroit, Denver, New York and
Chicago until 1898. As a general assignment reporter he covered the
whole contemporary repertoire: from court reporting to local reports and
theatre reviews. In 1898 he resumed his studies in Harvard, where he
attended lectures given by, amongst others, William James and Hugo
Münsterberg and, in 1899, he acquired his MA. In the winter term of
1899, he continued his studies in Berlin, where he attended lectures by
Simmel and Paulsen;[3] he then went to Strasbourg to study under
Windelband and Knapp and, finally, followed Windelband to
Heidelberg,[4] where he received his doctorate with a thesis on 'Masse und
Publikum' [The crowd and the public]. In the autumn of 1903, Park
returned to the United States: he was first of all an assistant lecturer in philosophy at Harvard; at the same time he worked as secretary to the Congo
Reform Association; and finally, in 1905, he became press agent to the
black civil rights leader, Booker T. Washington, for whom he also acted as
ghost writer. In 1914, at the age of 50, William Isaac Thomas called him to
the sociology department of the University of Chicago as a lecturer.

In this career, journalistic activity is evident as a kind of interruption;
however, given a duration of about 12 years, it can hardly be described as
a passing phase. The question arises, not only why did Park *become* a
journalist, but also, why did he not *remain* a journalist? Faris (1970, p. 28)
believes that the answer is to be found in Park's interest in getting under

---

[2] Those of Dewey's courses which Park attended included 'Empirical Psychology', 'Psychology
and Philosophy', 'Hegel's Logic' and 'Kant's Critique of Pure Reason'.
[3] Lectures given by Simmel which Park attended included 'Sociology' as well as 'Nineteenth-
Century Philosophy'; those given by Paulsen included 'Schopenhauer's World as Will and Idea'.
[4] Amongst Windelband's courses, Park attended 'Logic'. In Heidelberg, he also studied under
Hettner and attended 'Introduction to the Geographical Understanding of German Landscape
and Culture' as well as 'Geographical Exercises'.

2 Robert E. Park, Berlin, 1900; drawing by Clara Cahill Park

the surface of the subject he is concerned with (in this case, the big city and the news media). It is true that such an approach corresponds to Park's mentality, as will be shown later; in order not to paint an over-idealistic picture, however, account must also be taken of the precarious professional situation of journalists whose careers frequently come to a dead-end once a certain point in time or age is reached. In a letter to his fiancée and later wife, Clara Cahill, in 1893, Park wrote:

When I fall to worrying about the future – when I fear I am destined always to be a reporter at 25 dollars a week – when I have the moment of real dizziness and distrust, one thought of you has made them vanish. (quoted from Raushenbush 1979, p. 24)

The reference to earnings is an indication that Park was not in the first rank of reporters; in 1892, the average salary of a 'general assignment' reporter was $25 a week (see Mott 1950 [1948], p. 489). But, like many of his colleagues, Park did not want to remain a reporter all his life. This is not only because reporters were considered to be old and burnt-out by the time they reached the age of 40 at the latest.[5] More importantly, the activity of reporter was regarded as a kind of transitory stage on the way to becoming an editor or, as a more or less secret motive for those who turned to journalism, an interim step on the way to becoming an author. Someone who was still in the profession at 40 either had missed the boat or had not got out while the going was good; being a reporter, for the great majority of those who took up the profession in the 1890s, was part of a personal search for fulfilment. This motive is also central to the understanding of Park's career.

Park was undoubtedly dissatisfied or even disgusted, as he wrote while still close to his New York experiences, by the state of the contemporary press (REPA 1:3). This dissatisfaction, which is bound up with his hope in a *journalistic* alternative, finds expression in a short episode during his journalistic career, which nevertheless had a lasting effect. Around 1890, the journalist Franklin Ford put forward to the philosopher John Dewey a plan for a new kind of newspaper, which would be part of a gigantic intelligence trust.[6] Ford, who was described as an eccentric and a 'crank',[7] got the idea for this trust from his journalistic practice. While he was editor of the financial paper *Bradstreet's*, he received an inquiry from

[5] Park himself made a reference to this (to all appearances borrowed from Lincoln Steffens) in his 'autobiographical note', where he says: 'The life of the average newspaper man seemed, at the time, to be about eight years. After that if he remained in the profession his value steadily declined' (Park 1950a, p. v). Mencken expressed it even more drastically: 'The way out, perhaps, is to retire at thirty, or to slide a razor across the carotids at forty' (Mencken 1975 [1927], p. 57).

[6] My account of the *Thought News* episode draws on Coughlan (1975), Czitrom (1982), Feuer (1959) and McGlashan (1979/80) as well as unpublished seminar notes on the press written by Park (REP 2:8). Ford took the term 'intelligence trust' from Dewey. Kuklick (1980) classifies Dewey's 'intelligence trust' together with Veblen's 'Soviet of Technicians' and Ward's 'Sociography' as one of a number of contemporary concepts of a dictatorship of experts.

[7] McGlashan points out that the accusation of 'crankiness' came primarily from authors who were friendly to Dewey. The reason may have been that it was Dewey who became the butt of sarcastic comments in the daily press when the *Thought News* project was announced (see n10 below). Joas, too, makes the criticism that Coughlan turns the 'revolutionary syndicalists' Franklin Ford and Corydon Ford into mere cranks. The argument, however, that Ford not only appeared to his contemporaries to be odd, but actually was odd, is not so easy to refute. I am most convinced by the position of Oliver Wendell Holmes, who said in a letter to F. E. Pollock that Ford appeared to him to be 'half-crank', but added: 'He seems to have ideas' (Burton 1982, p. 12).

a businessman asking for further information on the economic situation of agriculture in a certain region in the West. Ford thereupon proposed to *Bradstreet's* the establishment of a 'National Bureau of Investigation', which would bring together supply and demand and carry out commissioned studies, e.g., for potential investors.

His plan, the ultimate aim of which was the realisation of the 'organic principle' of society on the basis of the new means of communication, was rejected by the management.[8] After trying in vain for several years to win over other newspaper publishers for the project, Franklin Ford and his brother Corydon (who is described as an even odder character) 'toured' the philosophy faculties of Columbia, Cornell, Harvard, Yale and other universities in search of a person who understood the scope of the principle and its practical significance, eventually having success with Dewey. Dewey was taken with the idea. In an enthusiastic letter to William James on 3 June 1891, in which he reported his 'wonderful personal experience' with Ford, Dewey explained that he owed Ford the insight that philosophy, which up until then had merely stated the unity of mind and outside world, was now capable of bringing about the conditions for its objective expression (Feuer 1959, pp. 548ff.). The project of the 'intelligence triangle' consisted in setting up three companies: (1) a news association, which would produce various newspapers, namely, a national paper (*Newsbook*), a local newspaper appearing in several regional editions (*The Town*) as well as an advertising paper (*The Daily Want*); (2) a 'Class News Company', which would publish specialist papers (*Grain, Fruit, Chemical News*, etc.); as well as (3) a news office called 'Fords', which would provide information mostly to bankers, business people and politicians. Ford also already knew the slogan he wanted: 'Buy your facts at Fords'.[9] The intelligence

---

[8] Franklin Ford spoke of the news-gathering and news-disseminating machinery of printing press, locomotive and telegraph. In the final analysis, the project amounted to standardisation of the social body by way of socialising knowledge: 'In place of writing about sociology so-called, we proceed to publish the sociological newspaper' (Ford n.d. [1892]). Some years later Dewey said in a lecture: 'Interpretation is the aim of social science. A proper daily newspaper would be the only possible social science' (noted down by Cooley, quoted from Matthews 1977, p. 28). Joachim Moebus has drawn my attention to Ford being in the tradition of the 'Saint Simonian' principle of association. I will not pursue this persuasive comment any further here.

[9] It may have been the mixture of detailed information (Ford not only produced the slogan but also announced in advance the New York addresses of the information offices – 'Wall Street, Broadway and Worth Street, Fourteenth Street, Twenty-third Street, Thirty-fourth Street, Fifty-ninth Street and Harlem') and a Utopian-sounding project that contributed to his proposals not receiving the attention they deserved. In retrospect, the media concept made up of traditional papers for the intelligentsia and what are now databases, journals for target groups and advertising papers seems to have been extraordinarily far-sighted, even visionary, 'too advanced for the

triangle was to be organised in such a way that a particular piece of information (for example, a discovery in chemistry) was to be disseminated to three types of public: 'The Social Rendering, meeting the Interest of the Whole through the News Association'; 'The Special Rendering, meeting the Class Need through the Class News Company', 'The Individual Rendering, meeting the Particular Demand for Information through Fords' (see illustration in Ford n.d. [1892], p. 4). The publication of the newspaper *Thought News – A Journal of Inquiry and a Record of Fact* (the proposed title) was planned as the inauguration of this information revolution. Park, who first wanted to leave the newspaper trade at the beginning of 1892, learnt of this project from Dewey and made a spontaneous decision to take part. What particularly impressed him was the concept of the press as a 'common carrier', a distributor and organiser of knowledge.

In April 1892, *Thought News* was announced as a journal

which shall not discuss philosophical ideas per se but use them as tools in interpreting the movements of thought; which shall treat questions of science, letters, state, school and church as parts of the one moving life of man and hence common interest, and not to relegate them to separate documents of merely technical interest; which shall report new investigations and discoveries in their net outcome instead of in their overloaded gross bulk; which shall note new contributions to thought, whether by book or magazine, from the standpoint of the news in them and not from that of patron or censor. (quoted from Coughlan 1975, p. 102)

Why the project failed is unclear. The first edition of *Thought News* was in fact set, but never printed. It may be that reactions to the public announcement had discouraged Dewey.[10] Nevertheless, the *Thought News* episode had a lasting effect both on Dewey (the resonance clearly comes through in *The Public and Its Problems* (1927)) and on Park. Park not only owed Ford the idea of 'Big News' which, like the idea of sociologists as 'super-reporters', became one of his catch phrases; above all, it was Ford's idea of communication as a cohesive

maturity of those who had the idea in mind', in Dewey's judgement, looking back retrospectively (Feuer 1959, p. 535). It may be the lack of recognition for his visionary ideas that stimulated an intellectual arrogance in Ford which developed features of megalomania. In later years he claimed 'to have done as much work as Darwin, with twice as much remaining to do' (quoted from Burton 1982, p. 12).

[10] The *Detroit Tribune* of 11 April 1892 wrote: 'Just how Mr. Dewey is to report thought no one seems to exactly understand, and Mr. Dewey has not yet explained . . . It is generally understood . . . that Mr. Dewey proposes to get out an "extra" everytime he has a new thought – in that case, the subscribers will be largely dependent upon the stability of Mr. Dewey's digestion for their news' (quoted from Coughlan 1975, p. 104).

principle of society which found expression in Park's theory of news and communication.[11]

The correspondence with and/or orientation toward Dewey's reflections on communication and society is very obvious here. Park's differentiation between physiological and instinctive order, on the one hand, and rational and moral order, on the other (Park 1940b), finds its counterpart in Dewey's differentiation between physical/biological and social/cultural aggregation. Furthermore, the linguistically mediated processes of foresight and empathy, which for Dewey form the basic pillars of community life, are already encompassed in the linking of 'rational and moral'. Foresight as a systematic and intentional process and empathy as the capacity to put oneself in the place of others are, however, two fundamentally different aspects of the human capacity for experience. It is the overemphasis on foresight as planning and the complete neglect of empathy which led Park, in his seminar 'The Press', to his criticism of Ford's model: 'Ford did not take account of what I have called the cultural process; the process by which we get such an understanding of one another, such a common understanding that we can differ, can have public opinion, can discuss' (Classroom plan, 'The Press', 25 February 1921, REP 2:8).

Even if his interest in the *Thought News* process is an expression of criticism of contemporary journalism, it would be a mistake to underestimate the influence of actual journalistic practice on Park's sociological career. Even though his professional activity did have a disillusioning effect because of the limited possibilities it ultimately offered him, the experience, above and beyond what he actually published, can scarcely be overestimated.

Both the *Thought News* project and journalistic practice seem to act like the conveying of systematic knowledge for the purpose of acquiring knowledge from experience. This distinction between 'acquaintance with' and 'knowledge about' is borrowed from William James,[12] though it has a much longer tradition, and plays a central rôle in Park's academic works, his teaching and his biographical self-inquiry. These all

[11] Apart from the various news essays and his essay 'Physics and Society' (1940b), I am thinking here particularly of his 'Reflections on Communications and Culture' from 1938, in which, taking up one of Sapir's reflections, he differentiates between referential and expressive forms of communication (e.g., science/literature). This distinction shows a striking similarity to Mead's differentiation between the informative and the aesthetic functions of the press.

[12] In *The Meaning of Truth* (1975), William James refers back to John Grote ('Exploratio Philosophica', 1865), which in its turn was inspired by Hegel ('Phenomenology of the Spirit', 1807). See also Merton (1972) in the context of a problematic which is stimulating in terms of this study.

reflect Park's way of thinking, the progress from experiences to concepts, a 'learning by experience' which to some extent became his life's programme, as is evident, for example, in the concept of the 'marginal man'.

The philosophy of forms of knowledge, as an abstraction, corresponds to Park's previous experiences; only in this way can the direct use of the distinction in his teaching be adequately assessed. 'Become acquainted with people' as an instruction means going out into the 'field' oneself. 'Acquaintance with' is the knowledge one acquires through experience at first hand, whereas 'knowledge about' means systematic knowledge, that which replaces concrete reality by concepts. For Park, 'acquaintance with' always precedes 'knowledge about': 'It is, in the last analysis, from acquaintance knowledge and nowhere else that we derive the raw materials for our more recondite and sophisticated ideas about things' (Park, 'The Sociological Method', typescript, p. 6; REPA 5:4).

Park was impressed by the number of examples where the social sciences owed some of their most profound insights to persons whose knowledge was based more on a broad and intimate acquaintance with people and their actions than on the methodically structured investigations of a systematic science. In such cases, 'ideas' may emerge from saturated experience. These ideas, Park believes, often give rise to important discoveries in the history of knowledge. As examples of scholars with a great breadth of experience, Park mentions Walter Bagehot, Adam Smith, William Graham Sumner and Georg Simmel:

None of these men, with the possible exception of Simmel, were systematic students of society. They were, however, men whose intellectual interests led them to range widely over the surface of events and to reflect deeply upon the human scene in the various aspects in which it presented itself to them. One might describe them, perhaps, as human naturalists, curious and interested observers of human relations, somewhat as Darwin and the naturalists of the last century were of the interrelations of the lesser organisms. (Park 1950b, p. 304)

The insistence on perception conceals an existential component which is reflected in his turning to journalism. Park finds his field of experience in his journalistic practice, which he understands in retrospect as an apprenticeship.

Since it was the usual practice of the daily press of the period not to identify the authors of articles, Park's journalistic activity would be difficult to reconstruct had not several documents survived that give an impression of its content and the range. Park himself gave an outline of his activity in his 'Newspaper' seminar:

I   Detroit. Going after the Rich. Writing Feature Stories.
II   Denver. Writing hangings and murders for six months.
III New York and the New York Journal. Essex Market Police Court . . .
     Jacob Riis' How the Other Half Lives . . . East Side News; Strunky's.
     Greenwich Village.
IV   Chicago. The Levee.

Another seminar sketch adds: 'Muckraking. Going after the Gamblers (Hunting up the Opium Dens). The New Journalism. The New York World's Crime Stories' (REP 2:8).

In addition to these notes, there is one of Park's scrapbooks[13] (a presentation book typical of the period containing newspaper cuttings) for the years 1893–4, from which we can gather that, besides literature and theatre reviews, Park wrote articles about a state school for the deaf and dumb ('Life in a World of Silence') and a poorhouse ('A City of Paupers'). As has already been indicated in his notes, Park, who was working during the heyday of city-beat reporting, covered the usual repertoire ranging from court reporting to exposure reporting. In 1934, he reported in an interview that he was put on the trail of gambling haunts and opium dens by Bill Brownlee, the chief editor of the *Minneapolis Journal*, where Park spent the first three years of his career as a journalist; in his own words 'This was the beginning of my interest in sociology, although at the time I did not know the word' (Paul J. Baker 1973, p. 254). In the interview, Park describes from memory the way he went about his job:

I got into the opium den with good luck and I had a few pipefuls of the awful stuff. The place was crowded with the riff-raff of the town, and they were talking openly about the gambling house that I wanted to get into. One of them, not knowing who I was, consented to take me to the place. We did get in, but we didn't get very far. One of them who owned the 'establishment' was well known at the police court, and in turn knew every reporter on the beat. He recognized me and you may be sure I was hustled out of the place on the spot. Scared? You can answer that! But I did get the story. (Taub 1934)

This description not only refers to some of the places in which the yellow press carried out its investigations; it is also an indication of the undercover research usual at the time. We shall see later that Park expected something similar from his students: 'This was one of the great thrusts in Chicago, because people had to get out and if they wanted to

---

[13] In the scrapbook, Park marked the unsigned articles he was responsible for with a 'REP', which does not exclude him from having had a hand in the other contributions (as a reporter or rewrite man).

study opium addicts they went to the opium dens and even smoked a little opium maybe' (Cottrell, JTC 1:6).

After his time in Minneapolis, Park worked, amongst other places, in New York (for him the Mecca of every ambitious journalist), where he was employed on the *New York Journal* and the Sunday edition of *New York World*, which suggests that he wrote longer feature stories. During his New York period and in his capacity as a reporter – he had been allocated the Essex Market Police Court as his 'beat' – Park frequently encountered Riis and was constantly being deprived of success ('scooped') by him, as he relates in the interview with the *Michigan Daily*. Forty years after the event, this may be a memory of an unforgettable encounter with a figure who has gone down in history; at the time, the fact that a rival was continually getting the better of him could hardly have been without consequences. The exceptional roughness of the New York newspaper scene (magnificently described by Dreiser 1922), in which rivals competed using both legal and illegal means, in all probability contributed to this phase in the Mecca of journalism being relatively short.

Nevertheless, his New York experience, or rather his experience of New York, seems to have had a formative influence on his later career. New York at the end of the nineteenth century was viewed as a gigantic spectacle and the reporter functioned as its connoisseur at first hand and as intermediary between it and the wider public: 'Walking on upper Broadway on a bright afternoon, or watching the oncoming and outcoming human tide as it poured morning and evening over Brooklyn Bridge, was always for me a thrilling spectacle' (Park, quoted from Matthews 1977, pp. 9ff.).[14] But, to Park, the big city was more than just a spectacle. For him, as for a number of his better-known reporter colleagues, it became a school, a college.[15]

The thing that made New York fascinating to the contemporary observer was not the big city in itself, not quantity, amount or number alone, but rather the variety contained within this quantity, which resulted from the position of New York as a reception area for immigrants from all over the world:

[14] A very similar picture, right down to the style, is to be found in Dreiser (1923, pp. 6ff.).

[15] Talk of the big city as a college was a contemporary stereotype amongst journalists: 'The area of the city in which Riis worked became the school he attended and the library he consulted' (Bigelow 1957, p. ix). Similarly Lincoln Steffens in his autobiography: 'Reporting at police headquarters was like a college education in this, that one had to take several courses altogether. There was the police news, police policies and politics: the Ghetto, with its synagogues, theatres and moral struggles: the strikes; and, on the side, Wall Street. It differed from college in this, that I was interested in each of these courses and could see that they belonged together. They all contributed to the learning of life as it is lived' (1931, p. 231).

one had only to wander casually and not at any great length to come upon the Irish in the Lower East and West Sides; the Syrians in Washington Street . . . the Greeks around 26th, 27th and 28th Streets on the West Side; the Italians around Mulberry Bend; the Bohemians in East 67th Street, and the Sicilians in East 116th Street and thereabouts. (Dreiser 1924, pp. vii ff.)

It is immediately obvious that it is only a short step from the idea of the big city as a college to the view of the big city as a sociological laboratory. On the basis of his apprenticeship in New York and other newspaper locations, Park developed his initial ideas on empirical urban research (illustration 3), as well as developing the first outlines of his conception of the city as a social organism with 'segregated areas' and 'moral regions' (see Park 1950a, p. viii). The constant arrival of new immigrant ethnic groups and the departure of the previous ones for other districts was a clear demonstration of those processes which are expressed in the ecological concepts of invasion and succession. The rapid and observable change unavoidably leads to thinking of the city in terms of process, instead of structure.

It is certain that muckraking journalism made Park sensitive to such themes as political corruption and the 'boss' system in local politics. The possibility that he found his way to urban sociology through Lincoln Steffens' book *The Shame of the Cities* (1969 [1904]), as Faris (1970, p. 28) suggests, can be discounted, for the simple reason that Steffens' exposés, which are supposed to have given Park the impetus to take up his studies again in 1899, only appeared in 1903. Park was not primarily interested in uncovering particular political irregularities, but in the principle of the uncovering itself; a new attitude to social facts is being heralded here. Park was interested in Steffens, above all, because he saw him as representing that intermediate generation, brought up in the spirit of puritanism, which had learnt to distinguish between morals and politics and accept the fact that moral standards are relative (Park 1933, p. 956; see also chapter 4, below). It was this new attitude which made it possible to recognise even the interests of the reformers as self-serving. Park shared this scepticism and even during his time as a reporter he was an impartial observer who took an interest in institutions and forms of life for their own sake.

The tendency to translate what is experienced into generalisable knowledge, in the course of the account, can be demonstrated by a newspaper article about a house for paupers and the mentally ill, dating from 1893, entitled 'A City of Paupers'. The article begins with a description of the landscape in which the asylum is situated. The location is

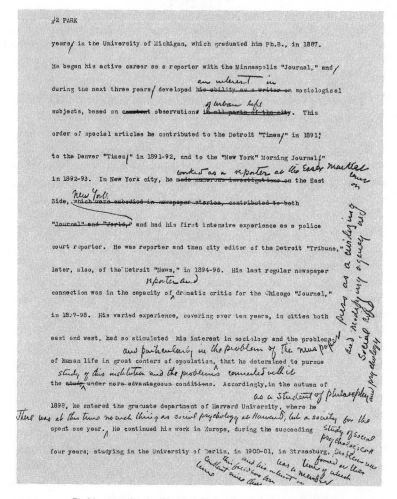

3 Park's entry for the *National Cyclopedia of American Biography*,
with his own handwritten corrections

described in detail in the manner of landscape painting ('The little station is but a dot in the landscape . . .') just as the later sociological monographs begin with a description of place ('Hobohemia', 'Gangland', 'The Shadow of the Skyscraper'). The Wayne County House is depicted as a 'little world all by itself', a sort of 'segregated area', far away from the troubles and burdens of everyday life. Having localised it, Park deals with the institution (the building, its furnishings, economy and administration), introduces the reader to individual inmates (the story of their lives, their fates, their present situations), reports observations and, as far as possible, gives an account of conversations. Just as he later progresses from the ecological to the cultural order, from an inventory of social facts to views and perceptions, so here Park moves from a description of the asylum's surroundings to a portrayal of the inner world of the inmates. The article then concludes:

Strange and incomprehensible is the fate that takes from man the mind that makes him human and leaves him a mere thing, governed by the passions that he knows not the sources of – out of all tune with his fellow men, no longer a social being, but a mere fragment of spiritual force torn from the life of the race to which it belongs and wandering about in indefinite space upon impulses quite its own, no longer a thing governed by the laws of ordinary human life. It is impossible to visit these two asylums, one of the insane who are no longer social beings, and one for the incompetents, the fragments of a defeated race, without perceiving that social disorder, no matter what its form, is a disease, a disease that manifests itself sooner or later in the individual in regularly recognized form. (Park in 1893; REP 8)

The manner of the conclusion is more important here than the conclusion itself. In the rapid jump from 'visiting' the asylum (i.e., acquaintance with) along with a portrayal of the fate of the inmates, to the 'perception' (i.e., knowledge about) that social disorder is a disease which has a visible effect on the individual, there already appears that tendency, which Bowdery, in an analysis of Park's sociological writings, describes as follows: 'Does Park use certain special words or phrases to verbalize generalizations which any thinking, observant individual, with or without sociological knowledge and training, can make for himself? It is my opinion that many of Park's concepts and generalizations are of this nature' (Bowdery 1951, p. 134). In considering this judgement, it must of course be borne in mind that Bowdery's analysis is in a doctoral thesis submitted to the Faculty of Political Science at Columbia University, so that it must consequently be regarded as a document which seeks to promote the position of that establishment. It must be emphasised, however, that Bowdery has touched on a vulnerable aspect of Park's sociology, which is already evident in his journalistic work, that is, his tendency to make rash generalisations from specific observations. This is not an argument against Park's epistemological division of forms of knowledge into 'acquaintance with' and 'knowledge about', into knowledge gained from experience and scientific knowledge, but it does point to the dangers involved in taking this distinction at face value.

'. . . A GOOD WORK AS LIEUTENANT': PARK IN TUSKEGEE

On 18 April 1904, Park wrote to the secretary of the black civil rights activist Booker T. Washington, Emmett Scott, as follows:

Your kind letter received yesterday and I note what you say about the material waiting for the right man to work it up. I hope that I am, as you suggest, the man to do it. I distrust my ability to perform any great original task in the world, but I believe that I can do a good work as lieutenant and have no other ambition except that of doing the best that lies in me under the direction of some first class man. (REPA 3:8)[16]

The resigned tone of the letter betrays more about Park's situation than the motive, mentioned retrospectively, that he had become tired of the academic world. That Park was seriously considering an academic position is clear from the correspondence with H. B. Ward, who tells Park in a letter dated 9 June 1904 that he had tried everything to interest the president of Hamilton College in him (REPA 2:8). The transition from his studies in Germany back to the United States did not take place quite as smoothly as the appointment to the post of assistant lecturer at Harvard, which Park held from the autumn of 1903 to the spring of 1905, suggests. The description 'assistant' is probably a euphemism; the Harvard files reveal that Park did not teach, but supervised students completing their graduation papers and taking examinations in Philosophy 1a; Hugo Münsterberg even accused him of exceeding his authority as well (REP 5:2; REPA 2:3). As he received a relatively low salary ($1,500 annually), Park was forced to supplement his income by working as external editor for the Associated Sunday Magazines. Whether Park wanted to keep a back door open with this job, one he also held on to during his years in Tuskegee, is an open question. In any case, it is clear that it would be wrong to see Park's journalistic activity, in the narrow sense, as being limited to the years 1887 to 1898. Moreover, during 1904–5, he was press agent for the Congo Reform Association, an organisation, with G. Stanley Hall as president, which was set up to combat the autocratic rule of King Leopold of Belgium in the Congo 'Free State'. His task was to educate the public about the situation in Congo; he did this, amongst other things, with three magazine articles,

---

[16] In making this case, Park corresponds exactly to the 'personal character requirements' in the professional make-up of the ghost-writer, 'which can be summed up as the "Eckerman complex"' (Peter 1985, p. 38).

which can be regarded as Park's only muckraking articles in the strict sense of the term.[17]

In 1905, Park finally became press agent and ghost-writer for Booker T. Washington, a position which he held until 1913. Whatever Park may have accomplished during this time, the position itself carried little prestige. This becomes clear indirectly from the fact that the post was at first offered to another black civil rights activist, W. E. B. DuBois, with the explicit assurance that accepting the offer would not mean sinking to the level of a ghost-writer. Internally, however, Park was at first regarded as just that (see Washington 1972–, vol. x (1981), p. 40).

A comparison with biographies of Park written from the sociological viewpoint reveals something of the conceptual retouching which Park later assigned as a theme for student term papers (Raushenbush 1979, p. 188). Whereas in the *Booker T. Washington Papers*, Park is described as a 'ghost-writer', in sociological biographies he is presented as 'secretary' (Odum), 'informal secretary' (Coser) or 'assistant' (Raushenbush). One reason for this conceptual retouching is that ghost-writing has little prestige because it is an anonymous activity; even today, it is considered a 'PR service without any standing' (Peter 1985, p. 33).

Park was very conscious of the low prestige of the official description of his position. In a letter to Washington on 20 July 1907, he said: 'I don't fancy wearing the title of a press agent but as long as you and I understand each other I shan't let that trouble me' (REPA 3:9). Park dealt with some of Washington's correspondence; he wrote speeches for him; he thought up topics which would have an effect on the public; he organised conferences and edited most of Washington's newspaper and book publications in the years between 1905 and 1912. For instance, he put together the two-volume *Story of the Negro* (1909) and conceived *My Larger Education* (1911), the second part of Washington's autobiography. *The Man Farthest Down: A Record of Observation and Study in Europe* (1913), a portrayal in the form of a travel account of the living conditions of the European lower class, deserves special attention. This book, which in the opinion of scholars was written primarily by Park, best reflects Park's journalistic past.

The title *The Man Farthest Down* is borrowed from the magazine series *Following the Color Line*, written by Ray Stannard Baker and first published

---

[17] 'A King in Business: Leopold II of Belgium, Autocrat of the Congo', 'International Brooker: The Terrible Story of the Congo' and 'Blood Money of the Congo', all of which appeared in *Everybody's Magazine* in 1906/7.

in 1907–8 in *American Magazine*, and as a book in 1908 by Doubleday, Page & Co.[18] Park and Baker had a reciprocal influence on each other as far as the 'race question' is concerned. For his series, Baker carried out research in Tuskegee, and Washington made some suggestions as well as giving him a list of interview partners. He corresponded with Park and gave Washington, Park and Scott drafts of his articles to look at. In his portrayal of the situation of coloured people, he placed particular stress on the relationships and conflicts between the races as well as on the situation of people of mixed race; it was precisely these questions which were also Park's main areas of interest in his work on the question of race.[19]

The Man Farthest Down is the result of a journey which Washington and Park went on together, which in eight weeks took them through England, Scotland, Germany, Austria, Hungary, Italy, Sicily, Poland and Denmark. The purpose of this journey was to form a picture of the conditions in which the European lower classes (especially the agricultural labourers and small peasant farmers) lived and to compare them with those of the black population in the United States. In making this comparison, there must have been disagreements between Washington and Park, since the civil rights activist was inclined to use the European lower class merely as a negative for the black population. Park accused Washington of not being at all interested in the people, of not really being curious (Harlan 1983, p. 292). The reproach is of interest to the extent that Washington's biographer Mathews deduces Washington's insatiable curiosity from reading the book (Mathews 1949, pp. 26off.). But the attitude which he attributes (because of the need to use the first person singular in the book) to Washington ('I find markets more instructive than museums') actually corresponds entirely to Park's usual approach. It can be assumed that the scenes in the book, where, according to Mathews, there is an expression of indefatigable joy in the

---

[18] The book edition was reviewed in the *American Journal of Sociology*. The review says, among other things: 'This is a study of the Negro problem remarkable for its objectivity and psychological insight. While a product of the higher type of modern journalism, it approaches the character of a scientific work in the painstaking carefulness of its investigations and in its accurate presentation of facts; and in the value of its interpretations it often indeed surpasses, in the opinion of the reviewer, many professedly scientific treatises' (Ellwood 1909).

[19] *Following the Color Line* was included in the Park/Burgess Reader (Park and Burgess 1924 [1921]) as recommended reading. In the section written by Park, entitled 'Race Conflicts', it says: 'Most of all that has been written [about the race conflict], however, is superficial. Much is merely sentimental, interesting for the attitudes it exhibits, but otherwise adding nothing to our knowledge of the facts. The best account of the American situation is undoubtedly Ray Stannard Baker's *Following the Color Line*' (Park and Burgess 1924 [1921], p. 646). For an analysis of the situation of the mulattos, see chapter 8, 'The Mulatto: The Problem of Race Mixture' in the reprint of the book version (1964, pp. 151–74).

observation of simple people (the description of market scenes in Catania, the portrayal of story-tellers and balladeers, the account of the lottery in Naples and others of a similar nature), are actually based on Park's observations.

The structure of the book reflects the journalistic genre of an article series, and in fact this report did first appear in series form in the magazine *Outlook* (1911); at the same time it shows formal similarities to the sociological plans of investigation which Park developed later in his teaching.

The importance which Park attached to this work, possibly also as a vehicle for a change of profession, can be seen from a letter he wrote to Washington on 26 April 1911, in which he insists on being named as co-author:

It seems to me the best thing to do would be to put my name on the book as a joint author. In case that is done, a statement could be made in the preface or in the introduction as to what my part in the book was. In case that is done I should not like to be represented as a professional writer who had helped you to put together the book. Rather I should like it to appear that I had been working at Tuskegee, interested in the school as others who are employed here. I would not want to [be] represented as engaged in any philanthropy or 'unselfish' work. (Washington 1972–, vol. II (1981), pp. 116ff.)

From this letter, which Washington completely complied with,[20] it is clear that Park was afraid of appearing as a hired hack. In fact he was very much more than a paid writer. He gave lectures at the Tuskegee Institute and made speeches to audiences of prospective patrons, he organised conferences and he used his stay in Tuskegee and the many journeys he made on behalf of Washington to the southern states to do an intensive examination of the issue of race. As with his period as a reporter, Park saw his time in Tuskegee not just as a professional activity but also as an opportunity for study in the sense of 'acquaintance with' (REPA 3:10; Raushenbush 1979, pp. 49ff.). During his travels he made notes about the country and the people, he spoke with officials and, in his notebook, he recorded the life stories of hundreds of black people.

In the spring of 1912, Park, in the name of Washington, invited William Isaac Thomas to take part in the International Conference on the Negro in Tuskegee (19 April 1912). Since this letter referred

---

[20] The author attribution reads: 'by Booker T. Washington' (in a 12-point fount) 'with the collaboration of Robert E. Park' (apart from the capitals, in a 6-point fount). On pp. 14–17 of the first chapter, 'Hunting [sic] the man farthest down', Washington emphasises the contribution which Park made to the book.

knowledgeably to Thomas' publications, the latter accepted the invitation, only to discover that the letter did not come from Washington himself at all, but from Park: 'This was the beginning of a long and profitable association' (Thomas, quoted from Raushenbush 1979, p. 68). Just four days after the conference, Thomas wrote an enthusiastic letter to Park, and in a further letter dated 6 May 1912, he says:

It has been the greatest thing that ever happened to me to meet you, and if we can pull this thing off, as we are going to, and eventually get together here and teach alongside, it will make life interesting . . . I have told Small of this thing. He said right off that he got a very fine impression of you. He is a very fine fellow, and will do almost anything I say within his power. It would strengthen our department greatly to have you here. We ought both to have a six months teaching arrangement, as I have now, and could go into the field then together half the time. (REPA 2:7)

In the autumn of 1913, Park received an invitation to join the sociology department of the University of Chicago as lecturer in racial affairs. The first course which Park delivered was entitled 'The Negro in America', with particular reference to race relations and racial conflicts.

Just as important, from the point of view of the history of sociology, is the fact that it was the experience of Tuskegee and the work with Washington that inspired Park to formulate the concept of the 'marginal man'. No other concept of his has had such a lasting effect. It appears for the first time in an undated note, probably written in the early 1910s: 'The Marginal Man: a study of the Mulatto Mind' (illustration 4). This concept, transferred to phenomena of social and spatial mobility, was later to become a significant heuristic principle for the investigation of socio-cultural marginality.

In the autumn of 1913 ended one of the longest apprenticeships ever completed by a scholar:

As a reporter I had learned a good deal about the city and I had used my position as a city and Sunday editor to make systematic studies on the urban community. During my connection with Booker T. Washington and Tuskegee, I had learned a great deal about the Negro. It was from these two sources mainly that graduate students found material for the researches which I directed after I went to Chicago. (Park, quoted from Odum 1951, p. 132)

THE BIG CITY AS *PARS PRO TOTO* FOR SOCIETY

The conception of the big city, not only as a geographical phenomenon, but also as a form of social organism, is given programmatic expression

4 Park's original manuscript jottings for *The Marginal Man: a study of the Mulatto Mind*

in Park's essay 'The City: Suggestions for the Investigation of Human Behavior in the City Environment'. In Shils' view, this essay, first published in the *American Journal of Sociology* in 1915[21] and described by Everett C. Hughes as a kind of inaugural lecture, is the source of the main principles which have influenced American urban sociology (Shils 1948, p. 9).

Before I go into the value this essay has, as both a source of ideas and a research agenda for urban sociology of the Chicago type, I would like first of all to examine its theoretical status. What is striking is the complete absence of the perspective based on ecological theory which became the trademark of Chicago urban sociology. In the first version of the essay, the concepts 'ecology', 'ecological' and 'human ecology' do not occur at all; thus, the whole conceptual apparatus adopted from the plant and animal ecology ('dominance', 'invasion', 'succession', etc.) is also missing. This does not mean that ecological processes are not considered, however. In the emphasis on the formation of areas segregated according to profession and ethnic membership (the concept of 'segregated area' precedes that of 'natural area' in the history of ideas, although neither term was yet being used), there is reference to the segregation of housing districts according to the price of land. This explanation is, however, much closer to observation than the developed ecology approach based on human ecology, as well as being founded on experience. The territorial structuring of the city, based on the specific distribution and segregation of business and administrative centres, job and population groups, had already been taken into account in the journalistic system of 'assignments/beats'. As a reporter, being assigned 'Broadway', 'Wall Street' or 'the Bowery', does not of course mean only being responsible for the theatre, the financial world or social welfare issues, rather that the assignment is based also on a quasi-ecological idea of the functional differentiation of the urban space. It was his knowledge, based on experience ('acquaintance with') of spatial differentiation, which made Park interested in human geography and human ecology. It can be assumed that Park became aware of Ratzel's

---

[21] The article was reprinted in 1925 in a revised form in the collection *The City* by Park, Burgess and McKenzie. Park had replaced 'City Environment' in the title with 'Urban Environment', undoubtedly a more sociological concept, one which implies the rural/urban antithesis. This subsequent change is not noticed by most authors, an indication that they have failed to compare the two versions. See, amongst others, Bell and Newby 1971, p. 92; Bulmer 1984, p. 246, n 3; Robert Burgess 1982, p. 23; Faris 1970, p. 52; Frazier and Gaziano 1979, p. 8; Goist 1971, p. 48; Hannerz 1980, p. 23; Everett C. Hughes 1971, p. 546; Madge 1963, p. 89; Oberschall 1972, p. 237; Raushenbush 1979, p. 79; Stein 1960, p. 15.

anthropological geography during his time as a student in Germany. In the summer term of 1903, Park attended Hettner's 'Geographical Exercises' course in Heidelberg, which suggests that he participated in map-making and field observation. During the 1920s the most important influences on Park in this respect were the French human geographers J. Vidal de la Blache and Jean Brunhes. The English translations of their works were reviewed by Park in the *American Journal of Sociology* (vols. 26 and 32 respectively).

Some initial elements of an approach based on a notion of human ecology are to be found in the Park/Burgess Reader, where there is an article by the plant physiologist Frederic E. Clements, who, next to Eugenius Warming, was the greatest influence on the development of human ecology. The Chicago sociologists owe the central concepts of 'invasion' and 'succession' to Clements; they also find in Clements' work the category of 'natural area', which takes the place of the concept of 'segregated area', which remained closer to observation.

In Park's view, ecology is a substratum of sociological analysis proper, both empirically as well as theoretically. It does not yet constitute an independent discipline, as was the case later. Theoretically, Park assumes a hierarchical model of human relationships – of an ecological, economic, political and moral (or cultural) order – to which distinct human and social sciences correspond: (1) human geography and human ecology, (2) economics, (3) political science and (4) social anthropology and sociology. Human ecology is about the basic processes of human co-existence (they are often erroneously termed 'sub-social' or 'pre-social') in a constantly changing environment characterised by limited resources. Park asks whether a functional mesh or matrix of interrelationships exists underneath what we term society (which for him, following Dewey, is constituted in and by communication). He finds such a matrix in the community which he defines as (sym)biotic or ecological, drawing an analogy with the world of plants and animals. This community is the result of interactions arising from the struggle for existence and the preservation of the species. In order to relate these interactions to the biological substructure, Park speaks of 'inter-stimulation', as opposed to interaction.

The distinction between the biotic substructure resulting from the struggle for survival and the cultural superstructure, which evolves in and through communication, is of fundamental importance to Park's social ecology. The ecological ('biotic') order forms the bedrock of what sociologists should actually be investigating, namely an edifice of customs and convictions, practices and traditions created by communication and interaction, in short, culture, that which distinguishes human society from plant and animal communities.[22]

The social and spatial structuring of the city is a result of competition for material and spatial resources which are in short supply. Hence, the technique of cartographic representation, which corresponds to the ecological distribution model – i.e., taking graphical stock of the spatial distribution of the characteristics and phenomena in question – enables us to construct a backdrop, a scenario, a stage on which the scenes that are actually of sociological interest unfold. This becomes clear when we look, for instance, at Thrasher's map of 'Chicago's Gangland', at Anderson's map of the institutions in 'Hobohemia' or at Cressey's map of the position of the dance-halls in Chicago. By means of these maps, the reader is informed about the situation and distribution of those phenomena within the confines of the city that are the object of sociological analysis. How close to observation Park remained in his illustrations can be seen from an example from his teaching, where he illustrated the process of segregation by taking a street in New York almost exclusively inhabited by revue girls as an example: 'On a bright afternoon it was a regular sunset of blond heads. In those days all chorus girls – almost all chorus girls – were blondes' (REP 8:21). This is a particularly good example of William O. Brown's assessment that Park 'was a master of the insight-giving story and anecdote' (REPA 6:6).

It should, of course, be remembered that the technique of cartographical representation (mapping) which became a trademark of Chicago urban sociology was not at all new; having been borrowed from epidemiology (see Frentzel-Beyme 1985),[23] it was already familiar in the field of social surveys. The 'Descriptive Maps of London Poverty' in Charles Booth's work *Life and Labour of the People in London* (1902–3), which Park gave as recommended reading for his 'Social Survey' course (along with works by Mayhew, Riis and Woods, amongst others) bear eloquent testimony to this. In his introduction to the volume containing selected works of Booth, in the 'Heritage of Sociology' series, Pfautz (1967) traces the ecological line of argumentation in Booth's work, up to and including the pioneering theory of concentric circles (Booth: 'rings') as well as

---

[22] 'Ecology was to Park a way of getting an underpinning for sociology in the narrower sense of interaction of people through their sentiments' (E. C. Hughes to W. Raushenbush, 20 July 1968; REP 7:7).

[23] The fact that this technique was also used in journalism can be shown by the example of Park, who as a journalist used 'spot maps' to discover the hot spot of a diphtheria epidemic.

considerations with respect to the process of succession (Booth: 'general law of successive migration'). It was through the agency of Jane Addams that this research perspective entered into Chicago thought. It is difficult to disagree with Anne Firor Scott (1967) when she insists that the staff of Hull-House Settlement were already carrying out ecological investigations into individual Chicago housing areas in the early 1890s, thereby paving the way for investigations at the Department of Sociology (see also Fish 1985; Deegan 1988). We must not forget, of course, that Burgess and Park themselves draw attention to this legacy (Ernest W. Burgess 1916; Park 1929a). The *Hull-House Maps and Papers* ('A Presentation of Nationalities and Wages in a Congested District of Chicago', 1970 [1895]) state that: 'The great interest and significance attached to Mr. Charles Booth's maps of London have served as warm encouragement.' The United States Department of Labor questionnaire on housing and living conditions (*Social Statistics of Cities*) dates in methodological terms at least back to the ones used by the Statistical Societies in Manchester (1833) and London (1834). This questionnaire was used as a basis for ground plans or area maps, exemplifying the ethnic mix of the district in the immediate vicinity of the settlement between Halsted Street in the west, State Street in the east, Polk Street in the north and Twelfth Street in the south, as well as illustrating the economic situation of the inhabitants (measured in terms of their wage levels). Mary Jo Deegan sees 'academic dishonesty' in the inadequate recognition of prior research on the part of the Chicago sociologists: 'Not only was this methodological technique first used in Chicago with *Hull-House Maps and Papers*, but Hull-House residents openly continued this tradition and practice' (Deegan 1988, p. 46).[24]

It is true to say that a number of students of sociology were among the residents; as far as they were concerned, the settlement was not only a place of social activity but also something resembling a sociological laboratory. Owing to this close link, mapping was included in the sociological researcher's tool-kit from an early date. In 1901, for example, Charles J. Bushnell compiled a doctoral thesis, published in the *American Journal of Sociology*, on the Chicago stockyards ('Study of the Stock Yard

[24] In her zeal, i.e., her diligence just as much as her vehemence, to rehabilitate the '"female" Chicago School of sociology', represented by Jane Addams, Edith Abbott, Sophonisba Breckinridge, Florence Kelley and others, from the point of view of the history of science, Deegan gets caught up in contradictions. The unnecessary virulence in her argumentation, with particular reference to Park's character, results in her arguments ultimately losing their persuasive power; this is all the more regrettable since the topics she covers fill a significant gap in the history of sociology.

Community at Chicago. As a Typical Example of the Bearing of the
Modern Industry Upon Democracy, With Constructive Suggestions';
published as 'Some Social Aspects of the Chicago Stock Yards', 1901/2),
complete with socio-statistical data and overview maps. The factors that
are illustrated graphically with the help of the city map (the geographical correlation between foreign population and child deaths; between
public establishments, such as churches, clubs and philanthropic institutions, and criminality; as well as others) shed light on the practical viewpoint from which the surveys were carried out. Bushnell's investigation
results logically in 'constructive suggestions' ('What the City
Government May Do'; 'What the Charities and Philanthropies May
Do'; 'What the Clubs and Settlements May Do'; etc.).

This practical thrust is also characteristic of the large-scale investigation into housing conditions in Chicago, directed by Sophonisba
Breckinridge and Edith Abbott, which appeared as a series of ten articles in the *American Journal of Sociology* (1910–15). Here, too, the maps serve
to point out (potential) danger spots: 'The red lines show the districts in
which vice is segregated and tolerated on the South and West Sides.' The
article on 'Families in Furnished Rooms' focuses on the question of the
effect housing conditions have on family life, 'through the lack of privacy
and dignity and the general irresponsibility of their mode of life'
(Breckinridge and Abbott 1910, p. 294).[25] The fact that life in furnished
rooms and families taking in boarders could come about as a result of
perfectly reasonable and family-orientated considerations, particularly
as far as immigrant families were concerned, was one which 'was often
completely unintelligible to social reformers', as Weidner shows, with
particular regard to Edith Abbott's work (Weidner 1990, p. 9).

As the *Hull-House Maps and Papers* expressly state, the primary concern
is to find a means of improving society ('constructive work'), and not to
make a contribution to sociology; today we might possibly call this
'action research'. As we shall see, rudiments (and occasionally, as shown
by Zorbaugh's spot maps, more than that) of this approach are still
present in the Chicago monographs, but in general it can be said that
those concerned are not content with mapping as a satisfactory way of
taking stock of and representing social facts: it is not the end point, but

---

[25] The excessive use of attributes to characterise problem families ('people of loose habits'; 'spend-
thrift, dissolute habits', 'shiftless families') is a sign that this study, at least as far as the categories
are concerned, is still in the tradition of the investigations carried out by the Charity
Organization Society (COS) which discriminated between welfare applicants (deserving/unde-
serving poor). For more about 'COS and the deformation of the gift', see Stedman Jones 1976.

rather the starting point, of sociological analysis. This is the basis for the distinction in Pauline Young's book (1939) between social survey and social research and forms the organisational principle underlying the methodology she puts forward there.

She interprets social survey to mean drawing up an account of social life, and social research to mean an investigation of values, norms, situations and processes. Mapping imparts information concerning the anatomy of the area studied ('base map') and the distribution of the phenomena of interest within that space ('spot map'); the actual activity of sociological investigation commences from this basis. The mention of the word 'stage' in this connection is deliberate. Park's ideas come very much closer to the literary procedure of introducing the sphere of action than to a social ecology which, in the final analysis, uses tautological arguments and at the same time sees its rhyme and reason as being in the existence in space of socio-pathological manifestations. The image of the stage makes sense in yet another respect: the physical factors, far from being ineffective, form both the foundation as well as the sounding-board of socio-cultural life.

As far as research into space is concerned, Park does differ from Burgess, a fact which up until now has been given too little attention. Overstating it, Burgess can be termed a 'social epidemiologist' in the sense of the Greek *epidemios*, while Park can be seen as a 'field researcher'. This is based on their differing models of 'field' assimilation – 'administration' vs 'reconnaissance' – and their differing models of professional orientation: the 'engineering' model, on the one hand, as opposed to the 'enlightenment' model on the other. Morris Janowitz, who first made this differentiation, emphasises that Burgess and Wirth were the two researchers in Chicago committed most strongly to the 'engineering' model, whereas Park was its most outspoken critic (Janowitz 1972, p. 117). This difference becomes glaringly obvious when we look at Park's introductions to the monographs and the summaries provided by Burgess.

Not only can different lines of Chicago sociology tradition be traced here (Henderson → Burgess; Thomas → Park), but I am also of the opinion that these differences reflect Burgess' and Park's different careers: put as ideal types, the one was a 'reformer' figure, and the other a 'reporter' figure. I will be going into more detail about this distinction, which seems to me to be the key to understanding Chicago sociology, in the second part of this book.

The reference to a difference of opinion with respect both to how they accessed the field and to their professional orientation should not be misunderstood as implying there was any animosity between Burgess and Park. Park and Burgess complemented each other in an ideal way, as far as the institutionalisation and implementation of the Chicago experiment are concerned. It was precisely that mixture of reconnaissance and administration, of 'enlightenment' and 'engineering', which enabled Chicago sociology in the 1920s to assert itself and give itself a stable organisational form. Seen in the context of the history of institutions, Burgess and Park formed a tandem similar to that of Lazarsfeld and Merton at the Bureau of Applied Social Sciences at Columbia.[26]

If we consider that the perspective based on human ecology in 'The City' of 1915 was primarily a product of observation and not of theoretical processing, then another influence emerges throughout the whole text, an influence not evident in the references, namely that of Georg Simmel. Donald N. Levine has drawn attention to Simmel's effect on American sociology on several occasions (Levine, Carter and Gorman 1976, 1981; Levine 1984). It is hardly surprising that such an influence existed, if we remember that Simmel's thought found its way into American sociology at a very early date. As early as 1895, just a year after their first publication in the *Jahrbuch für Gesetzgebung, Verwaltung und Volkswirtschaft* [Legislation, administration and national economy yearbook], Simmel's fundamental statements on the 'Problem of Sociology' were available in translation, in the *Annals of the American Academy of Political and Social Science*. Simmel is regularly represented in the *American Journal of Sociology*, published by the sociology department of the University of Chicago, from the second year of its publication (1896) through to the sixteenth. Material which was published includes large parts of his 'Sociology' (1983 [1908]; chapters 2, 3, 4, 5 and 8, as well as chapter 1 in a version annotated by Small) as well as extracts from his 'Philosophie des Geldes' [Philosophy of money].

In spite of this, Levine maintains that Simmel's rôle in American sociology might well have been forgotten had it not been for Robert Park (Levine 1971, p. xlix). Park not only played a significant part in introducing Simmel to a wider audience by incorporating selected passages from his works (including the first American publications of, for example, his excursus on 'The Stranger') in the Park/Burgess Reader,[27] thus bringing Simmel's thought to the attention of several generations of

---

[26] On the importance of combinations of persons in understanding the reality of institutions, see Lepenies 1981.

[27] Simmel is represented in the Reader by ten reading selections.

American students; in addition, by throwing his weight behind the publication of Nicholas Spykman's *The Social Theory of Georg Simmel* (1964 [1925]), he promoted the discussion of Simmel's work.[28]

To a certain extent, we can see this intervention as an act of gratitude, since Park, in his reply to a question asked by C. C. Bernard in 1927, confessed that 'with the exception of Simmel's lectures I never had any systematic introduction in sociology' (Paul J. Baker 1973, p. 257). The influence of these lectures, which he compiled during the winter term of 1899 and published in 1931 (in German),[29] thus becomes all the more evident.

Without this being made obvious by references, various of Simmel's main notions are in evidence throughout 'The City'. Indeed, the essay can be taken as an example of Levine's assertion that Park found in Simmel a fundamental form of thinking about society, which in American sociology has led to Park and Simmel up to a point being mentioned in the same breath.[30]

Now what does this kind of thinking about society consist of? In his search for a separate and new object, the investigation of which would make sociology a science in its own right, Simmel rejected both the contemporary ideas of society as a real entity on the one hand and as a mere abstraction on the other. He came up with the notion of society *sensu strictissimo*, which exists where several individuals interact:

This interaction always arises on the basis of certain drives or for the sake of certain purposes. Erotic, religious or merely associative impulses; and purposes of defence, attack, play, gain, aid or instruction – these and countless others, cause man to live with other men, to act for them, with them, against them and thus to correlate his condition with theirs. In brief, he influences and is influenced by them. The significance of these interactions among men lies in the fact that it is because of them that individuals, in whom these driving impulses and purposes are lodged, form a unity, that is society. (Simmel 1983 [1908], p. 4; translation by Wolff 1959)

Human beings, who co-exist in space, follow each other in time and pursue their respective interests, interact in clearly defined, identifiable

[28] In a letter to Gordon Lang of the University of Chicago Press, in which he made the case for Spykman's study, Park stressed that Simmel: 'has written . . . the most profound and stimulating book in sociology . . . that has ever been written': letter written on 8 July 1924 (REPA 2:1).

[29] 'The sociological lectures of Georg Simmel. Given at the University of Berlin in the winter term of 1899 (Society for Social Research, Series 1, Number 1). Containing: Origin of sociological research. Extent of sociology. Definition of the task of sociology. First topic: The self-preservation of society. Second topic: Precedence and subordination.'

[30] The citation tables which Levine and others have compiled from selected textbooks can be regarded as an indication of this. In both textbooks in which Park leads the rankings, Simmel is also mentioned relatively the most frequently (Levine, Carter and Gorman 1981, p. 75).

ways. The product of these interactions is society: 'If, therefore, there is to be a science whose subject matter is society and nothing else, then it must exclusively investigate these interactions, these kinds and forms of sociation' (Simmel 1983 [1908], p. 6; translation by Wolff 1959).

Park followed formal sociology both in his dissertation as well as in the selection and classification of his material for the Park/Burgess Reader, *Introduction to the Science of Sociology* (1924 [1921]). 'Mass' and 'public' can be construed as two forms of sociation, which come about when a large number of persons interact. Nowhere else in his work does Park seem to be closer to the sociology of pure forms than in his dissertation (Levine 1972). But also the four types of interaction which Park believes are most important – competition, conflict, accommodation and assimilation – and to which he gives pride of place in his *Introduction*, can be read as forms of sociation in Simmel's sense, just as the bringing together of the material under the umbrella of abstract concepts (the most elementary scholarly form) corresponds quite precisely to formal sociology.

It is not so much the concept of the *form* of the interaction, rather the concept of *interaction* itself which is the guiding principle of Park's sociology and it is borrowed from Simmel. In a notebook dating from the years 1929–30 Park jotted down those basic concepts, together with their originators and/or advocates, which were in his opinion sociologically relevant. This collection is an excellent example of Park's eclecticism, but put positively, it is also an example of the degree to which, for him, concepts functioned as tools; moreover, it can be used to reconstruct the scholarly influences (on Park) with a clarity otherwise rarely encountered. Amongst those quoted are Comte and Spencer ('social organism'), Durkheim ('collective representation'), Ross ('social control'), Thomas ('attitude'), Sumner ('mores') and Dewey ('communication'). Simmel is represented in this list by two concepts, those of 'interaction' and 'social distance' (REPA 4:7). In the view of Levine and others, these concepts are the ones which form the nucleus of Park's appropriation of Simmel, as is evident in the Park/Burgess Reader:

a concern with distance as the key dimension of society and with specific forms of interaction as they appear in varying circumstances. (Levine, Carter and Gorman 1981, p. 48)

But, at the same time, the differences between the two men emerge in the way in which Park manipulates these concepts. In Simmel's view, proximity and distance are essential elements of any form of sociation, where distance may be conducive to nearness, while nearness may be prejudicial to distance (exemplified by acquaintances made while travelling on the one hand and by the figure of one's neighbour on the other), so that people can be near to and far from each other at one and the same time. Park, by contrast, is more concerned with the common features created by interaction, which through the medium of communication overcomes both social and spatial distances. Even when both Simmel and Park answer the question, 'How is society possible?' in the same way, namely 'by processes of interaction', they differ from each other to the extent that Simmel is content with this answer as such, whereas Park emphasises commonly shared action as an ideal. Sociology is meant to uncover the conditions which induce individuals to corporative existence; these include the processes of communication, by means of which individuals who are in the process of interacting with each other reach a consensus.

Park goes along with Simmel to the extent that he thinks of society in terms of the category of process instead of the category of structure. In this respect he shows himself to be more 'in tune' with Simmel than does Albion Small, who in his commentaries on Simmel's 'The Problem of Sociology' (1909) takes up the concept of 'form', which he then contrasts with the concept of 'process'. However, to Simmel's way of thinking, 'form' means nothing more than a momentary pin-pointing of processes; Simmel records processes by abstracting them from their specific contents and describing them as processes in pure form. In Park's view, society, as he said in one of his seminars, might 'be visualized as like a table, which was only a complex of atoms in motion' (Matthews 1977, p. 134). This is an image which brings to mind Simmel's idea of 'microscopic-molecular processes within human material', those 'interactions among the atoms of society', which 'explain all the toughness and elasticity, all the colourfulness and consistency of social life, which is so striking and yet so mysterious' (Simmel 1983 [1908], p. 15; translation by Wolff 1959).

The differences in sociological perspective, mentioned in passing, emerge with exceptional clarity if Simmel's essay 'Die Großstädte und das Geistesleben' [The metropolis and mental life] (1957 [1903]) is compared with Park's programmatic article. These differences are apparent even in the titles: 'Mental Life' versus 'Investigations of Human Behaviour'. Simmel sees the big city as one of those products of modern life which raise the question of the adaptations made by the personality 'in its adjustment to the forces that lie outside of it' (Simmel 1957 [1903], p. 227). There are two reasons for the big city causing adaptations: first of all there is the difficulty 'of giving one's own personality a certain status within the framework of metropolitan life' (Simmel 1957 [1903], p. 239) and secondly, the city is characterised by the preponderance of what can be called the objective spirit or objective culture. Both of them suggest, as a form of resistance and a means of personal self-preservation, a drive toward the development of emphatic individuality or even 'exaggerated subjectivism'.

Simmel saw the big city as an example *sui generis* of a development in which relationships are objectified owing to the dissolution of traditional bonds and where social levelling occurs as a product of individualisation; this ambivalence is in his view the hallmark of modern life. Park follows Simmel in understanding the big city not only in the context of alienation, as was usual amongst his contemporaries, but also in the context of emancipation; indeed, he sees alienation as a crisis which at the end of the day proves to be fruitful. It is thus a grave misunderstanding to ascribe Park as belonging to the anti-big city wing of the American intelligentsia (White and White 1964). On the contrary, with his reflections as regards the big city – as Goist (1971) convincingly shows – Park was one of the first not to think in terms of the antithesis of community (rural) and society (urban). Park sees big cities, precisely because they are destroyers of tradition, as laboratories of modern subjectivity.

In the dialectics of disintegration and liberation, which form the dynamics of the big city, we can detect Simmel's thinking. But whereas Simmel's reflections have little to do with empirical research and nothing to do with the resolution of practical problems, the special sort or exceptional type (of person) who evolves as a contrast to the general levelling is seen by Park as providing one reason why the big city is especially suitable as a sociological laboratory for the study of human behaviour. Closely bound up with this is Simmel's view, which Park shares, that the citizen of the metropolis 'is "free", in contrast with the trivialities and prejudices which bind the small town dweller' (Simmel 1957 [1903], p. 237; translation by Edward A. Shils). In the extravaganzas which are specific to the big city, both the possibility and necessity of individualisation within the metropolis come together as if in a condenser lens. However, the 'strangest eccentricities' which are to be encountered in the big city are, in Simmel's view, only exaggerated illustrations serving to show that the big cities 'thereby attain a quite unique place, fruitful with an inexhaustible richness of meaning in the development of the mental life' (Simmel 1957 [1903], p. 242; translation by Edward A. Shils).

Park reads Simmel's historico-philosophical reflections in a naively empirical manner. That is precisely why, in his view, the big city, which in the dialectics of disintegration and liberation facilitates freedom from prejudices and enables the formation of a exceptional type of individual, becomes the ideal place to carry out sociological research; it is a place where human behaviour and social processes can be studied *in situ* and *in the making*.

Because of the opportunity it offers, particularly to the exceptional and abnormal types of man, a great city tends to spread out and lay bare to the public view in a massive manner all the characters and traits which are ordinarily obscured and suppressed in smaller communities. The city, in short, shows the good and evil in human nature in excess. It is this fact, more than any other, which justifies the view that would make of the city a laboratory or clinic in which human nature and social processes may be most conveniently and profitably studied. (Park 1915, p. 612)

In the final analysis, Simmel's sociological discussions culminate in cultural and philosophical reflections on the fate of the personality in the modern world, which he was only able to countenance in terms of its being cultivated, i.e., including the objective structures in its own process of perfection. By contrast, Park is concerned with diagnosing social processes on the basis of empirical data, processes which give the individual greater structural scope and thus open up a field of possibilities which does not exist in small communities. In his view, the big city is a 'human laboratory' that not only releases aspects of human nature which would otherwise remain suppressed, remoulding both the character and essence of the human being, but also brings forth completely new 'varieties'. Simmel's covert agenda is dissociation, while Park's is heterogeneity. This difference emerges overtly in the way the consequences of the growing trend toward a division of labour are evaluated. Whereas Simmel fears a crippling of personality as a whole, Park sees an opportunity for individuals released from the constraints of tradition to find a place in society which corresponds to their temperament, talents and ambitions and, thus, to make a contribution to the common good. This difference is made clear by the different ways in which they emphasise or handle empirical data. Whereas Simmel tends to rummage through his stocks of knowledge to find a suitable anecdote in order to illustrate an abstract point,[31] Park attributes a greater value in sociological cognition

[31] For instance, Simmel illustrates his idea that cities are places where the highest level of economic division of labour is to be found, by using the example of the *quatorzième*, i.e., the person who makes a living from taking part in functions to which thirteen guests have been invited.

to direct observation, to recording life stories and to reading autobiographies (e.g., of immigrants). In essence Simmel is not curious about
things new, whereas Park certainly is.

Park is indebted to Simmel for a theoretical schema which enables
him to classify and categorise the problems he is concerned with. In
terms of perspective, however, the two have different ideas. Simmel
represents the German approach to sociology, one which brings
philosophical arguments to bear, whereas Park stands for the American
brand of sociology which proceeds empirically: a 'Simmel
Americanized' (Cahnmann).

In Norman Hayner's study 'Hotel Life and Personality' (1928), which
presents findings from his doctoral thesis (it was published, under the title
Hotel Life, only in 1936), one can clearly see, almost line for line, the influence of Simmel's 'Die Großstädte und das Geistesleben' [The metropolis and mental life], which serves as the theoretical framework for
Hayner's empirical data.[32] After introducing, in the first paragraph of
his treatise, statistics and census data relating to the number and location
of the hotels as well as to the hotel population, Hayner in the two subsequent sections ('Characteristics of Hotel Life' and 'Personality
Patterns in the Hotel Environment') goes into detail about the peculiarities of life in hotels and their effect on the person of the hotel guest. In
Hayner's study, the hotel is a micro-cosmos (and thus at the same time, a
social laboratory), in which all those peculiarities and idiosyncrasies
which characterise the big city and the big city dweller resurface.
Throughout large parts of the study, we could easily replace the terms
'hotel' and 'hotel guest' by 'big city' and 'big city dweller'. This is not to
say that the analysis of hotel life is wrong; on the contrary, the hotel guest
can be perceived with some justice as the ideal type of *homo urbanus*.
Nevertheless, what does give rise to some unease is the way in which
Hayner transplants Simmel's reflections concerning the spiritual
manifestations of the big city, seen by Simmel as reflexes of the 'all-per-
vasive money-based economy', on to the empirical object 'hotel life'.

Hayner interprets the hotel as an anonymous location, in which the
relationships between landlord and guest, in contrast to the personal
relationships in the taverns of earlier times, are de-personalised, more
matter-of-fact and indifferent. Indifference also characterises the relationships between the hotel guests themselves; physical proximity in the

---

[32] The first official translation of this essay was produced in 1936 by Edward A. Shils, under the title
'The Metropolis and Mental Life', but Hayner had prepared a translation for his own purposes at
the beginning of the 1920s (JTC 1:9).

hotel goes hand in hand with social distance. But the anonymity which is characteristic of hotel life also makes possible a high degree of personal freedom. Free of the constraints which predominate in small and intimate circles, the hotel dweller is able to follow his own impulses, a tendency which Hayner illustrates by the example of the prohibitionist who was found drunk in the hotel.[33]

Over time, the hotel guest develops a style of his own. He becomes either blasé or cosmopolitan and he feigns indifference ('blank faces') in the face of the multitude of different impressions so as to protect himself against them by withdrawing into himself. In conclusion, Hayner makes a distinction between four different personality patterns which, with Simmel, we can understand as being specific emanations of the personality, by means of which it comes to terms with forces external to itself, namely: restlessness, i.e., the difficulty or incapacity to adjust to the anonymous and impersonal atmosphere in the hotel; individuation, i.e., the free play of impulses freed of constraints; a blasé attitude, as a defensive reaction against the irritations and emotions which are part and parcel of hotel life; and finally, refinement or 'behaving as a man of the world', as a way of immunising oneself against the influences of the hotel milieu.

In his introduction to the selected volume of Park's writings *On Social Control and Collective Behaviour*, Ralph Turner (1967, p. xvii) describes the widely held view that Park's procedure is inductive, 'guided by intuition rather than systematic concerns', as an extremely distorted picture. In his view, Park developed a refined conceptual apparatus in order to create a reference system which would enable him to observe significant regularities. The pattern sketched out by Turner, one which is followed by all Park's work, actually seems to bear out the critics: searching for creative conceptual structures that illuminate empirical observations and making use of concepts which shed light on a wide range of observations. The changes to be observed in the second edition of 'The City' in 1925, compared with the 1915 edition, are an example of this procedure. Apart from some insertions within the text itself, these changes are all contained in the introductory passage which precedes the outline of the fields of investigation and primarily concern the conceptual apparatus. It is clear that Park had come to see society in the meantime as a 'hierarchy of relationships', the fundamental stratum of which is formed by an ecological structure. The ecological terms ('ecology',

---

[33] This anecdote could equally be one of Park's, corresponding as it does to reporter folklore, where the eye and the feeling for paradox play a central rôle.

'human ecology', 'natural area', etc.), which we found were missing in the first edition, now make their appearance in the introductory passage, admittedly without their leading to any changes within the research programme.

The reference to Spengler's *The Decline of the West*, which had been published in the intervening period and which Park had become acquainted with during his visit to Germany in 1922, is also new. The mention of this work is important to Park to the extent that Spengler, whose cultural and philosophical deliberations Park utterly misunderstands, provided him with a catch-phrase which becomes vital to the justification of his research programme. That is to say, out of Spengler's phrase 'What his house is to the peasant, the city is to the civilised man', Park extracts the key notion of the big city being the natural habitat of the civilised man. In this way, Park had found the missing link in a chain of argumentation which was aimed at claiming the big city as a genuine field of research for sociology and at the same time appropriating it as a *pars pro toto* for society as a whole. Since by this time the areas investigated by the social sciences ('primitive man' on the one hand, 'civilised man' on the other) had become cleanly divided from each other into different disciplines, Park is moreover now in a position to draw on anthropological (ethnological) methods, without encroaching on the preserve of the neighbouring discipline.

As an appendix to Park's reference to Spengler, there follows that famous passage which led to the adoption hypothesis (the hypothesis that he borrowed from anthropology):

Anthropology, the science of man, has been mainly concerned up to the present with the study of primitive peoples. But civilized man is quite as interesting an object of investigation, and at the same time his life is more open to observation and study. Urban life and culture are more varied, subtle, and complicated, but the fundamental motives are in both instances the same. The same patient methods of observation which anthropologists like Boas and Lowie have expanded on the study of the life and manners of the North American Indian might even be more fruitfully employed in the investigation of the customs, beliefs, social practices, and general conceptions of life prevalent in Little Italy on the Lower North Side in Chicago, or in recording the more sophisticated folkways of the inhabitants of Greenwich Village and the neighbourhood of Washington Square, New York. (1925a, p. 3)

This passage, which is inserted into the second edition, is of central importance to the history of sociology, to the extent that a number of authors make reference to it in order to prove that sociological field research as a method was borrowed from anthropology. This hypothesis is introduced in a legitimating manner specific to the discipline, as a way of establishing its own historical tradition and also substantiating the cognitive identity of sociology as a subject. For example, Girtler (1979, p. 51) quotes the hypothesis in order to claim that the methodological strategy of the Chicago School was 'an eminently "cultural anthropological"' one. In this way, he wishes to underpin his suggestion that cultural anthropology must not be limited to studying oral cultures. This is a strategic move in the argument which has become necessary because of the loss of the traditional subject matter for cultural anthropology, the so-called primitive peoples and tribal societies (see Lindner 1987). Hannerz (1980, pp. 30ff.) cites the same hypothesis in his comprehensive attempt to lay the systematic foundations for urban anthropology, in order expressly to incorporate Chicago urban sociology into the tradition of the new discipline.[34]

The most interesting thing, as far as we are concerned (because of its inadvertently being closest to the original intention of the insertion), is the context of the argumentation within which Jim Thomas (1983) refers to the borrowing or adoption. In the justification he gives for a critical ethnography, Thomas cites a 'friendly debate' with a positivistically orientated colleague, who emphasised the advantages of 'hard' data when compared with ethnographic 'stories'. Ethnography, in the view of the critic, is not much more than 'hanging around'. To refute this and similar criticism, Thomas cites the above hypothesis in order to show that the criticism is only justified inasmuch as contemporary researchers (whose criticism Thomas is particularly concerned about) have watered down the Chicago sociologists' original position. The latter, he implies, entailed not only a method (direct observation) and an epistemology (realism) but also concealed a critical potential with respect to the social circumstances being investigated.

The passage which was subsequently inserted must therefore be given an important status in a wide variety of contexts, whether it is in substantiating a legitimate claim to a specific subject-matter and method, in marking disciplines off one from the other, or in bringing into play the 'true' story of the discipline *vis-à-vis* 'false' contemporary interpretations. In this way, the supporters of the hypothesis give the passage a double logical status: by using it as a form of legitimation for the proximity between sociological field research and ethnological field research, in

---

[34] Hannerz does, however, mention Park's journalistic experience and literary Naturalism as being an impulse for the ethnographic approach.

order to cover up its considerably less prestigious relationship with journalistic investigation.

In his introduction to Zorbaugh's *The Gold Coast and the Slum*, Park resorts again to a comparison between the procedure adopted by the urban sociologist and that of the anthropologist: '*The Gold Coast and the Slum* offers an example of a kind of investigation of urban life which is at least comparable with the studies the anthropologists have made of the cultures of primitive peoples' (Park 1929b, p. xx). The first thing that impresses a reader of this study is its literary quality; we are involuntarily reminded of Steffens' ideal of literary journalism.[35] However, in contrast to the dry terminology of the ecological studies in the narrow sense or the dutiful use of ecological terms in ethnographic studies, here, the ecological perspective is woven into a literary depiction:

> Here change has followed fast upon change. With the growth of the city [a reminiscence of Burgess' essay of the same name?], commerce has encroached [invasion] upon residential property, relentlessly pushing it northward or crowding it around the lake shore, until now the Near North Side is chequered with business streets. Into this area, where commerce is [completing] the conquest [dominance] of the community, has crept the slum. Meantime great industries have sprung up along the river, and peoples speaking foreign tongues have come to labor in them. The slum has offered these alien peoples a place to live cheaply and to themselves [natural area]; and wave upon wave of immigrants has swept over the area – Irish, Swedish, German, Italian, Persian, Greek, and Negro – forming colonies, staying for a while, then giving way to others [succession]. But each has left its impress and its stragglers, and today there live on the Near North Side twenty-nine or more nationalities, many of them with their Old World tongues and customs. (Zorbaugh 1983 [1929], pp. 3ff.)

The ambivalent reception given to this particular study once again shows not only its closeness to journalistic reporting, but, if we connect the angles of the different points of view with each other, it also indicates the actual relationship between a style of naturalistic and realistic reporting based on observation and an analysis of urban life and urban living based on an ethnographic approach. The view of both Shils and Matza is that Zorbaugh's study embodies Park's interests in the best possible way, although whereas Shils emphasises this in a rather more critical way, Matza stresses it approvingly. Matza even describes Zorbaugh's book as the most influential contribution to the Chicago School: 'Zorbaugh documented in a manner still unsurpassed the variation in

---

[35] Contemporary reviewers saw it in a similar way: 'The whole study is illuminated by a literary style, vivid, crisp, and alert. It is worthy of a title once used by Theodore Dreiser, "The Color of a City"' (Vance 1929).

customary behaviour as it occurred within several areas in one small part of Chicago. Zorbaugh achieved the aspiration of Robert Park' (Matza 1973, p. 57). As far as our area of interest is concerned, the following sentence is particularly informative: 'It was as if an anthropologist let loose in Chicago had discovered urban America in its full diversity.' However, it is precisely this study which other sociologists see as being a perfect example both of the descriptive form of presentation and the illustrative use of concepts, a procedure which corresponds to that of an observant journalist (see, e.g., Faris 1970, pp. 66 and 83). Finally, Bowdery's view is that the greatest part of Zorbaugh's book is 'devoted to a reporter type of investigation and research' (Bowdery 1951, p. 131).

A MASSIVE RESEARCH PROGRAMME: *THE CITY*

The world had been discovered. This adventure is finished. But the world is still young, still eager for adventure; what next? There are other worlds to be discovered; even more interesting. The world of great cities. The immigrant colonies. The Ghettos and the Chinatowns.   Robert Ezra Park

Irrespective of whether *The City* is described as a massive research programme (Madge), as the definitive account of the Department of Sociology (Kuklick), or as a manifesto and programme of what the Chicago School should become (Bell and Newby), there is unanimous agreement in stressing the programmatic character of the book and in emphasising the wealth of empirical issues it contains.

Notwithstanding its thematic range, it is hardly surprising that the Chicago School is identified with urban sociological investigations. As Bulmer remarks, *The City* acts as a blueprint for these. This is indeed plausible from the point of view of a sociology of the discipline: to a certain extent, the character of Chicago sociology as a 'school' in its own right is already preordained by this concerted programme of investigation.[36] What do the 'suggestions for the investigation of human behaviour in the city environment' actually consist of? Park deals with the 'big city' as an object of study by dividing it into four sections:

I   The City Plan and Local Organization
II   Industrial Organization and the Moral Order

---

[36] This assumption is indirectly confirmed by the fact that it is the period of 1920 to 1932, i.e., the period most strongly influenced by Park, which is considered to be the 'classical era of the Chicago School.' Bulmer (1984, p. 205) sees the main reason for the decline of Chicago sociology in the 1930s as the departure of Park.

III   Secondary Relationships and Social Control
IV   Temperament and the Urban Environment

All sections follow the dualism I have already referred to, namely that of structure (physical organisation) and culture (moral order). In section I, Park comes out against the prevailing view that the big city is an artificial product of town planning, an idea that seems so obvious precisely because of the geometrical shape of the American city, one which follows the model of the chessboard. Maurice Halbwachs, in his large report on Chicago sociology (1932), compared Chicago and Paris. Paris, he claimed, was an old city which had grown slowly and which faced problems in adapting the old infrastructure to the new requirements (in this context the politically motivated Haussmann plan set a dramatic new direction); Chicago he considered an adolescent, almost brutal city, that consisted of a regular lay-out of straight streets which cross one another at right angles. The differences between the old and the new can scarcely be better illustrated than on the basis of the differing understandings of what is meant by a 'corner', when referring to a street: the geometrical angles of the scientifically designed American city, and the picturesque, idyllic or dark corners of the European city where the term is used more as a metaphor.

What particularly interests Park is the subversion of the prescriptive architectonic (block) and administrative (district) lay-out by processes of human nature, leading to the formation of unplanned 'natural' areas. On the basis of economic, professional, ethnic and cultural interests, the populations (like species) become distributed in a quasi-natural way into certain quarters and residential districts, the ones they 'belong to'. In this respect, natural areas are implicitly always first-order social formations. The adjective 'natural' at the same time implies a natural science of the area, in the course of which the population in question forms its own norms, traditions and behavioural patterns, so that the observer perceives a natural area that he can localise topographically and define spatially as a cultural space:

Each separate part of the city is inevitably stained with the peculiar sentiments of its population. The effect of this is to convert what was at first a mere geographical expression into a neighborhood, that is to say, a locality with sentiments, traditions, and a history of its own. (Park 1915, p. 579)[37]

[37] For more on 'natural areas' as 'distinct cultural areas' see Park 1929c, pp. 36ff. Although Park had already described the processes in *The City*, we may assume that the influence of cultural anthropology is reflected in his referring back to the concept of 'cultural area'.

The real theme of the first section is 'cities within cities', i.e., the 'colonies', 'districts' and 'segregated areas', which Park later on embraces in the concept of 'natural area'. He is concerned here with analysing both the urban structure (history of the area and population distribution according to economic, professional and ethnic criteria) and the culture of the segregated districts (tradition, moral code and social rituals).

In its rôle as the home of business life and the money economy, the modern big city promotes the individualisation and specialisation of its inhabitants. The growing division of labour, the genesis of organisations which function as regulative agencies for the interdependency of individuals in the market economy, as well as crisis situations which arise from individual mobility, are all characteristics of the big city. At the same time they are the essential theme of section II.

Using the German proverb 'city air makes you free' as a starting point, Park first of all goes into the possibilities which the big city offers individuals as a living space. It is the big city which first affords the opportunity for individuals to develop their particular talents; it is the big city which has a market for these special abilities; and it is the big city where every job, 'even that of a beggar', tends to take on the character of a profession. That is why the study of new jobs and professions is central to urban research; Park puts forward a list of types of jobs and professions which seem to him to be worth investigating.

The ongoing division of labour – in the sense of Spencer's notion of competitive cooperation – at the same time increases the interdependency of individuals who are thrown back on their own resources. This interdependency first of all produces new forms of social solidarity which depend not on a community of feeling but rather on a community of interest (professional associations, trade unions, interest groups). Secondly, this calls for tools which serve to rectify the lack of balance; Park cites amongst others the market, the stock market and the chamber of commerce, as well as professional and trade publications which inform the representatives of the individual branches of professions about new methods and techniques.[38]

A typical feature of societies with a high degree of mobility is the appearance of crisis situations which seem to be psychologically based – this applies just as much to panics on the stock exchange as it does to mob activity. In the final part of the second section, Park takes up the

---

[38] There are clear echoes of the *Thought News* project here.

motifs from his doctoral thesis 'The crowd and the public'. Park is interested in forms of collective behaviour and how they are controlled, e.g., by political bosses and worker-agitators.

In section III, Park again assumes a dualism of space and behaviour. Changes in the organisation of industry go hand in hand with changes in the relationships and customs of the urban population. The general character of these changes is indicated by the fact that primary (face-to-face) relationships are gradually replaced by indirect, secondary ones, a situation which produces problems of social control. Park advocates studying traditional institutions (church, school and family) and the changes to them (adaptation) prompted by the influence of the big city. He also calls for the investigation of traditional forms of moral control (customs, moral codices, religious beliefs) and the way these change or disintegrate, primarily giving way to political and legislative measures. Park pays particular attention to the modern mechanisms of consensus formation, which appear important to him because of the (social and ethnic) heterogeneity of the big city. The seemingly Babel-like confusion of languages, world views and moral codes requires a unifying medium to help break down prejudices and find a way to a common 'universe of discourse'. Park believes this exists in the form of modern communication media (the news and press services, agencies for researching and disseminating public opinion), with whose help the 'fabric of life' that interlinks individuals is given greater communicative strength.

In section IV, finally, Park turns to the distribution of the population in accordance with its natural disposition, 'tastes' and 'temperaments'. This section is of particular interest because it is here that the tension between segregation of groups and mobility of individuals, which permeates Chicago sociology and which at first sight seems to be a contradiction in terms, is dissolved in the sense that Park claims it is segregation itself which seems to be the precondition for the mobility (and thus the freedom) of individuals:

The processes of segregation establish moral distances which make a city a mosaic of little worlds which touch but do not interpenetrate. This makes it possible for individuals to pass quickly and easily from one moral *milieu* to another and encourages the fascinating but dangerous experiment of living at the same time in several different contiguous, perhaps, but widely separated worlds. All this tends to give to city life a superficial and adventitious character; it tends to complicate social relationships and to produce new and divergent individual types. It introduces, at the same time, an element of chance and adventure, which adds to the stimulus of city life and gives it for young and fresh nerves a peculiar attractiveness. (Park 1915, p. 608)

More than in the other sections, the focus here is on other specific characteristics of the big city in Simmel's sense: the personal freedom which the big city affords the individual; the intensification of living on one's nerves which is inherent to the urban experience; the evolution of a specifically urban individual with his or her own particular mentality and the development of that special sort of person who turns up at the specifically big city extravaganzas.

If we compare Park's proposals with the research work that was carried out in the department later, it becomes clear that not only was research conducted into jobs and professions (Frances R. Donovan, *The Saleslady* (1929); Martha H. Hall, *The Nursemaid* (1931); Edwin H. Sutherland, *The Professional Thief* (1972 [1937])) as well as institutions which are specific to big cities (Norman S. Hayner, *The Sociology of Hotel Life* (1923); Ernest H. Shideler, *The Chain Store: A Study of the Ecological Organization of a Modern City* (1927)), but also into topics, which, although outside the strict confines of urban sociology, are nevertheless central to Park's sociology. Examples here are the research into the news business (Carroll De Witt Clark, *News: A Sociological Study* (1931); Helen MacGill Hughes, *News and the Human Interest Story* (1940)) and into collective behaviour (Ernest T. Hiller, *The Strike as Group Behaviour* (1924); Lyford Edwards, *The Natural History of a Revolution* (1927)). Beside these, an important place is occupied by the research into the symptoms of social disorganisation, which concludes that it leads to individual disintegration, e.g., Robert E. L. Faris, *An Ecological Study of Insanity in The City* (1939 [1931]); Ernest R. Mowrer, *Family Disorganization* (1924); Ruth Shonle Cavan, *Suicide: A Study in Personal Disorganisation* (1926).

Nevertheless, when people speak of the legacy of Chicago sociology, they always mention the same studies: *The Hobo* (1923), *The Gang* (1927), *The Ghetto* (1928), *The Taxi-Dance Hall* (1932), *The Gold Coast and the Slum* (1929) and *The Jack-Roller* (1930). What is it that makes these works stand out, what is it that makes them, in retrospect, into classics of Chicago sociology? None of these studies applies to a particular problem (such as divorce), a distinct job group (such as saleslady) or a specific institution (such as hotel), but they all attempt to unravel the relationship between urban space and behavioural patterns as a whole. With the exception of *The Jack-Roller*, which occupies a special status as a document of biographical method, they all take their ethnographical claim seriously; they investigate human behaviour within a constantly changing urban environment. The ecological model serves here primarily to locate the scenery and to provide a theoretical superstructure for the classification and systemisation of the insights yielded by the research. This is clearly shown in the use of ecological terminology in the classic monographs, where they appear almost compulsive. Downes and Rock (1982, p. 60) are correct to speak of a 'pro-forma obeisance' shown by many people to a theory of which they know absolutely nothing.

The question then arises as to whether we are in any position to speak of a unified ecological approach in the context of Chicago sociology. René König, in his brief survey of social ecology in Chicago, made a distinction between the 'original Chicago School thought in its pure form' and the later statistical ecological investigations (René König 1978, pp. 62ff.). The 'original thought', i.e., the idea that the big city is fragmented and segmented into a mosaic of small worlds, was, with a pinch of salt, something like a starting-point for explorations of urban social worlds. The classics are a model for this. By contrast, the extension, i.e., the generalisation and systematisation of the ecological conception, goes hand in hand with a narrowing of the sociological aspects. Instead of linking the ecological and cultural analyses, interest is now focused on a sort of social symptomatology. Only once they are freed from the all-embracing context of the Chicago department that connects them do these two subjects take on independent form and function as two disparate disciplines that scarcely take any notice of each other: namely urban anthropology and social ecology.

Becker (1966), in his introduction to the new edition of *The Jack-Roller*, emphasised that the individual researchers in the Chicago group were well aware of the fact that they were taking part in a large-scale research enterprise called 'Chicago' and that their studies were being used to provide set pieces to help fill in the mosaic. The references which the individual authors make to other investigations, either completed or in progress, testify to their being conscious of this. However, when we look more closely at the overall project, as it is presented in the 'Sociological Series' and when we place the fields of investigation within Burgess' ideal-typical diagram of the big city, then the claim that the object of all their interest was Chicago becomes considerably more relative. According to Burgess, the modern American big city, as an ideal type, takes the form of five concentric zones (Ernest W. Burgess 1925). Zone I, in Chicago the Loop, is home to the business and administrative centre.

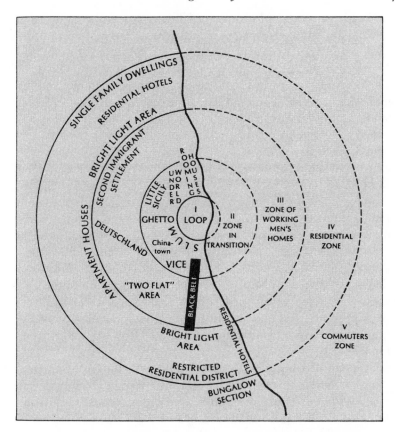

5 Ernest W. Burgess' diagrammatic representation of the paradigmatic city

Zone II is the so-called transition zone which includes the slums, the ethnic enclaves and the niches of voluntary or involuntary outsiders (Bohemia/Hobohemia). Zone III is where the first wave of immigrants settled, with 'Deutschland', the quarter of the acculturated Jews, representing a miniature version of the whole. Zone IV is the residential district of American-born middle-class citizens and, finally, Zone V is the commuter zone.

If we give the fields of investigation their due place within the diagram, then it becomes clear that, if we ignore the investigations of typical urban institutions and job groups, the major topic of interest was not Chicago as a whole, but rather the second zone, the 'zone in transition'. All the classic studies focus on this zone (illustration 5). Only Zorbaugh's *The Gold Coast and the Slum* is to a certain extent an exception, when in his panoramic description of Lower North Side, he also goes into detail about the elegant residential area on Lake Michigan, which was known in Chicago as the 'Gold Coast'. He does this primarily in order to show that the Lower North Side is the area with the greatest social and cultural contrasts: only a 'stone's throw' from the concentration of wealth to be found on the 'Gold Coast' lies the district with the greatest poverty, 'Little Hell'.

There are scientific, political and personal reasons for this concentration on the zone in transition:

1. The 'zone in transition', as its name suggests, is the ideal-typical laboratory for a type of sociology concerned with investigating change in human behaviour in the urban environment. As the place where the immigrants first settle, as the district containing the ethnic enclaves and as the niche for social outsiders, this zone offers a wide variety of areas for a form of sociological research concerned with the interdependency of ecology and culture and with the symbolic construction of social space. Chombart de Lauwe's designation of the second zone as a *zone d'acculturation* (Chombart de Lauwe with collaborators 1952, pp. 40ff.) is a better description of what is meant than the term 'transition', which is primarily orientated toward the expansion model.

2. The 'zone in transition' is considered to be the problem area of Chicago. For a type of sociology which is linked in a variety of different ways with foundations and reform organisations, it is precisely this area which has to be the focus of research.

3. But, and this is by no means a trivial factor, the zone in transition, seen from the viewpoint of the middle-class observer, is the most exciting and most colourful part of the city. Exploring this area satisfies a culturally conditioned appetite for the exotic, a subjective aspect of research which people usually like to keep quiet about:

   the sheer delight of discovering a lot of things you never dreamed of, all sorts of things going on in the world and you found out you could get close to them, and understand the criminals, or the addicts or these prostitutes, all the seamy sort of thing that you were sort of protected from in your conventional life. (Cottrell, JTC 1:6)

To summarise, 'The City' proposes three major themes for an empirically based urban sociology:

   – The city as a constellation of geographically specific social worlds;
   – The evolution of new types of jobs, personalities, mentalities and behavioural patterns specific to the big city; and

– The changes to institutions, including the problems of social control, which go hand in hand with this.

How little this research programme had need of the strict ecological terminology of the later phase is shown by a syllabus from the year 1918, which follows the guidelines laid down in the essay:

The mobility, local distribution, and segregation of the population within the urban and suburban areas of the city of Chicago; the cultural differences and relative isolation of different classes, racial, vocational, and local groups; resulting changes in institutions, e.g., the family, the church, etc.; in organization and expression of public opinion, and in the traditional forms of social control. (quoted from Bulmer 1984, p. 95)

Once again, we encounter the research programme introduced in *The City*, in a concise form. Against this background and in view of the classic monographs, Shils' statement that *The City* was the source of many of the prominent ideas which have influenced American urban sociology seems to be somewhat of an understatement. In essence, the 'inaugural lecture' of 1915 already contained everything which was later to constitute the cognitive identity of the Chicago style of *urban sociology*.

Refracted through the lens of journalism, Park's proposals take on a different quality. I have already pointed out that, to the eyes of the attentive and circumspect reporter at the turn of the century, big cities such as New York and Chicago inevitably appeared as mosaics of small communities. Thus it is no surprise to find an expression such as 'cities within cities' already being used in journalistic descriptions of urban life shortly before the turn of the century as a metaphor for the spatial segregation of ethnic and social variety. The chapter entitled 'Mixed Crowd' in Riis' *How the Other Half Lives* (1957 [1890], pp. 19–25) is an excellent example of a view of the big city which perceives it as a mosaic of nationalities and cultures. Not only is ethnic variety mentioned ('The cosmopolitan character of Lower New York'), but also the ecological processes of invasion, dominance and repression ('forcing its way'; 'possessing the block'; 'crowding out') are all talked about in the language of everyday speech. Moreover, this chapter shows that the 'spot map' technique for designating specific populations was already well known in journalism:

A map of the city, colored to designate nationalities, would show more stripes than on the skin of the zebra, and more colors than any rainbow. The city on such a map would fall into two great halves, green for the Irish prevailing in the West Side tenement districts, and blue for the Germans on the East Side. But intermingled with these ground colors would be an odd variety of tints that would give the whole the appearance of an extraordinary crazy-quilt. From

down the Sixth Ward, upon the site of the old Collect Pond . . . the red of the
Italian would be seen forcing its way northward along the line of Mulberry
Street to the quarter of the French purple on Bleeker Street and South Fifth
Avenue, to lose itself and reappear, after a lapse of miles, in the 'Little Italy' of
Harlem, east of Second Avenue . . . On the West Side the red would be seen
overrunning the old Africa of Thompson Street, pushing the black of the negro
rapidly uptown . . . occupying his home, his church, his trade and all, with
merciless impartiality . . . Hardly less aggressive than the Italian, the Russian
and Polish Jew . . . is filling the tenements of the Old Seventh Ward to the river
front and disputing with the Italian every foot of available space in the back
alleys of Mulberry Street . . . Between the dull grey of the Jew, his favorite color,
and the Italian red, would be seen squeezed in on the map a sharp streak of
yellow, marking the narrow boundaries of Chinatown . . . And so on to the end
of the long register. (Riis 1957 [1890], pp. 20ff.)

It is not the case that the journalists of the day, lacking a scholarly
apparatus, saw the big city as chaos; it is rather that the logic of the
assignment system already completely conformed to the logic of regularities and systems of natural laws in its spatial differentiation of functions and populations. Moreover, in order to arrive at an appropriate
appraisal of the rôle of the journalist, the following should not be forgotten: no other group of professional people of the time had available a
comparable spectrum of knowledge of the big city gained from direct
observation; no other group of professional people was conscious of the
co-existence of populations of diverse social and ethnic origin to such an
extent; and finally, no other group was involved in a similar way, by virtue
of its profession, in the big city in its guise as a 'laboratory for urbanistics
and urbanity', to use Korff's phrase. The journalists themselves are the
product of the big city *par excellence*; being both reflectors and protagonists of urban life, they embody the mentality which Hellpach
ascribes to the urban dweller, where 'emotional indifference' goes hand
in hand with 'sensual vigilance'.

The energy-laden sensual vigilance characteristic of the journalist
takes on an objectified form in the press world. An allegory of modern
life, it is characterised by 'speed and deadlines' (and the structure of its
editorial and technical apparatus becomes a model for the organisation
of factories and government departments) as well as by an insatiable
curiosity and appetite for news which is kept on the boil by the editorial
apparatus. This trade was clearly aware of its special position, as is
shown not only by its self-referential style of reporting, but also by the
gigantism of the press headquarters buildings, which for a long time set
the standard for metropolitan architecture. In this context, one thinks,

for instance, of the Tribune Tower in Chicago, the result of the biggest and most sensational competition in modern building history. It is therefore no surprise that a sensorium for urbanistics was developed in such an environment; the buildings which are regarded as typical of urban life, such as skyscrapers, department stores, office blocks, hotels and blocks of apartments are all typical themes of reporting.[39]

Proof of the dynamics of urban living is shown in an exemplary fashion in the evolution of new jobs and professions, which form part of the usual journalistic themes of the period. In this context, particular attention is paid to the evolution of jobs and professions for women, since they form a contrast to the traditional rôle model; among these are the single professional woman as a general type or special jobs or professions such as that of the waitress or the female men's barber.

Park's list of vocational types reads like an excerpt from a city editor's file of potential stories.[40] Job types such as the 'shop-girl' or the 'pawn-broker' are all part of the repertoire of journalistic reporting around the turn of the century, not to mention the 'vaudeville artist', as representative of an entertainment culture which, in the form of the 'variety show', corresponds to the urban experience (see Barth 1980).[41]

In 1893, Park published an article in the *Detroit Tribune* entitled 'Life in a Flat' (REP 8). This is an account of some particular aspects of modern life, namely 'Civilized People Who Have No "Homes"', as the subtitle reads. Park begins his account with the statement that the rapid growth of apartment blocks in Detroit can be regarded as an indication of the city having changed into a modern metropolis, a change which leads to a growth in the population group which no longer has no permanent home in the traditional sense. Translated into the language of the 'proposals', his theme is the mobility of individual people so characteristic of modern society, the constant coming and going which is reflected in

---

[39] Just to mention a few examples taken from one periodical, *Scribner's*: Samuel Hopkins Adams, 'The Department Store' (vol. 21, 1897); Jesse Lynch Williams, 'A Great Hotel' (vol. 21, 1897); Lincoln Steffens, 'The Modern Business Building' (vol. 22, 1897).

[40] 'Among the types which it would be interesting to study are: the shop-girl, the policeman, the cabman, the nightwatchman, the clairvoyant, the vaudeville performer, the quack doctor, the bartender, the ward boss, the strike breaker, the labor agitator, the school teacher, the reporter, the stockbroker, the pawn-broker; all these are characteristic products of city life' (Park 1915, p. 586). See also the proposals in the contemporary instruction book for journalists written by Bleyer (1923 [1913], p. 275). Types of jobs and professions were popular themes for student term papers in the sociological department. Nels Anderson, for instance, wrote about 'panhandlers', 'clerks in flophouses', 'landladies', 'bartenders', 'mission workers' and 'policemen'.

[41] Park's former colleague and long-time friend Hartley Davis published an article in *Everybody's Magazine* (August 1905) about vaudeville ('In Vaudeville').

establishments such as hotels, houses with furnished rooms (rooming-houses) and apartment blocks.

With his sketch of the apartment block as a symbol of life-style in the modern big city – in a literary journalistic style – Park anticipates thematically as well as interpretatively the studies of Chicago urban dwellings and their users which were carried out by Conway ('The Apartment House Dweller'), Hayner ('Hotel Life and Personality' (1928)) and Zorbaugh ('The Dweller in Furnished Rooms' (1926a)) in the 1920s.

Park plans his description as a guide. The visitor to an apartment house is first of all confronted with a new type of profession, that of janitor: 'He is one of the most recent products of modern society. He came with the messenger boy and the elevator man, three professions that have been created within a couple of decades.'[42] In what follows, he sketches the typical working day of a janitor, explaining his tasks, referring to his monitoring function, one which has an adverse affect on individual freedom, and sheds light on the janitor's character, the main weak point of which is his fondness for tips, or more exactly, bribes. After portraying some aspects of life in apartment houses, paying particular attention to the anonymity which prevails in them, Park goes into the question of what type of people live there. In a sort of house guide, he quotes different types, which include commercial salesman, newly married couples, but above all, as typical apartment dwellers, single men and women (with a touch of the bohemian)[43] as well as wealthy childless couples (in a similar fashion to the subsequent Chicago studies, childlessness is noted here as being characteristic of people who live in apartment houses). The whole thing has something of the literary cross-sections taken through a typical Berlin or Paris house, such as were customary around the middle of the nineteenth century. It includes a suitable illustration, which is remarkable for the fact that it provides the observer with a view of the inner life of the apartment house, not by the artifice of taking off its roof, but, up-to-date, using X-rays ('What the X-ray would disclose if directed to a modern flat').

The journalistic reports written shortly before and after the turn of

---

[42] How close Park stuck to such typologies in his teaching is shown by a note from Hayner's diary, in which he reports on a lengthy conversation with Park about possible themes, mentioning amongst others: newspaper boys, lift-boys and janitors (Faris 1970, p. 80).

[43] The tendency toward the bohemian, the unattached element, is already accounted for in the new phenomenon of the single woman living alone, the object of many journalistic exposés in the 1890s. See as an example Mary Gay Humphries, 'Women Bachelors in New York', in *Scribner's*, vol. 20 (1896), pp. 626–36.

the century, if we take Burgess' zone model as a guide, also concentrate thematically on the first zone, the actual urban space, as well as on the second zone, the so-called zone of transition or zone of acculturation. The motives for journalistic investigation may well be widely different. What they do have in common, however, seen from the logic of news value, is an eye for the new as well as an eye for what, from the point of view of the reporter as well as that of the reader, is different. In short, even journalists use the big city as a laboratory, one in which human nature and social processes can be studied in a particularly profitable way.

Some of the volumes of journalistic reportage which have resulted from series of articles, like the sociological monographs, have become classics in their field. Some that spring to mind are Lincoln Steffens, *The Shame of the Cities*, (1904, reprinted 1969); Hutchins Hapgood, *The Spirit of the Ghetto* (1902, reprinted 1967); Josiah Flynt (Willard), *Tramping with Tramps* (1899, reprinted 1967); as well as Jacob A. Riis, *How the Other Half Lives* (1890, constant reprints). But we should by no means forget the series of reportages which were important to the further spectrum of topics covered by Chicago sociology: Ray Stannard Baker, *Following the Color Line* (1908, reprinted 1964), for instance, or Will Irwin, *The American Newspaper* (1911, reprinted 1969), a series about the American newspaper business, which was highly esteemed by Park. The importance of these and other works of journalism for Chicago sociology is shown, amongst other things, by the fact that they were included as recommended reading in bibliographies: Baker, Hapgood, Riis, Steffens and Willard in the Park/Burgess Reader, for instance; Hapgood, Riis and Steffens in Wirth's 'Bibliography of the Urban Community' (1924, reprinted 1967). In the 1920s, reviewers occasionally compared individual Chicago monographs with their journalistic predecessors. Such comparisons may have contributed to the reproach that Chicago sociology was only journalism in disguise. They do, however, point to the fact that the work of the reporters around the turn of the century set a standard by which sociological investigations would have to be measured.

Journalistic reportage	*Sociological investigations*
Josiah Flynt (Willard), *Tramping with Tramps* (1899)	Nels Anderson, *The Hobo* (1923)
Hutchins Hapgood, *The Spirit of the Ghetto* (1902)	Louis Wirth, *The Ghetto* (1928)

Jacob A. Riis, *How the Other Other Half Lives* (1890)

Hutchins Hapgood, *The Autobiography of a Thief* (1903)

Harvey W. Zorbaugh, *The Gold Coast and the Slum* (1929)

Clifford R. Shaw, *The Jack-Roller: A Delinquent Boy's Own Story* (1930)

Edwin H. Sutherland, *The Professional Thief: By a Professional Thief* (1937)

George K. Turner: 'The City of Chicago: A Study of the Great Immoralities', *McClure's*, vol. 28 (April 1907), pp. 575–92[44] (1933)

Will Irwin, 'The American Newspaper', *Collier's*, vol. 46/7 (January–July 1911)[45]

John Landesco, *Organized Crime in Chicago* (1929)

Walter C. Reckless, *Vice in Chicago* (1933)

Helen MacGill Hughes, *News and the Human Interest Story* (1940)

THE SOCIOLOGIST AS CITY EDITOR

Put yourself in their places, be a good reporter, that was what Park was trying to tell me and trying to tell the rest of us. Hell, that's what I've been ever since, a reporter.

Norman S. Hayner

In her reminiscences about the 'golden era', Ruth Shonle Cavan described the methodological preferences of the Chicago sociologists and said of Robert Park that he was primarily concerned not with case studies or statistical surveys, but with investigation and observation (Cavan 1983). In the history of sociology, it is field observation, the essence of ethnographic procedural technique, that has turned out to be characteristic of the Chicago approach, even if, as we have seen, other methods were also used just as widely. Against this background, it may come as a surprise that there were no courses on field research. The course in 'Field Studies' offered by Park and Burgess, which might lead one to suppose that such instruction was given, resembled more a practical research project, where possible fields of investigation were outlined and tested. Measured by today's standards, the instruction in techniques of field-work happened in an informal and unsystematic way. Students

---

[44] Park knew about the article. It is mentioned in a letter written by the editor of *Everybody's* (1 April 1907). Park must have made a proposal with respect to this article (REPA 2:2).

[45] Park: 'The most complete and candid account we have of the modern newspaper was written by Will Irwin, and is buried away in *Collier's Weekly* for 1911' (REP 3:7).

were encouraged to explore the city on foot, to talk with the people and to note down their observations in detail; this type of field investigation has found its expression in the 'As one walks . . .' style of the opening chapters of several studies.[46]

'Get the feeling' was one of Park's maxims with respect to the exploration phase, a peculiarly vague conceptual basis for characterising a research process that has made a decisive contribution to the cognitive identity of a sociological school of thought. But even so, concepts such as 'sense' and 'feel' do have a certain plausibility when they are read against the foil of journalism. It is the newsman's 'instinct' for news, his proverbial 'nose' for news, which makes a good reporter – though it must be said that it is an organ which is not present from birth, but rather something which has to be carefully nurtured:

However, what is known in the newsroom as a 'nose for news', is not an original trait of human nature. On the contrary, it is usually a hard-won acquisition and one which is more likely to be learned on the job than in the classroom, even of a school of journalism. What the reporter learns, finally, in the course of his newspaper experience is *the art of looking* at events as evidence of things in progress, the full significance of which he does not seek to assess. (Park 1955c [1940], p. 110; my italics)

These statements on the reporter immediately bring to mind Park's demand that the first thing sociology students had to do was to go out and observe and note down their observations exactly. What they also intimate – and this was the decisive methodological step taken by Chicago sociology under Park's guidance – is that the observation paradigm will assert itself as the means of acquiring knowledge: 'the art of looking'. As a starting point, this has little to do with what we describe today as field observation, with its arsenal of rules and techniques. Park, who frequently strolled through Chicago with his students, insisted that observation was just as important as rummaging around in libraries.

A statement of Park's which Howard Becker noted down makes this clear; at the same time it includes caustic criticism of the way official records come about, together with an apparently unavoidable dig at the finicky 'do-gooders':

You have been told to go grubbing in the library, thereby accumulating a mass of notes and a liberal coating of grime. You have been told to choose problems wherever you can find musty stacks of routine records based on trivial schedules

---

[46] See, for instance, the first chapter of Thrasher 1968 [1927] ('The Gangland') and of Zorbaugh 1983 [1929] ('The Shadow of the Skyscraper').

prepared by tired bureaucrats and filled out by reluctant applicants for aid or fussy do-gooders or indifferent clerks. That is called 'getting the hands dirty in real research'. Those who thus counsel you are wise and honorable; the reasons they offer are of great value. But one thing more is needful: first-hand observation. Go and sit in the lounges of the luxury hotels and on the doorsteps of the flophouses; sit on the Gold Coast settees and on the slum shake-downs; sit in Orchestra Hall and in the Star and Garter Burlesk. In short, gentlemen, go get the seat of your pants dirty in *real* research. (McKinney 1966, p. 71; italics in the original)

'Go into the district'; 'get the feeling'; 'become acquainted with people': Park's instructions, as reported by his students, seem at first sight trivial; they can, however, only be understood against the background of the 'sociology of the library'. They are aimed at first-hand observation, at sociology 'on the hoof' as Hughes called it, and seen in context, these instructions do have an intrinsic logic. Hughes (REPA 1:5), for example, states that the custom was to keep a sort of research diary, in which impressions from the area of investigation were noted down and interviews as well as life histories were collected, similar to the way in which Park kept a diary during his time as a journalist, and at a later date, on his travels.[47] The students were also required to prepare regular research reports, as well as detailed statements on the next steps in the research. The student research papers which have been preserved in the E. W. Burgess Papers are a rich source of material for illustrating the procedure adopted. This led to the development of an exceptionally multifaceted form of research, which used a wide variety of procedures and a multiplicity of perspectives. Let us take, as an example, the investigation into hotels as a form of dwelling and life.[48] The ideal-typical procedure

[47] The following excerpt from Park's travel diary gives us an impression of the value of the 'notebook method' and Park's feel for hypotheses:

Tokyo, Sunday [Nov.] 17, 1929. 'Conflict of Cultures'. The Ginza, the jass thoroughfare of Tokyo, the street of smart shops, restaurants and night life as well, is busy, but not as crowded as usually today. On the corner of the Ginza and . . . Street I am suddenly aware of familiar music, and recognise the thrilling notes of 'Onward Christian Soldiers' which is being broadcasted from a building across the street . . . On the Ginza across the street there is a shop selling postal cards. There are pictures of Japanese actors and actresses in the decent formal and . . . decor of the Japanese theatre, posing in the theatrical attitudes and with the dramatic traditional gestures of the traditional Japanese drama. Side by side with these pictures but occupying more space and filling more completely the eye of the spectator are the pictures of American actors and actresses, most of the chorus girls, scandalously draped or undraped from the traditional Japanese point of view . . . This scene is a symbol of the turmoil in Japanese life and culture (Park's 1929 travel diary, REPA 4:7)

[48] Although I am referring here to some of Hayner's statements concerning the way he went about the hotel study, the example is altogether fictitious; thus, for instance, I have transferred the methods of procedure used in other studies on to the example of 'Hotel Life'.

could be as follows: obtain census data about the hotel trade (how many hotels in the city; how many rooms, how many overnights per year); classify hotels by size and type; enter the position of the classified hotels on the map of the city; mark areas of hotel concentration ('hotel areas'); stroll through the area, investigate the surroundings (bars, restaurants, cinemas, theatres), form an impression of the hotels (surface area, height of the building, entrances); question the manager (seasonal occupancy trends, average length of stay, profession and civil status of the guests); in addition, consult the hotel trade press; hang around in the hotel lobby, or in the hotel bar, book yourself in as a guest, conduct observations, engage the guests and the staff in conversation, obtain the life histories of the guests and staff, read novels to supplement all this (*People in the Hotel*);[49] where possible, slip into different functional rôles (porter, reception clerk, barkeeper, chambermaid, etc.).[50]

On the basis of these explanations, we can indeed concur with Jennifer Platt (1983) in doubting whether the instructions are actually aimed at participant observation in the strict sense of the term, or, and this is what Platt is getting at, whether the research resulting from it is indeed appropriate to a reflective methodology of participant observation. It certainly does not provide the basis for the latter. What we have before us corresponds more to the techniques of observation and research used by a reporter or detective.[51] It was not by chance that the Californian group of neo-Chicago Schoolers, who met in San Francisco in 1969, gave themselves the name of 'Chicago Irregulars', 'reminiscent of the "Baker Street Irregulars" of the adventures of Sherlock Holmes – but having an additional significance for "field-oriented" devotees of "Chicago sociology"' (Lofland 1980, p. 252).

Within this comprehensive repertoire of techniques, participant observation in the strict sense probably came about more by chance. Nels Anderson, who is frequently quoted as an example, had – to paraphrase the Malinowski dictum on the appropriate conditions for ethnographic work – probably set up his tent in 'Hobohemia' more by chance, namely because of the cheap lodgings (Anderson 1983, p. 403). Cressey,

---

[49] In the course of his investigation, Hayner went to see the musical *Hotel House*, for example (Faris 1970, p. 82).

[50] For his study into the roadhouse, Daniel Russell worked in a cloakroom, as a night watchman and as a bouncer in two of the biggest Chicago dance halls (EWB 135:1).

[51] These techniques of observation also include the enjoyment of playing a rôle. Hayner reports that he once acted as a fictitious management assistant and, together with the manager, he took complaints from hotel guests: 'that is the way according to Park that you learn about these institutions that you don't know' (Hayner, JTC 1:9).

who likewise is often quoted, certainly frequented the 'Taxi-Dance Hall' as a guest, as a way of getting a glimpse inside. But much more impor- tant to his investigation was the 'participant observer' in the original sense, as developed by Lindeman (1924), i.e., insider informants who conduct observations on behalf of the sociologist or who act as his sources.[52]

Platt speaks of the Chicago 'origin myth', but the problem she raises is merely of secondary importance in our context, because we are con- fronted with it only against the background of a differentiated qualita- tive methodology. The problem of the refined methodology is one imposed by the quantitative approach on the qualitative method and, particularly in the case of sociology, it led to a pseudo-scientific method- ology which for a long period ignored the fundamental questions result- ing from the interactive character of qualitative research; this pseudo-scientific methodology is something which Park, who was a pragmatist not only in this respect, would certainly not have agreed with. Park's position was clear: in his view, statistical data without some 'acquaintance with' the subject matter was worthless, and might just as well be collected by a more or less bright secretary, as he once remarked sardonically. Bulmer, in a letter to Winifred Rorty (Raushenbush), was right to point out that Park's type of field research did not make use of any pre-set pattern nor did it in any way call for unthinking compliance with 'what is so frequently spoken of these days as "research design"' (Bulmer, 11 April 1966; REPA 6:6). What was important, during this founding stage of field-orientated sociology, was to get away from pure book study, the so-called 'sociology of the library' (Kurtz), not from any of the competing methodologies: 'I think the big push in the 20's was toward getting actual concrete data and facts and making some kind of an analysis of them' (Cavan, JTC 1:3, p. 16). What was required, or rather, what was stimulated, was imagination and resourcefulness in research; how people actually went about implementing this – whether by more participation or by more observation – was a secondary consideration. Park emphasised not methodical rigour but rather

[52] There is even a journalistic precedent for the sociological rôle of insider informant, the so-called 'collaborative technique', which was applied, amongst others, by Riis (with Max Fischel as insider informant) and by Hapgood (with Abraham Cahan as informant). A manuscript discovered by Bulmer (1983b), written by Cressey probably in 1927, shows that a method similar to that of par- ticipant observation, developed from the sociological analysis of urban relationships, does indeed play a rôle, the researcher rôle of 'anonymous stranger' (see Cressey 1983, pp. 102–10). The risk that this type of conversation in the field, described by Cressey as an 'anonymous confessional relationship', may also be misunderstood as deliberately sounding someone out, is shown by Cressey's report of a conversation with a visitor to the dance palace (see EWB 129:6).

sociological imagination. Finding the best way to gain access to the field was a test in itself. One thing was obligatory, though, and that was to go out into the field. Such a demand followed logically from the idea that the techniques of exploration could not be learnt from books (in Park's view, a contradiction in itself) but only in the field. This is a clear case of translating journalistic experience ('is more likely to be learned on the job than in the classroom') into sociological training. By carrying out small research tasks (e.g., describing the activity of a bartender), which are very like the 'test assignments' that were customary when checking the suitability of cub reporters, the novice researcher acquired a feel for the procedure, learnt the art of looking and developed a nose for those distinctive features of a situation which, even in a sociological study, constitute its 'news value'.

Guidance and teaching a feel for the thing in question also has a journalistic equivalent, namely the activity of the city editor. The city editor, later also dubbed 'metropolitan editor', guides the activities of the staff reporters. His desk forms the heart of the local editor's office. Here, plans are drawn up (and rejected), themes developed, tasks assigned to the reporters and texts edited. The city editor controls the process of local reporting, from finding the topics via research to the actual writing of the articles. He takes the part of 'devil's advocate', as it says in one guide to journalism, by checking the exactness and consistency of the story, editing the article, revising the text and altering the headline. He keeps an 'assignment book' about his reporters, a 'futures file' on events, people and institutions which serves as a source for future reporting assignments, as well as an 'ideas file' with suggestions as regards possible reporting themes.

It is tempting (and not out of place, bearing in mind that the big city press forms a model for the *modus procedendi* of modern organisations) to imagine the Chicago department in the 1920s as the editorial office of a big city newspaper (let us say, *Chicago News*): Albion Small, until 1925 the managing editor, would thus be entrusted with the management and finance and is personally responsible to the owners for the smooth functioning of the business; he would be supported in this by Ernest Burgess, who, as family editor, maintains contact with the social welfare establishments. In the midst of all this is the 24-hour city editor Robert Park, drawing up the line to be taken by the paper (*The City*), dreaming up and rejecting topics and giving the reporters their assignments. In this editorial office, a staff of news specialists is being trained, each person having his own lengthy training in, and expert knowledge of, a

specialist area: hoboes or gangs, organised crime or individual delinquency, hotels or apartment blocks. The seminar, in this fictional
context, becomes an editorial meeting, at which the reporters who had
been sent out into the field report back to the assembled editors and
Wirth, the editorial assistant, on what they have done, their experiences
'on the beat' and the pieces of news they have brought back with them.
What will the verdict of the city editor turn out to be? 'Remarkable
stuff' or 'It's no news'?[53]

The analogy is not as far-fetched as might seem at first sight. The reminiscences of former students draw a distinct picture of Park as editor. In
a letter to Fred Matthews, Winifred Raushenbush characterises her relationship to Park as that 'of a green cub reporter to a city editor. I was
handled and damned out on precisely that basis' (Raushenbush, 30
September 1963; REPA 9:3).

At the beginning of this century, the structure of the relationship
between cub reporter and city editor still greatly resembled that of the
apprentice to master craftsman (Duncan 1948, p. 231). The cub reporter
received little theoretical training; instead the craft was learnt 'on the
job', under the constant supervision either of the editor responsible or
an experienced reporter. The seminar reports written by the students
about their experiences in the field, together with the discussion or
analysis of these reports, resemble this structure. The main thing, above
all, was whether the students had developed an eye for the essentials and
whether their explanation of what they had seen and what had happened was consistent.

If it was not, then they could be almost certain that it was 'the art of
looking' that was underdeveloped. The city editor took the trouble to
find out the particular inclinations and talents of cub reporter and
having discovered them, he went on to develop them systematically. Park
proceeded in a similar way. He regularly asked first-year students about
what experiences, previous knowledge and interests they had. In the
Park Papers, there is a draft 'questionnaire' (more a sort of subject index)
for a seminar on social problems, in which he questions the students,
amongst other things, about their reading (*not* specialist texts), their experiences and their interest in particular issues (REP 5:3). Sounding out the
students' interests formed the basis for selecting the themes which they
then addressed, themes which sometimes remained with them throughout their lives: thus, Thrasher became an 'expert' on gangs, Hayner a

[53] Werner Cahnmann recalls that 'the worst verdict of Park's about a valueless contribution was that
"it's no news"' ('My Relation to Robert E. Park'; REPA 6:7).

specialist on hotels. Only a few managed escape this type of attribution; one of those who succeeded in choosing his own topic was Everett C. Hughes, as he himself emphasised.

Just as the city editor sounded out the particular talents of the cubs (one person would happen to be a better society reporter, another a better police reporter), so, and this was the reverse side of the apprentice–master relationship, he was also in a position to assign to one of the cubs a topic that had just sprung to his mind. The erratic changes of interest in topics are evident in the reminiscences of the students; a situation could arise where the very next student who came into the office was given Park's new interest as the theme of a final-year project.[54]

The way in which Park treated his students corresponds at times exactly to the myth of the fight of the young assiduous reporter with his editor:

The reporter, a deracinated stranger in the big city, who has chosen not to follow in his father's footsteps,[55] creates a father of the man whose footsteps he does follow. Then the myth is played out between father and son: the son dares to express himself and the father punishes; the son conforms to the father's demands and the father comes to trust him; the son rebels to express himself again, with some maturity this time, and triumphs over the father; the father grows old or dies, becomes a memory, and the son forgives, acknowledging that he had, after all, taken his father's admonitions to heart. (Schudson 1978, pp. 84ff.)

Memories of Park show more than just a hint of this dramatic flair. Since it is customary for only the successful students to be asked what their memories of him were and for these to be evaluated, the fact that they took Park's admonitions to heart played a large part in their retroactive descriptions of their careers. But the father–child relationship did not always end happily. The fact that many of Park's students did not contribute anything worth mentioning to sociology after completing their projects (Shils 1981, p. 189) is explained, to a not insignificant degree, by the fact that the students were carried along by Park's own enthusiasm. Park kept at them until the project was successfully completed; by then, figuratively speaking, 'the air had been let out of the tyres'. Nels Anderson expressed this state of affairs somewhat more dras-

[54] The erratic change from one topic to another and from him saying something to its being written down is, in Shils' view, the reason why Park's own work, though admittedly keen-sighted, is often incoherent (Shils 1981, p. 190). The erratic change of tack is clearly derived from the need to be topical; this particular attitude corresponds to the picture of the hectic reporter.

[55] I shall return later to just how great an impact this assumed deracination, mentioned in passing, has on our understanding of the new generation of reporters.

tically. According to him, Park had two sorts of students: 'Some he drains so dry, they can never piss another drop.'

Everett C. Hughes, who quoted these words in a letter to Raushenbush ('these are Anderson's words'), admittedly does not share the criticism they contain. In his view, Park got the optimum out of his students, 'more indeed than their ability would otherwise have produced . . . Those who never p—d another drop, had at least had their big day with Park, and most of them remember it as a great thing in their lives' (REPA 7:5).

Herbert Bulmer expresses himself in a very similar way. He stresses that Park's achievement as a teacher and research tutor showed itself in the very fact that he succeeded in stretching students beyond their actual limits:

> He succeeded in getting a large number of them to develop an unflagging interest in concentrated work on their topics, resulting, it should be noted, in a very impressive series of publications. These publications were by and large excellent; they frequently represented achievements which the individual students would, under other conditions, never have been able to realize. (REPA 6:6)

Similarly to the way in which Lazarsfeld was later characterised as a 'managerial scholar', Park saw himself as a 'captain of inquiry with a company of men and women who must be directed to a worthwhile topic, then given the energy required to complete their work' (Matthews 1977, p. 107). Such a captain of inquiry, someone who leads a team, is at the end of the day only a variation on that new type of profession whose other representative is the city editor.

Details are precisely what a good editor takes very seriously. In his obituary of Park, Erle Young writes that practically all the students also experienced Park as someone who gave instructions for editing manuscripts: 'Choice of words, economy of expression, word order, paragraph construction, and the minutiae of composition were sometimes illustrated on the student's manuscript so fully that it remained hardly legible' (1944, pp. 437ff.). He remorselessly pilloried 'poor English' and pointed out grammatical errors: ' "What many writers need, and some of them badly", he would say, again recalling his days as a reporter, "is the discipline of an editor's blue pencil" ' (Pierson to Matthews, 7 November 1964; REPA 7:3). Park's lessons often took the form of editing students' papers. With respect to his editing final-year project reports, a passage from Anderson's autobiography is particularly enlightening.

When Anderson wanted to discuss his research report on 'The

Homeless Man in Chicago' with Burgess, he went to see Park at the office:

Park turned to make some compliment, not much, but much for him; the worth of it was the tone, which flattered me. He began, 'I hope you don't mind' and went on to say he had transposed words here and there or had written occasional suggestions with lead pencil. He added that he had already been to the University of Chicago Press: 'They will publish it as soon as we can get it ready!' 'But it was not written to be a book', I protested. 'It's just a report for the committee.' He and Burgess exchanged smiles. In the manner of Let's-get-on-with-it, Park began explaining changes he had made, mentioning at the outset a quotation he took from an article written by Harry M. Beardsley of the *Chicago Daily News*, 20 March 1917, a man who knew the West Madison area as he knew the hobo and his special culture. It was more than an ordinary main stem and he suggested 'Hobohemia' would be a more fitting identity. This may have suggested *The Hobo* as the title, which I didn't see until the book appeared. My title was something like, *The Homeless Men In Chicago*, the social workers' identity for all hobohemians. In about an hour we went through some hundred pages. A better word than mine he would put in here and there, I think most of the changes called for switching the sentence order in paragraphs. Some sentences which said little could be blanked out. I think no whole paragraph had to be removed, but on some pages the order of paragraphs needed to be changed. What was especially flattering, he raised no question about the content of paragraphs, sections or chapters. (Anderson 1975, p. 169)

Anderson is painting the classic picture of an editor here. A particularly revealing indication of this, but something woefully neglected in the literature to date, is the alteration to the title. As far as is known, the working titles of none of the classic studies was retained; in some cases, the title was changed several times until the final version came into being ('A Problem Boy' → 'The Delinquent Boy's Own Story' → *The Jack-Roller*). Park attached a great deal of importance to a pithy title which expressed the object of the investigation graphically, in the way a headline does. In the classic texts such as *The Gang*, *The Ghetto* or *The Gold Coast and the Slum*, the titles emulate the literacy practice of the period; Dos Passos' *Manhattan Transfer* (1925), Lewis' *Main Street* (1920) or Sinclair's *The Jungle* (1906) come to mind as only a few examples. This approach can be seen as an indication that the eye-catching title was chosen so as to reach a reading public well beyond the bounds of scholars, social workers and students. This guidance was in evidence even during the writing process itself: 'Watch if these sentences march along! . . . You are not writing for the professors; you are writing for the general public' (Park, according to Pauline Young; REPA 7:4).

Titles such as 'The Homeless Man in Chicago' (*The Hobo*) and 'A Problem Boy' (*The Jack-Roller*) would have limited the circle of readers to the above-mentioned groups from the outset. In fact, they would even have signalled to the reader that what he had before him had something to do with a sociology orientated toward social reform. Substituting a title such as 'The Homeless Man' by a title aimed at catching the attention of the public, such as 'The Hobo', must thus be understood as being part of the publication policy of a sociology aimed at achieving a public profile. Park was responsible for the realisation that even scholarly works can be sold to a general public beyond the narrow confines of the specialists. *The Gang*, *The Taxi-Dance Hall* and *The Gold Coast and the Slum* all make headlines in the daily press, they become the topic of leading articles and they find their way into the scandal columns of the Sunday papers; this is all illustrative proof that the Chicago studies are 'news' in a journalistic sense as well.[56] Zorbaugh's book becomes a bestseller in Chicago; the first edition sold out within ten weeks. The rules for social advancement in Chicago 'society' contained therein, conveyed by a member of the 'top 400', were for obvious reasons reprinted in all the Chicago daily newspapers. Individual studies were printed as excerpts in the daily press, one example of these being Cressey's *Taxi-Dance Hall* (1932), which makes taxi dancers into the latest journalistic sensation.

The efforts made to publicise the classics reinforce still further the impression of a shift from a sociology aimed at reform to one directed at the general public. For *The Hobo*, there are order forms headed 'I am curious about *The Hobo*'; this is a form of propagating a serious theme that would have been unthinkable for the reform-oriented literature. The prospectus for *The Hobo* unashamedly uses the fascination of the topic to advertise it, emphasizing that the book enables the reader to take a look behind the scenes. In this announcement, the principal theme of reform sociology is marginalised; there is only casual mention of the possibility that the reader might be interested in the problems which the hobo creates for his community. At all events, what seem to be more important are the insights into the hobo's way of life, his comradeship, moral code, and philosophy, insights that are the product of the author's participant observation – which thus becomes the sales argument. Even though we must assume that these texts were written by the advertising department, the fact still remains that they were intended to announce

---

[56] It is reasonable to assume that it was the reaction to these studies, not the studies themselves, which gave rise to the criticism that Chicago sociologists were indulging in journalism.

"Speaking of Books~

and especially those published by the University of Chicago Press

WHAT DO YOU KNOW ABOUT THIS MAN?

Has he begged of you at your back door, or slept under your porch?

Nels Anderson, who has tramped with him, eaten his handouts, worked (occasionally) with him, loafed with him "on the stem," and slept in his "jungles," will tell you about him.

In THE HOBO you may peer behind the scenes, as Anderson points out the intimate details in the vagrant's life. You will learn why he prefers to be homeless, what comradeship he seeks on the road, and what codes he lives by.

You may be surprised at the hobo's philosophy, be diverted by the poetry in his songs of the road, or you may be seriously interested in the problems that he is making for your community. In any case, you will like this strange, new book. Ask your dealer for it, or send your order to us.

The Hobo
by Nels Anderson

"THE TRUE UNIVERSITY IS A COLLECTION OF BOOKS" — CARLYLE

6 University of Chicago Press publicity for *The Hobo*, by Nels Anderson

scholarly works put out by a university publishing house. A line from the *Chicago Daily News* review is used to advertise Zorbaugh's *The Gold Coast and the Slum*: 'as thrilling as a best seller, as specific and apt as a book on etiquette, and as intimate as a diary'. Even *McClure's* could not have done it better!

That Park is playing the role of city editor becomes evident in the meeting between Anderson and Park – 'pushing, suggesting, inquiring,

needling, rewriting, scolding' (Matthews 1977, p. 108). Park's quick
temper and grumpiness, something that has been remarked on by
former students, as well as the unacademic forthrightness with which he
informed students that their ideas were worthless,[57] can in this context be
interpreted as elements of a type of rôle behaviour borrowed from
journalism, just as can the cynicism which Park all too frequently displayed, particularly with respect to the 'damned do-gooders'.[58] Clearly,
this cynicism served primarily to set the research and theoretical programme of scientific sociology off from the evangelical school of the
social gospel. But it is just as important to note that the way in which Park
expressed his criticism *vis-à-vis* the reformers was entirely consistent with
the tone prevalent amongst journalists. In his memoirs about his time as
a reporter, Theodore Dreiser writes that when people had a conversation with a journalist, they could at least be sure of speaking with
someone who was free of 'moralistic mush'. Park used this attitude in
order to offend the students – his talk of 'damned do-gooders' was not
exactly a mild provocation – and in this way scare them away from the
'Big D-Sociology (Drink, Desertion, Dependency)',[59] which was still
prevalent in the colleges of the 1920s.

'A moral man cannot be a sociologist', Park once said, and in reply to a
student's question about what good he himself had done in a problematic case under consideration, he said somewhat brusquely: 'Not a damn
thing' (Hughes, REPA 9:2). Park once stated to a reform-minded student
that the greatest damage perpetrated to Chicago was not as a result of
corrupt politicians or criminals, but of women reformers (Noss, REPA
7:2). It can be assumed here that Park had in mind the militant movements such as the Anti-Saloon League. But it cannot be completely ruled

[57] See, for example, the anecdote which Shils relates (Shils 1981, p. 189).

[58] What is significant is the cynicism which was *put on show*, because as is well known, Park was not
against (social) reformers as such, but against those reformers who combined their commitment
toward 'the other half' with an attitude of the know-all who claims to be able to lead the rest. In a
lecture manuscript on the subject of 'The Newspaper in America', Park states, in this context:
'Most newspapermen who have come up from the ranks of the reporters have a wholesome distrust of opinions, programs and reform, and if not of reform, then at least of reformers' (typescript, p. 14; REP 3:7).

[59] The process of disillusionment to some extent forms part of the informal training which journalists had in the newspaper editor's offices of the period. In his autobiography, Dreiser depicts a
conversation with his editor in this connection: 'You're just a cub yet, Theodore . . . full of college
notions of virtue and charity, and all that guff' (1922, p. 339). Apart from this, it seems to be the
rough way of speaking borrowed from journalism which led Anderson to believe that Park, like
himself, was from the 'wrong side of the tracks': 'When he [Anderson] read my chapters [about
Park's family background] he was disappointed about this. He said something like: our back-
grounds were not alike. His father was a businessman, mine was not' (Raushenbush to Hughes, 26
January 1967; REP 7:6).

out that Park was attacking the people he loved to hate, Sophonisba Breckinridge and Edith Abbott of the School of Civics and Philanthropy. This deep-seated enmity is borne out in detail in the interviews which James T. Carey conducted with former members of the sociology department. In a letter to Winifred Raushenbush dated 13 August 1966, Mrs Louis Wirth writes that Park 'disliked professionally trained social workers and was anathema to the two distinguished ladies who were the School of Social Service Administration . . . He once called Miss B. "that elderly spinster" in public – or rumor had it something worse' (REPA 4:4). To what extent personal reasons – relating to Mrs Park – are a factor, as is hinted at in the correspondence between Mrs Wirth and Raushenbush, is something I would like to leave as vague as it is to the letters (REPA 7:4). The fact is that an intellectual animosity (Diner 1975) arose between the two departments from the moment the School of Social Service Administration was set up in 1920 (replacing the School of Civics and Philanthropy which was previously supported by private patrons) and this animosity apparently went as far as the SSSA refusing access to 'case studies' files, claiming that the sociologists did not belong to the profession (REPA 9:2).

Behind all this, of course, lurked a controversy about the status of sociology and probably also a struggle for resources. But it is significant that Park conducted his end of the controversy using the argumentative tools of the newspaperman. In conversation with Carey, Mowrer characterises Abbott and Breckinridge as rigid anti-sociologists. Mowrer goes on to say that even Burgess still had a decided leaning toward social work: 'Park had no use for it at all.' Mrs Mowrer: 'Well, he was a newspaperman' (JTC 1:16).

Without doubt, the ostentatious demarcation *vis-à-vis* a type of sociology which had taken up the banner of the 'social gospel' did contribute to bringing forth a generation of students who were able to approach social reality without prejudice. The questioning of self-evident (class-) cultural truths (including the understanding of oneself as a beneficiary), the insistence on taking a close look for oneself as a starting-point for all real knowledge of social reality, as well as the emphasis on capturing varying perspectives so as to avoid ethnocentric distortions, all contributed to the image of a sociologist whose primary concern was not to find out what should be done, but rather to understand what people were actually doing.

The significance of the teacher's *habitus* or attitude in transforming sociology into an empirically based science has not been taken into account in the research to date. Understood in Bourdieu's sense as a generative grammar of patterns of action, the *habitus* to some extent runs like a scarlet thread through all forms of experience, so that each individual experience can become the 'metaphor' for another. In the case of Park, the scarlet thread is his characteristic attitude of reporter and editor. Robert Darnton (1975), in a sociological reflection on his own work as a reporter, has traced this characteristic attitude graphically, emphasising Park's understanding of himself as the editor in the rôle of 'ideas man', his contempt for preachers and professors as 'do-gooders' and 'egg-heads',[60] and his development of an ethos that rested not only on enthusiasm for work, punctiliousness and speed, but also on shrewdness, tenacity and a certain earthiness.

To summarise, Park's activity as an 'impresario in research' (Matthews) can be characterised as being that of a city editor in an academic milieu. His behaviour in this rôle – his understanding of himself as a 'captain of inquiry', his allocation of 'test assignments', his 'rewriting' of students' texts, etc. – all correspond to the behaviour of a city editor, as does the exhibitionist side of the rôle he played: his cynicism, his expressively performed contempt of 'do-gooders' and the intimidating side of his 'impression management'.

His curiosity and undisguised interest in others seem to be the elementary precondition for an unprejudiced approach to social reality. 'Perhaps what impressed me most about him', writes Donald Pierson to Fred Matthews, 'was his constant and absorbing interest in and curiosity about all kinds and conditions of people and in the ways in which they live. It should be remembered that he began his productive years as a reporter, and he never lost the reporter's curiosity about the world around him. He seemed to like nothing better than to wander the streets of a strange city, like he did, for instance, in Bahia, "poking his nose", as he once said, "into everything", observing, pausing to ask questions and to talk with anyone whose person or work or other activity interested him at the moment' (REPA 7:3). His ability to find topics for investigation in the immediate vicinity, which so impressed students, also fits this picture. Good examples of these are the 'Topics for Investigation', printed in the book by Raushenbush, which he compiled in the context of a 1925

---

[60] The fact that this attitude was not alien to Park is shown by an anecdote from Werner Cahnmann, who gives an account of a conference at University of Chicago at which Park reacted to a remark made by a European refugee scholar that the matter under discussion be analysed logically, by going 'red with rage' and saying: 'We don't give a damn for logic around here! What we want to know is what people do!' Cahnmann puts down these sorts of outbursts to the influence of Park's pragmatism as well as to his journalistic background (REPA 6:7).

conference organised by the Institute of Pacific Relations in Honolulu, Hawaii (Raushenbush 1979, pp. 127ff.). Formally speaking, such a plan of investigation corresponds to the notion of a 'series' in journalism. A comparison of these topics with the structure of the series of articles written by Washington and Park, *The Man Farthest Down* (1913), shows this clearly. Again, it would be particularly appealing, not only from the formal angle but also from the point of view of content, were a comparison with the three-part Hawaii series by Ray Stannard Baker (which appeared in *American Magazine*, vol. 123 (1911/12)) to be made.

A final area where his work resembled that of the editor is manifested in the fact that Park published very little, apart from essays and reviews. If we leave aside his reviews, then one-fifth of his scientific publications are introductions to the works of his students, the scientific equivalent of the programmatical editorial note. The fact that this status did not displease him is shown by an autobiographical sketch: 'I have been most successful, I suspect, in my introductions to other men's books – books which represent the problems I have been most interested in' (Paul J. Baker 1973, p. 260).

An anonymous poem written by a student, which was presented to Park on the occasion of his retirement from Fisk University on 12 February 1938, celebrates him as an author of introductions. Perhaps nowhere else is Park's true significance, namely that of an innovator, better summed up than in this poem. And not only that: the poem, which presents Park as a 'tramper through cities', as a 'man of the senses', as a 'teller of stories', and as a 'writer of introductions', projects – admittedly from the point of view of an enthusiastic student, but nonetheless – an impressive picture of Park's personality.

To Robert E. Park

I

You are the tramper through cities:
London, New York, and Chicago,
Honolulu, Calcutta, Berlin
Respond to you,
Acknowledge you,
As friend and confidant;
Openly declaring their life to you,
Communicating their secrets,
In esoteric tones.
You, the interrogator!
The insistent questioner!

Steeped in the poets,
Whence came the first insights
That made you curious about life
And sent you in search of the news.
That is why you love the city,
With its massed and varied humanity;
Where life whirls to a vortex,
Where life moves,
Through conflicts, through changes,
Of persons and cultures.
Like Darwin,
You go prowling and seeking,
Unhasty and tentative,
Patient yet eager,
Your mind alive
In the streets of the city;
You, the listener and interpreter,
Absorbing through all your senses,
Absorbing through your very pores!
Filled with immense enjoyment,
You, the tramper through cities.

II

You are a man of the senses;
No adamantine figure is yours,
But one quick to react;
The warmth of the sun in your smile;
Olympian wrath in your temper
That you have not cared to control.
You have not aspired
To be a gentleman, you say,
And laugh quietly
At the notion
Of institutionalized civility,
Sense and sensory meaning:
These are the elements,
The honest basis of life,
The source of our culture!
This you have never doubted.
The immediacy of your living
Shows in your face:
The child is there,
And the Negro:
Those simple impulsive reactions
Declare themselves eloquently;

Yet the breadth of the world is there,
And the depth of the soul,
You are
What you have known and appreciated;
You have cast out pretensions,
Preferring humanity,
The strong appetites, the wants,
That you have seen in others;
That you have recognized in yourself:
You, a man of the senses.

III

You are the teller of stories,
To old and young alike.
You are a kind of oracle,
Your smile and gentle manner
Inspire warm confidence,
While the story is told
With splendid zest
And a smiling remembrance
As if, in the end,
There was nothing in life
But humor.
Pathos and tragedy disappear
As if by magic
Because, to you,
There is no tragedy in life –
Only unintelligible things –
And your task is to know,
To get understanding.
Being wise, you cultivate wisdom;
Transmitting your insights
By indirection.
No hint of the preacher
Nor of the moralizer;
No story of yours to frighten,
No tale to hurt or offend:
You aim only to stimulate,
To educate, to make clear.
Yours is the gift of the ages,
The sensitive mind of the artist:
To those who have learned to listen,
You are impelling, inspiring,
You, the teller of stories.

IV

You are the writer of introductions:
Like the architect of a building
Who does not himself
Lay the brick on the mortar,
But who knows the meaning
Of basic design or method,
So you present a study
Of friend or colleague –
You write the introduction:
Better, oft-times, than the book itself,
A finished essay,
Suggesting approach or direction!
Always expanding, not closing a subject.
To introduce:
That, in truth, is your function:
These prefatory chapters
To a score of volumes
Are your biography –
The various aspects,
Each in some essential way,
A phase of your own experience,
A thought you have explored,
And would explore further.
You are no prophet,
No reformer, no academic priest;
You are the sceptic of formulas,
The scorner of dead institutions.
You look to life itself,
To the warm impulses
Of men and women.
You are the true philanthropist:
You, the writer of introductions.

ADOPTION OR STIMULUS? A SUMMARY

When I took Dr and Mrs Park for a sightseeing trip through the city we stopped at a museum. While I took Mrs Park in, Dr Park stayed in the car and said something to the effect 'Mrs Park likes pictures. I like to watch the people.'

Bernard L. Hormann

The scholarly community undoubtedly took note of the journalistic influence on Park's sociology, and yet the systematic import of this influence has hitherto scarcely been considered. The space taken up by the

years of journalistic experience in the Park biographies is itself symptomatic of the 'oblivion' to which this less prestigious background has been
consigned.

A mere thumbnail sketch of this period within the overall biography
of his career as a sociologist would be quite in order if it had had no
effect, or at best an insignificant effect on his scientific activity – if, as it
were, we could speak of two completely separate phases of his life. But
Park's activity in research and teaching cannot be interpreted adequately without taking account of the imprint left by his years of journalistic apprenticeship. Above all, his view of reality was shaped by these
years. The essential elements of this approach to reality were his insistence on direct observation, coupled with his demand that people con-
front social facts without prejudice and question things which seem to
them to be a matter of course, which means looking behind the scenes.

In practice, such an approach to reality leads to a teaching atmosphere where sociology becomes 'work in progress' and the seminar
becomes a sociological workshop where the raw material gained in the
field is conceptually processed. Park's idea was that the students should
become 'reporters in depth', 'so as to "enter as fully as possible into the
social worlds they studied, participating in them sufficiently to understand the attitudes and values of these worlds"' (Bulmer, quoted from
Matthews 1977, p. 108). This description shows very clearly that the
'reporter in depth' is nothing more and nothing less than a sociological
field researcher. Park's recourse to cultural anthropology, irrespective of
how similar the approach was, would therefore not have been necessary
unless it was being used to justify his case by covering up a considerably
less prestigious relationship with reporting. *That* there was a need for this
is shown from the criticisms made by fellow specialists of the day, who
dismiss Chicago sociology as a 'journalistic school of sociology' and
'journalism in disguise'.[61] Nels Anderson has quite rightly interpreted
this criticism as a spiteful allusion to Park's past (REPA 6:6). Just how
common the suspicion was that he was merely presenting a variant on
journalistic reporting is shown by a collection of critiques by Louis
Wirth in the *Kölner Vierteljahresheften*. There, the theme of cultural anthropology as a justification for Park's brand of sociology was taken up
again, this time for the benefit of the German experts. In this critique,

---

[61] I have unfortunately not succeeded in reconstructing from whom the criticism came. Edward
Shils, in a conversation, did actually mention the names of sociologists who possibly come into
consideration, but since this must remain a matter of speculation, as he himself emphasised, I
would not care to reproduce these.

Wirth presents Zorbaugh's *The Gold Coast and the Slum* as one volume
from the series of urban studies which were carried out by Park's students and which he compares to the investigations 'conducted by
anthropologists into the culture of primitive peoples'; Wirth continues

There are certainly sociologists who consider this sort of work beneath their
academic dignity and reject it as a form of journalistic reporting. However, for
as long as the representatives of sociology do not concern themselves with such
studies as these, there will be no scientifically based sociology. In other words:
unless future sociological research bases its generalisations on the patient collection of concrete material and verifies its hypotheses by repeated observation of
the same phenomenon, sociology will remain a pointless sort of armchair philosophy and its claim to be recognised as a science mere pretension. (Wirth
1930/1, p. 547)

Only in old age did Park make it clear that, when compiling his essay
'The City', he had, to a not inconsiderable extent, made use of information and experiences he had gained whilst a reporter; he does this using
arguments which show how far-sighted Pulitzer's statements were with
respect to sociology in the context of the planned curriculum for a
College of Journalism. In the house bulletin of the Society for Social
Research in 1939, Park tells us that:

In the article I wrote about the city I leaned rather heavily on the information I
had acquired as a reporter regarding the city. Later on, as it fell to my lot to
direct the research work of an increasing number of graduate students, I found
my experience as a city editor in directing a reportorial staff had stood me in
good stead. Sociology, after all, is concerned with problems in regard to which
newspaper men inevitably get a good deal of first hand knowledge. Besides that,
sociology deals with just those aspects of social life which ordinarily find their
most obvious expression in the news and in historical and human documents
generally. *One might fairly say that a sociologist is merely a more accurate, responsible and
scientific reporter.* (Park 1982 [1939], p. 338; my italics)

Referring to the passage, Bulmer remarks that we should not exaggerate the influence of Park's journalistic background, 'with the connotations of imprecision and casual and unsystematic inquiry that this
carries' (Bulmer 1984, p. 91). It bears mentioning that the conventional
argument against empirical sociology in the Chicago mould, which is
based on connotations of 'imprecision' and 'unsystematic inquiry', is
used here as an argument to claim that the influence of journalism on
Chicago sociology was relatively insignificant. This reasoning, which
implicitly borrows the arguments put forward by the critics, can be compared to exorcism. Park's statement, however, makes it clear that what
was involved was not primarily the connotations of imprecision and

unsystematic inquiry, which were only introduced later as a competitive argument between different sociological orientations, but 'first-hand knowledge', i.e., a view of reality based on the principle of observing human behaviour and social processes where they actually happen.

Park's demand that the investigation be done in an unprejudiced and purpose-free way is of central methodological importance as evidence of the assertion that a relationship existed between journalistic inquiry and sociological research. Park constantly made his students aware of the connection between empathy and objectivity as a research standard. In so doing, he formulated something as a methodological principle of sociological research which had already been considered as the ethos of journalism. Bleyer writes, in his instruction manual for journalists (which, by the way, Park made use of in his teaching), that young journalists frequently insist on making known their own views concerning the topic they are questioning someone about: 'The reporter should remember that he is an impartial observer, not an advocate of one side or another' (Bleyer 1923 [1913], p. 52).

It is amazing how closely the combination of objectivity and inner knowledge ('empathy and distance'), presented here as the characteristic attitude of the reporter, corresponds to the ideal path to be trodden by scientific field research.

As should have become clear by now, my attempt to reconstruct the influence of Park's journalistic past on his draft for a programme of urban sociology has nothing to do with any repudiation of this programme and the associated research methods. The importance of Park for the emergence of an empirically based urban sociology can scarcely be underestimated; René König, making use of a superlative, describes him as the 'Chicago School's greatest pioneer.'

Also, this attempt to emphasise his journalistic background is certainly not intended to gainsay the influence of ethnology on Park's thinking; the very manner in which he referred to it in justification makes it clear that Park saw in ethnology a kindred scientific discipline. In the 1920s, when sociology and anthropology in Chicago were still linked together in one department, the two disciplines had a mutually stimulating effect on each other; as Fay-Cooper Cole writes,[62] their common denominator

---

[62] Fay-Cooper Cole refers to this common ground in a letter to university president Woodward, in order to emphasise the things that divided them (archaeology, physical anthropology and linguistics) as an argument in favour of the establishment of an independent anthropology department (see Stocking 1979, p. 16).

lay in their concentration on people and their culture. Cross-fertilisation also means that the influence was not only in one direction. If I have said that ethnologists refer to the adoption hypothesis when searching for the subject they have lost, as a means of justifying a historic claim to complex societies as a field of study, the argumentation can just as easily be turned around. By referring to the usefulness of the methods developed by the ethnologists for investigating 'primitive' ethnic groups, for the study of urban life and manifestations of urban culture, Park becomes willy-nilly the catalyst or indirect founder of a type of ethnology devoted to research into local communities and big cities. Girtler, who, as has been shown, quotes the adoption hypothesis in his essay on cultural anthropology in order to justify the claim that cultural anthropological methods can also be used to investigate the complex societies of European and American culture, cites W. Lloyd Warner and his 'Yankee City' studies (Girtler 1979, p. 52) in his defence. Warner, an ethnologist who had previously carried out research in Australia, was not only influenced by Radcliffe-Brown, but he confesses to having been inspired by the sociological series (Warner cites *The Gold Coast and the Slum, The Gang,* and *The Ghetto*; see Raushenbush 1979, pp. 144ff.) while carrying out his study of Newburyport, Massachusetts. Beside this, he corresponded with Park and had a detailed discussion with him.

When Emilio Willems, in his encyclopaedia entry 'Ethnology', stresses that ethnological exploration of non-primitive cultures is 'particularly due to the initiative of Robert Redfield and William Lloyd Warner' (1967, p. 65), then there is a third person behind the two, functioning as a common reference point, namely Robert Park. This connection is indirectly suggested whenever Park, Warner and Redfield are periodically mentioned in the context of recapitulating the history of community research using ethnographical procedures, although commentators fail to see the specific structure of this relationship (see, e.g., René König 1984, pp. 27ff.).

The influence of Chicago sociology on the modernisation of ethnology can be traced directly to Robert Redfield, Park's son-in-law. The correspondence between Redfield and Park is an eloquent testimony to the encouragement and stimulation which Park gave his son-in-law when he was planning and carrying out his Tepoztlán study. Redfield wrote to Park on 2 December 1926:

We are at least on the brink of our exploit, because tomorrow very early we intend all of us to go down to Tepoztlan together . . . our interest in the job has been very brightly rekindled by my two glimpses of Tepoztlan. The whole history of Mexico appears in the walls, the streets, the talk of the people. Over the ancient foundations of the precolumbian Indians stands an old and crumbling colonial town with its church and ruined monastery. The adobe houses . . . are about one-third in ruins due to the revolution of 1910. In those years Tepoztlan was perhaps the most dangerous place in Mexico, a center of Zapatista warfare . . . They are still very Zapatista in sentiment, but it is going to be difficult to get them to talk about it . . . Without this Sr. Conde I could have done very little. He is educated, ambitious, clever, temperamental and very poor. I think eventually I will get him on the payroll. He speaks Aztec fluently. The Aztec is in part kept up as a self-conscious nationalistic point of pride, in part spoken as the natural idiom of the less civilized individuals. Sr. Conde did the introducing, the arguing, the cajoling, the bargaining, while I merely patted the babies' heads and murmured polite sentiments to everybody.

In his reply of 8 December 1926, Park wrote:

Your description of the country and the people of the country you are in delighted me and made me envious. I think you have a great chance to write an account of the life that will be at once scholarly and humanly interesting . . . Tell Daty [Margaret Park] that I hope that she will have time to make a rather complete collection of the songs of the people, their ballads, love songs and their hymns if they have any of their own. But do not hurry . . . Learn the language, learn the Aztec language if you can but do not work . . . If you just manage to live there one year and write down leisurely what you learn you will have enough. I suggest that you study the ruins; study the Aztec language; the Zapata revolution, but do not worry getting things about the country and the people in one year. I think you will want to return to that country many times and the main thing is to see that everyone lives outdoors a good deal and sleeps a good deal and has a good time. (REPA 2:2)

What makes Redfield into what Firth has termed 'one of the international pioneers of modern work in social anthropology' is, firstly, his extension of the field of study to include rural communities ('peasant societies'), which he regards as an 'intermediate stage' between primitive society (the traditional terrain addressed by ethnologists) and urban society. Under the influence of Robert Park, writes George Stocking Jr in his essay on the history of the Chicago anthropology department, Redfield moves away from Boasianic historicism toward a sociological anthropology with evolutionary undertones (Stocking 1979). It is probably undeniable that Park's urban sociological exposé, where he deploys the particular characteristics of urban life against the foil of the rural community, was just as important in prompting a change of direction toward the rural community as a field for research as was Thomas and Znaniecki's *The Polish Peasant* (1974 [1918–20]), where the main themes are actually the conflicts which arise from the differences between the original Polish peasant culture and American urban life. This influence is glaringly obvious in the choice of 'community' as an object of inquiry ('a true laboratory') in studying whole cultures – a parallel to the urban environment as a paradigm for modern society. It is not possible here to reconstruct the influences in detail, but some of the elements can be cited: the holistic approach, which at the same time, and this is where it differs from traditional ethnology, sees the whole ('community') as part of a greater whole ('a community within communities' = 'a city within cities'); the interlinking and juxtaposition of ecological systems and moral order; the analysis of social processes and socio-cultural change; the value of secularisation, individualisation and socio-cultural disorganisation and, above all, the methodical approach, the biographical method ('life history') and the observation paradigm, something which is used frankly and imaginatively, in keeping with community research's claim to be holistic (Redfield 1955, 1962). To date, there have only been rudimentary attempts to study the line running from Park – via Redfield – to ethnology and its modernised form. It is not possible here – in fact it would be presumptuous in this context – to make up for this omission, but I would, however, like to make a brief reference to a particularly interesting chapter in the history of science, namely, to Chinese sociology/social anthropology, as represented by Fei Xiaotong (Fei Hsiao-Tung). This chapter is particularly interesting because Fei Xiaotong, considered to be the founder of Chinese field research and one of the pioneers of Chinese community research, was directly influenced by Park.

In his acceptance speech when being given the Malinowski Memorial Award, Fei refers to the historical watershed in the mid-1930s, when young students such as himself refused to accept purely textbook knowledge relating to Chinese society, such as was taught at university: 'So we walked out of our schools, left our textbooks behind, and went to the countryside, to communities in cities and townships to observe and experience society as it was' (Fei 1981, p. 3). Fei acknowledges Malinowski, with whom he studied from 1936 to 1938, as the person who had shown him this path for research. Such an acknowledgement, in the context of the official acceptance at the presentation of the Malinowski Memorial Award, may not be surprising. However, as far as both time and persons are concerned, there is another and more obvious influence. This influence, which is hinted at in the specific way the observation paradigm is worded ('left our textbooks behind . . . to observe and experience society as it was'), is that of Robert Park, who spent some time in the autumn of

1932 as guest professor at Yenching University. The mere fact that Park was invited itself speaks in favour of an influence derived from Chicago sociology, which was taken to China via former students: 'At Yenching University I found many students who had earlier studied in America and were now attempting to use the ideas and conceptions we had given them to understand and study their own society and civilization' (Park, quoted from Raushenbush 1979, p. 134).

During the quarter he taught at Yenching University, Park introduced the students to ecological thinking; he gave a course in 'Methods of Social Research', a course which was received with particular interest because of the Chinese tradition of pure book study; and he conducted small field projects with the students.[63] We can only guess at the way in which Park proceeded to give instruction in field work; however, it can be assumed that his proposals resembled those which he made at the turn of 1932/3 to Bernard Hormann, who was teaching English and German at Lignan University and who was planning an investigation into a nearby village:

Now, regarding your own research, you seem to be succeeding in getting acquainted with the people: Writing down your immediate impressions is also valuable . . . You should use all of Honan island as a setting for your study. Get a good map of the island. Then locate all the villages and plot other interesting information. Make the map graphic. Somehow or other you must make your village real to yourself and to your readers . . . Then, coming to your particular village, make a map of it, showing in some graphic way how the houses are clustered together, how the narrow lanes cut across the semi-circle, so that from above it may look almost like a pie. In a third map locate all the temples, gods, shrines, and other objects around which there is or has been sentiment. Start with the public objects. Later get those in the homes. Then in the coming year you must get all kinds of information. Speak to everyone. Use everyone. Find out every-thing you can about the history of Honan, the boat people and this particular village. In the village you will have a difficult task. But you must try to discover what exactly are the sentiments of the various groups of people towards the objects of worship. You will find that their sentiments vary according to the groups, the time, and the occasion . . . You must live with the people. You must put yourself on their level. Only thus will you be able to understand them. (REPA 7:1)

In a letter dated 15 November 1943, Fei, who was staying as a guest of the State Department in Chicago, acknowledges Park's influence on his studies:

Dear Professor Park: This is from a student of yours when you were teaching in Yenching, China. At that time I was a small college boy and I remember nothing

---

[63] A volume in Chinese, entitled *Robert E. Park and His Sociology*, was put together from his lecture notes and papers.

outstanding that could attract your attention. But I was not the last one that had been very much inspired. Since you came back, we had edited a little book entitled Park's Sociology and I was the one who translated our articles on China and on Sociology. This was in the year 1933, just ten years ago. To-day I am working in your office in Chicago. I am overpower by a feeling of human fate. It is something like a dream but the dream is in someway true . . . I am sending you several copies of the summaries of our work and a book I wrote in London about five years ago *Peasant Life in China*. I hope you will be glad to see how the seeds you had sown in China have grown in some shape. I am extremely flattered when I met your daughter, Mrs. Redfield and learnt that she is willing to help me in preparing my manuscript. She is so like to me that I cannot find any word to describe. Dr. Redfield allows me to work in this university, . . . in your old office on the fifth floor. A man coming from a folk society will certainly be bewitched by the history behind the walls. I feel all the time I am working under your spirit. I hope your inspiration will be transferred into the work I am now engaging in. (REPA 1:15; grammatical errors in the original)

As far as I am aware, Park, who died on 7 February 1944, never replied to this letter. But the influence of the Chicago department survives, via Margaret Park Redfield and Robert Redfield. In 1953, Fei's *Essays in Rural–Urban Relations* appeared in the University of Chicago Press, published by Margaret Park Redfield and provided with an introduction by Robert Redfield (Fei 1980a [1953]). As far as the reconstruction of the (Chicago) influence is concerned, this volume is especially noteworthy for the six 'life histories' which were collected by Chow Young-teh, probably an assistant of Fei's. As far as I can judge from what was accessible to me in English, the Chicago understanding of research finds constant expression in Fei's writings, as does the influence of Malinowski's functionalism at the theoretical level. When Malinowski, in his foreword to Fei's community study *Peasant Life in China* (1980b [1939]), by way of marking a new beginning, emphasises the fact that Fei is directing our attention, not to a 'small, insignificant tribe', but to one of the greatest nations on earth, while at the same time examining and coming to terms with the change in its traditional culture due to Western influence, then he is once again merely expressing the essence of the pioneering achievement of Robert Park.

COMMUNICATION AND SOCIETY: PARK'S THEORETICAL CONCEPT

> Society really begins with communication.   Robert Ezra Park

It initially sounds odd when Herbert Bulmer asserts of a sociologist who was being introduced as a city editor that: 'Dr. Park was tremendously interested in analytical theory; he was always seeking to go beyond mere descriptive depiction and to make generalizations' (Bulmer, REPA 6:6). This endeavouring to go beyond mere descriptive depiction manifests itself vividly in Park's travel diaries, where detailed observations are to be found alongside analytical considerations, on the very next page, as it were. For example, in the same diary in which we come across his observations relating to the Ginza,[64] we also find his thoughts on the relationship between communication and social distance as a process that functions to constitute society:

Communication is always a matter of overcoming distance – physical distance first and then social distance – anything that is an obstacle to complete understanding. Social distance is a term in which one attempts to describe abstractly and in terms of degrees of difference these obstacles. So far as one individual is able to communicate with more or less ease . . . the social distance is more or less transcended.

Communication is social, since only so far as communication is possible does social life exist. (REPA 4:7)

We can agree with Bulmer when he stresses that it would be a great mistake to see in Park someone merely striving to attain a higher level of journalistic reporting: 'Instead he was always seeking to extract from the down-to-earth descriptive accounts meaningful characterizations and generalizations' (Bulmer, REPA 6:6). Park is a genuine social scientist; the appreciation Frazier and Gaziano (1979) give, of him being the founder of communication and media sociology, misses the point, notwithstanding all the recognition of Park's work embodied in this acknowledgement. His sociology always revolves around the question: how is society possible? This fundamental question was posed by Simmel in his famous excursus on the first chapter of his *Sociology*, and even if the question 'How is society possible?'[65] is not posed by Park in so many words, it nevertheless best describes the thrust of Park's thought, albeit with the characteristic, pragmatic undertone which differentiates him from Simmel. Just as Simmel presents his seminal arguments by means of sociological miniatures, namely 'The Argument'/'The Meal'/'The Adventure', Park, whether concerned with the news world, racial prejudice or strikes, is also aiming beyond concrete analysis at generalisations. Park is no sociologist of some specific subsector (although he is possibly more knowledgeable than the specialist – simply because he is not a

[64] See n47 above.
[65] This was the title of Simmel's 'Excursus on the Problem: How Is Society Possible?' when it appeared for the first time in English, in the *American Journal of Sociology*, in 1910.

specialist), but someone who takes social situations and institutions as sociological source material: to cite one commentator, 'his essays on race relations are, in fact, essays on social processes and social interaction in general' (Everett C. Hughes 1950, p. xiv).

As I have already attempted to show when outlining Simmel's influence on the conception of 'The City', for all their agreement, there are also substantial differences between the two men. Sociology, as Park understands it, is meant to uncover the conditions which cause individuals to lead a cooperative existence. He sees these primarily in the processes of communication by means of which individuals reach consensus. An extract from his travel diary is actually a perfect example of this, for here we encounter Park's key concepts with regard to both the theoretical and practical strands of his work, 'communication' and 'understanding':

What is achieved by communication is understanding and the ability of one individual to understand another is the measure of the distance between them. This differing ability to understand one individual or another is a matter of observation but it is also a matter of feeling. We can see the distance that separates A from B, but we can *sense* the distance that separates us from others. This individual seems reserved and distant and insofar incomprehensible. There is always a certain amount of vague apprehension of the one we do not understand; but we are at ease with the person who is completely understandable. This sense of being at ease and at home or the absence of it is what we mean by distance. (REPA 4:7; emphasis in the original)

It is clear from this entry that Park's thoughts are not only of a theoretical nature; they are at the same time the expression of the sociologist comprehending himself as someone who uses the method of understanding in order to arrive at a better comprehension of things. Donald Pierson, who was apparently particularly impressed by this characteristic, gave any number of examples in his letter to Fred Matthews of Park's ability to communicate, indeed his liking for communication, the interest and curiosity he showed toward others, be this in conversation with students or in the field (Donald Pierson letter, 7 November 1964; REPA 7:3). The travel diary itself is an expression of this attitude, travel being for Park a particular form of communication.

Park develops his theory of society similarly to the way in which he made his case for the 'city' as an subject of sociological investigation.[66] He puts forward a substructure (the physiological conditions, so to

---

[66] Or perhaps to put it more precisely, the city as an example of society.

speak), on the basis of which the structure, which we can denote as society in the real sense, the social *sui generis*, is erected. The following approach to the issue is the starting-point of his considerations:

From the point of view of sociology and human ecology the question is twofold: (1) Does there exist below the level of what is ordinarily called society a system of vital and functional relationships between human beings which can properly [be] described as symbiotic or ecological; (2) How does one distinguish between those relationships that are symbiotic and ecological and those which are political and moral, i.e., social in the narrower sense of the word? (REPA 6:3)

By means of this two-fold question, Park varies a distinction which runs through his macro-sociological work and which he had made early on in his dissertation 'The crowd and the public', namely, that between biological and sociological processes (Park 1904, pp. 70ff.). Park's draft theory of society repeatedly focuses on the distinction between two different kinds of order, while constantly endeavouring to give a precise sociological definition of the relationship between them. Drawing an analogy with animal and plant ecology – the work of Eugenius Warming was the model here – Park labels the social substructure 'community', a community being an entity which gradually takes spatial shape and is thus geographically definable, providing all those conditions which are necessary for societies to put down roots:

The essential characteristics of a community, so conceived, are those of: (1) a population, territorially organized, (2) more or less completely rooted in the soil it occupies, (3) its individual units living in a relationship of mutual interdependence that is symbiotic rather than societal, in the sense in which that term applies to human beings. (Park 1936, p. 4)

This visible spatial dimension, and the fact that we can pin-point its territorial boundaries exactly, also yield a methodological advantage, which allows the community thus defined to be taken as an object of sociological research. The community is the point of departure, because the elements which go to make it up, the respective groups of population and their institutions, can all be recorded cartographically and statistically with great precision. Here once again, it is clear where Park saw the necessity for (but at the same time also the limitation of) statistical procedures, namely, in collecting spatial indices, that is to say in cases where the correlation of spatial and social facts is actually possible. To take up Park's dualistic way of thinking, we could say that quantitative procedures are appropriate to the ecological order, while qualitative procedures are appropriate to the cultural order.

The structure that is sociology's subject of investigation proper, namely society, in the sense of a cultural order, is created on the foundation of the ecological order:

The fact seems to be, then, that human society, as distinguished from plant and animal society, is organized on two levels, the biotic and the cultural. There is a symbiotic society based on competition and a cultural society based on communication and consensus. (Park 1936, p. 13)

This last quotation indicates precisely from what origin Park derived his dual concept of society as 'community' and 'society', on the one hand, and symbiotic 'base' and cultural 'superstructure', on the other, namely those elementary relations, conceived by Spencer for one and by Comte for another, which serve to constitute society in the first place. What I mean is, the view of society as a system determined by the division of labour, which makes competitive cooperation necessary on the basis of growing interdependency, and the idea of society as a spiritual order, a system of what Comte termed 'common moral ideas'.

A biotic (ecological) order, on the one hand, and a cultural (social) order, on the other, are each distinguished by specific forms of interaction, namely, competition on the one hand and communication on the other:

Communication and competition seem to be the two fundamental processes, or forms of interaction, by which a social order is initiated and maintained among the individuals whose life in common is the life of society. Communication is, on the whole, an integrating and socializing process. It creates the loyalties and understanding that make concerted and consistent collective action possible. (Park 1955c [1940], p. 314)

It is astounding, but probably symptomatic of the low esteem in which Park's sociology is held in Germany, that Habermas, in his theory of communicative action, at no point considered Park's ideas. Habermas' distinction between work and interaction, between instrumental and communicative action, which he derives from Marx's differentiation between the forces of production, on the one hand, and the relations of production, on the other, corresponds to Park's distinction between competition and communication. In a similar way to Habermas, who views instrumental action as corresponding with the compulsions of external nature, Park sees competition as both an expression and a means of what the social Darwinists considered the struggle for survival, something which finds a social corrective in processes of communication. Competition, as Park sees it, is the principle of individuation, whereas communication operates as an integrating and communitising principle. Communication engenders that consensus by means of which a social group becomes a cultural unity. Put differently, communication is, if not quite identical to, then nevertheless indispensable to the cultural process of reaching understanding, i.e., that which Habermas terms 'interpretative schemas on which a consensus can be reached'.

The dualism[67] of community and society, of biotic and cultural order, admittedly allows the subject of the investigation and the course of the investigation to be specified more precisely, but as a theoretical construct it runs the danger of naturalising social situations. As Joas rightly remarks, Park does not succeed in creating a viable theoretical bridge between economy and society; instead, the cracks are papered over with 'evolutionistic assumptions about the gradual transformation of the unplanned and competitive sector of society into a democratic and self-determined one' (Joas 1988, p. 434). The result of this is a 'mere combination of democratically orientated macro-sociology with background assumptions about naturalised competition and the struggle for survival' (Joas 1988, p. 434). The gradual transformation takes the form of stages in the process of developing community, territorial → economic → political → cultural, which each correspond to a specific social science dealing with the subject area in question: human ecology, economics, political science and social/cultural anthropology (see Park 1955c [1940], p. 309; REPA 5:10). I am not in a position to judge whether this construction involves Comte's well-known model of the hierarchy of sciences – from the most general to the most complex – being applied to sociology. What does become clear, however, is that Park thinks decidedly in terms of stages and cycles which he often merely posits deterministically, rather than creating an empirically informed theory of mediation between economy and society.

On the other hand, the dualistic model, and this is something not usually seen by critics, makes clear in an especially cogent way the outstanding rôle which Park attributes to communicative action, not only from the standpoint of social theory, but also from the viewpoint of the politics of society, i.e., both as a socialising principle *and* as a medium of

---

[67] Dualism is *the* characteristic figure of thought as far as Park is concerned, whether used to distinguish between forms of society (community–society), forms of interaction (competition–communication), forms of collective action (crowd–public) or forms of knowledge (ecology–sociology). Matthews – and I concur with his arguments – sees Park's dualism on the one hand as transferring a philosophical experience to sociology (to some extent as a principle of classification), and on the other, as an attempt to synthesise different contemporary attempts to explain human action.

democratic self-understanding: 'I have said that society exists in and through communication. By means of communication individuals share in a common experience and maintain a common life' (Park 1926, p. 14). Society exists in and through communication (an insight which Park gained from Dewey), because in the final analysis, it consists of individuals with a clear consciousness of themselves.

This consciousness of self (the term 'subjectivity', according to Park, in fact means nothing more than this) always includes a knowledge of individual differences and distance – in fact it even presupposes this (see Park's Honolulu travel diary, 6 January 1930, REPA 4:7). The condition for successful communication is not the identical nature of members of society, but rather their diversity. It is precisely this diversity which makes communication in the sense of reaching understanding not only necessary, but also possible, because only subjects with individual experiences have anything to say to each other:

It is this diversity in the experiences of individual men that makes communication necessary and consensus possible. If we always responded in like manner to like stimulation, there would not be, as far as I can see, any necessity for communication, nor any possibility of abstract and reflexive thought. The demand for knowledge arises from the very necessity of checking up and funding these divergent individual experiences, and of reducing them to terms which make them intelligible to all of us. (Park 1936, p. 15)

Here, the task of communication goes far beyond what we might term that of providing a correction to rampant biotic growth, i.e., the harmful consequences of unplanned competition. It becomes a cultural ideal which transcends traditional bonds, in order to arrive at a common *universe of discourse*. This common quality does not actually mean the sublation of diversity; on the contrary, it is a case of diversity appearing irreversible.

Communication enables individual experiences to be integrated, but not sublated. It is also the task of science to contribute to this ideal, which, in the final analysis, is the ideal of global citizenship, for in essence science is nothing more than a particular form of communication:

It is the business of science to reduce the inarticulate expression of our personal feelings to a common universe of discourse and to create out of our private experiences an objective and intelligible world. (Park 1936, p. 15)

'To a European observer,' writes Park in 'The Problem of Cultural Differences', 'the outstanding characteristic of American life, as compared with that of Europe, is the extraordinary mobility and restlessness of the American population' (Park 1950b, p. 10). This mobility and inherent restlessness are also the characteristic features of Park's model of society. His theory of society portrays the image of a society in movement, 'in constant flux', as he once said, 'a complex of atoms in motion'. Stability is to some extent an illusion; in reality it is always relative, a relatively constant form of change. It would be a serious misunderstanding to interpret Park's so very characteristic way of thinking in stages and cycles as something arresting and finalising. Certainly evolutionistic in origin, as well as being intended to serve as an instrument of analysis and a principle of classification, it is at the same time proof of a thinking in categories of movement: the individual stages and cycles form schemata so that movement can be frozen for a moment, in order to direct the view toward fixed patterns, which, as it were, lie underneath the current.

Park's model of society is not only dynamic and processual, it is also, in the words of Ralph Turner, 'a dynamic disequilibrium model', a concept which appears to shy away from all that is fixed, immobile and encrusted:

Unlike equilibrium theorists, Park tells us little about the hypothetical states of equilibrium. He seems to be little interested in the characteristics of states of assimilation and institutionalization, and when he does take time to describe them, his characterizations are contradictory and sound more like states of disequilibrium. These states merely serve as points of reference, and his preoccupation is with the movements, the sequences, that take place. (Ralph H. Turner 1967, p. xxii)

Only when society gets out of balance does it enter flux: the crisis, in which the old is no longer (unquestionably) valid and the new has not finally achieved a breakthrough, establishes social *momentum*, i.e., motion *par excellence*. Yves Schemeil (1983) has termed Park's macro-sociology a sociology of crisis. Instead of, as usual, seeing crisis as a phase of destabilisation, which must be rectified with everything at one's command as quickly as possible, Park conceives the period of crisis as being productive, i.e., as being a catalyst of emancipation in the literal sense, unleashing us from traditional bonds. 'There is a crisis in the boy's life when he leaves home. The emancipation of the negro and the immigration of the European peasant are group crises' (Park 1915, p. 596). Just as communication only seems sensible where we can presume a diversity of experience, so social change is only conceivable where the self-evident, which is always the spontaneous, reaches its limits, thus giving rise to upheavals, collisions and collapse.

Crisis situations are situations of clarity (and therefore actually the only ones which should be made permanent). In crisis situations the individual becomes conscious of himself, he relates reflexively to himself, he 'makes up his mind': '*A crisis is the most favorable moment for objectivity and abstract thought.* It is the most fertile moment for social knowledge, a moment at which the scholar is able to achieve a certain distance from the mores, the customs and the representations of his group'[68] (Schemeil 1983, p. 642; emphasis in the original). The 'natural' state of society is not a peaceful one, in spite of, or precisely because of, the emphasis on social consensus; rather, it is thoroughly fraught with conflict. Conflict is in a certain sense the normal state of society. The idea suggested by Park's cycle of basal forms of interaction–competition–conflict–accommodation–assimilation – namely, that competition and conflict dissolve into pleasure, i.e., end up in unanimity – conflates logical and historical finality and misunderstands the infinite course of historical processes: the end of a cycle is at the same time the beginning of a new one. Given that stasis at the same time equates to mental immobility, or naiveté, as Park puts it in a letter to Thomas (see Raushenbush 1979, p. 71), it would seem that he himself was never able to 'rest'. His constant urge to travel, his thinking in cycles and his life as an ever migrant intellectual must all be seen together. Shils describes Park as a searcher: 'I had the impression that he cared more for the search for answers than for the answer itself. It was the journey, not the destination, that mattered. Perhaps that is the right attitude of a great scholar' (Shils 1990, p. 127).

---

[68] The original reads: '*La crise est le moment le plus favorable à l'objectivité et l'abstraction.* Elle est le moment le plus fécond pour la connaissance sociale, moment ou le savant peut prendre ses distances avec les moeurs, les coutumes, les réprésentations de son groupe.'

CHAPTER 3

Reporters in depth: a comparison of journalistic and sociological studies

WANDERLUST AND JOURNEYWORK: ON THE ETHNOGRAPHICAL METHOD

'The Wanderlust is a strange malady which rarely is cured.'

Mary Earhart about Josiah Flynt Willard

Josiah Flynt Willard, whom van Wyck Brooks termed the Audubon[1] of the tramp world, was a small, thin and fragile man. It remains a mystery whether he owed his nickname 'The Cigarette' solely to his smoking habits or to his physical size as well. At any rate, the nickname which tramps gave him identified him as an insider and, given that for all his wanderlust, he was quite down-to-earth, he made it into his trademark.

He was born in 1869 the son of a Chicago newspaper publisher, and after the death of his father in 1878 he grew up with his aunt Frances E. C. Willard, the co-founder of the Woman's Christian Temperance Union (WCTU) and a woman of strict morals, resolute character and strong will.[2] It may have been this family background which later induced Josiah F. Willard to emphasise the rôle alcohol abuse played in people becoming tramps, but he clearly did not let this trouble his own life-style at all. Willard, who ruined his own health by excessive alcohol consumption, died at the age of 38. It must have been especially painful for Frances Willard, as a pioneer of the temperance movement, that in her eyes her nephew was 'a common vagabond and drunkard'. But at the same time it is worth asking whether the course Josiah Willard's life took was not influenced by the stiff puritanical atmosphere in his aunt's house. At any rate, it was quite early on, if we are to believe the biographical

---

[1] John James (Jean-Jacques) Audubon (1785–1851), ornithologist and ecologist.
[2] Frances Elizabeth Cochran Willard (1839–98) was a passionate supporter of women's rights, and in addition to founding the WCTU in 1874, founded The World's WCTU. The Frances E. Willard Memorial Library for Alcoholic Research is named after her. For more about Frances Willard, see Earhart 1944; for more about the WCTU, see Gusfield 1955.

notes, that Willard began to show traces of a restless character. He ran away from home on several occasions and roamed around,[3] gripped by what the Americans, using the German word, call 'wanderlust'. In his autobiography (Flynt 1908), Willard, who published under the pseudonym Josiah Flynt,[4] never tires of claiming to have been filled with wanderlust and portraying himself as a fickle, restless character, as someone who cannot stand being in one place for very long. But wanderlust is, initially, nothing more than 'running away', escape from circumstances that appear intolerable. All his life Josiah Flynt Willard held the respectable puritanical society in contempt and he showed a passion for everything which lay beyond this world of strict morals. His wanderlust has to be understood as both escape and protest. Spending his life doing nothing as a tramp and turning to everything that appeared to be unseemly and useless was for Willard the *ultima ratio* of escaping from the narrow confines of his puritan surroundings.

According to Bremner, Willard, who in later life liked to stylise himself a noble hobo, was only a 'bona fide hobo' for a period of around eight months; after his first hobo article in 1891, he went on his excursions primarily in order to collect material. Nevertheless, this self-stylisation harbours an important motif, one which not only helps to explain Willard's ambivalence, but also provides the key to interpreting this genre of literature. Willard made into his profession those desires to which the general public scarcely dared to admit. He succeeded in combining and yet at the same time cleanly separating the two sides to the image of the tramp, i.e., that of 'social parasite', on the one hand, and that of 'voluntary exile' from bourgeois society, on the other: 'Flynt seemed to live easily the dual existence which Dr. Jekyll and others found impracticable' (Filler 1968, p. 71). In Europe, where he travelled from 1891 to 1898, he led a double existence: one life was as an 'amateur tramp' who observed German, English and Russian tramps, the other was as a person who frequented literary circles, where he was acquainted with Aubrey Beardsley and Arthur Symons, amongst others.

Willard was an adventurer, a person who went on 'travels into the poor man's country', to borrow the title of a book on Henry Mayhew (Humphreys 1977). His inner motive is probably most clearly expressed in his admiration for Richard Burton, who travelled widely in Arabia and

---

[3] It is supposed that Willard's melodramatic story *The Little Brother* (Flynt 1968), about the life of a boy tramp, exhibits autobiographical features.

[4] Earhart refers in a footnote to the fact that Willard used the pseudonym out of respect for his aunt (Earhart 1944, p. 401).

Africa. He shared with Burton the love of dressing-up,[5] an exceptional ability to step into a rôle, linked with an above-average gift for languages,[6] as well as that non-conformist approach to bourgeois life-styles which drove him again and again to new wanderings and trips into the underworld. Occasionally immersing oneself in foreign life-styles does mean breaking out of, but in no way does it mean making a complete break with, one's own culture, as Karl-Heinz Kohl emphasises in his essay on people who defect from one culture to another (Kohl 1987, p. 30). This can be seen in the case of Willard, who toyed coquettishly with the tramp's life-style all his life, for it emerges in the discrepancy between description and interpretation which runs through his studies of tramps and vagabonds. As an author, he could never completely free himself from the conventional morals of his time. The fascination which the life of tramps obviously held for him goes hand in hand with a moralistic judgement which sounds like paying lip service (Hutchins Hapgood 1939, p. 163).

This ambiguity is not the only thing that makes Willard into a typical representative of the rebellious young generation at the end of the Victorian era. Even the combination of vagrancy, bohemian life and journalism, all three being milieus 'free of ties' and 'unseemly', is not unusual. As will be shown, the orientation toward the bohemian life and toward journalism (in some cases both) is, for this generation, synonymous with turning their backs on the puritanical culture from which they originated.

Willard had more or less a publishing monopoly on the subjects of hoboes and tramps in the 1890s. In 1899, a collected volume of his writings appeared under the title *Tramping with Tramps* (1967 [1899]), making him an authority on the field, even in scientific circles. And he maintained this reputation until long after his death. Many reviewers compare Nels Anderson's *The Hobo* with Willard's *Tramping with Tramps*, making it advisable for us to take a closer look at his work and compare it with Anderson's study.

In an obituary of Willard in the *Literary Digest* of 2 February 1907, his writings were described as a sort of 'realistic sociology'. Willard owes his reputation as a realistic sociologist probably not least to the methodological reflections with which he prefaced his book *Tramping with Tramps*:

---

[5] There is a photo of Willard dressed as a Russian tramp – 'In his "Garb of the Road"' – both in his book *Tramping with Tramps* (Flynt 1967 [1899]) as well as in his autobiography, which appeared posthumously (Flynt 1908).

[6] Hodder (1908) describes Willard as an accomplished actor, a person who, on taking his first step into the 'side-streets', changed his whole demeanour and the tone of his voice as well as his vocabulary.

During my university studies in Berlin I saw my fellow-students working in scientific laboratories to discover the minutest parasitic forms of life, and later publishing their discoveries in book form as valuable contributions to knowledge. In writing on what I have learned concerning human parasites by an experience that may be called scientific in so far as it deals with the subject on its own ground and in its peculiar conditions and environment, I seem to myself to be doing similar work with a like purpose. (Flynt 1967 [1899], p. ix)

In Berlin, Willard had studied during 1890–1 under Schmoller, Wagner and Virchow, amongst others. His reference to these studies, and the comparison with scientific procedure, was quite obviously intended to underline the seriousness of his undertaking. The use of the term 'parasite' in this context has a dual function: on the one hand, Willard is drawing pejoratively on prejudices which have effective public appeal, while on the other he confirms in a seemingly naive way the tendency to transfer scientific methods (see Lepenies 1978). His recourse to the term 'parasite' in this case has the function of a rhetorical figure meant to justify his thesis, which is supposed to suggest to the reader that he himself had adopted scientific procedures.

Admittedly, if this is indeed what is happening, we would not actually be dealing with a transfer of scientific methods in the strict sense, but merely with an imitation of scientific methods. In fact, however naively, Willard is formulating an alternative to the traditional transfer of scientific methods on to the human sciences. Actually, Willard is explicitly objecting to the procedures for carrying out measurements and conducting experiments, as used by the criminology of the day:

Up to the present time the criminal has been studied exclusively behind prison-bars, after he has been caught, tried and convicted. Out of durance he is his own master, and is naturally averse to being measured and experimented upon by scientists; hence the criminologist has been forced to await the almost certain vicissitudes which bring him once more inside a prison-cell. Here he has been subjected to the most minute examinations; and there exists a bulky literature on the results which these examinations have brought to light. We have volumes for instance, about the criminal's body, skull, and face, his whimsical and obscene diet in his deportment, the workings of delicate instruments, placed on his wrists, to test the beat of his pulse under various conditions, the stories he has been persuaded to tell about his life, his munderings when under the influence of hypnotism, and numerous things, anthropological and psychological, which have been noted down, compared, and classified. (Flynt 1967 [1899], pp. 1ff.)

In contrast to this transfer of scientific procedures over to the investigation of criminals, Willard, judged from a modern standpoint, is advocating an ethnographic approach. Willard considers the situation in

prison to be so out of the ordinary that it does not allow any valid statements to be made about the way the subjects of the investigation actually
think and act. A scientific investigation, as Willard understands it, would
have to start by asking the question as to when we may assume we might
meet the criminal in his most natural physical and mental state, in detention or at liberty:

It is now more than a decade since I became acquainted with tramps. My
purpose in seeking them was to learn about their life; and I soon saw that, to
know it well, *I must become joined to it and be part and parcel of its various manifestations.*
At different times during this period, – some of them lengthening out into
months – , I have lived intimately with the vagabonds of both England and the
United States . . . My desire is to tell of the impressions they make on one *who
studies them in their own habitat,* that I may be able to show how different is the
outdoor criminal from his convicted brother shut in behind prison bars. (Flynt
1967 [1899], pp. 2ff.; my italics)

Given that he was working at a time when criminology was dominated by the positivist school of Lombroso, with its emphasis on
anthropometric procedures, Willard's suggestion that vagrants be
studied in their own natural surroundings, something which anticipates
the reasoning behind sociological field research, must be regarded as
absolutely remarkable. Given that he may possibly have been less than
serious in the scientific claims with which he prefaced his work and irrespective of the fact that his procedures may possibly have been
unsystematic, he nevertheless intuitively heralds the transition from
physical anthropology to cultural anthropology.

On the strength of his experiences, Willard arrived at a revision of the
findings of anthropogenetic criminology, which is all the more surprising, since it was not until 1913 that Lombroso's theory was finally proven
false, by Goring's control investigations. In Willard's view, there is no
such thing as the born criminal, someone who can be identified by definite features or combinations of features. Abnormalities which are supposed to identify criminal persons, such as lack of beard, sloping
forehead, strong jaw, pronounced cheek bones, jug ears, insensitivity to
pain and unusual vision, were encountered by Willard, as he himself
stresses, no more frequently among criminals than in so-called normal
citizens. What is more, Willard perceives than the scientist who is hooked
on 'abnormalities' has an inclination to draw analogous conclusions as
to the defective mental state of the object of his investigation (Flynt 1967
[1899], p. 11).

Even today, it is worth noting that Willard not only refutes the claims of the Italian school concerning the psychological features of the criminal, such as lack of will power, epilepsy and mental illness, he also offers an alternative heuristic, based on interpreting the experimental situation between criminologist and criminal as an interactive situation. Inadequate intelligence, sensory deprivation and epilepsy, in Willard's view, can all be manifestations of an anti-performance consciously being staged by the prisoners themselves. The diagnosis 'inadequate intelligence', for example, can result from the investigator having been taken for a ride by the person being investigated. Given that, in American prisons of the day, prisoners' learning successes were rewarded, many of the newly arrived detainees, when asked about their abilities, deliberately pretended to be stupid.

By emphasising the interactive constituents of the investigation situation, Willard proceeds intuitively to provide fundamental criticism of such behavioural research as is based on experimental procedures. Thus, by constantly stressing that the criminal is fooling the criminologist and that in many cases he is more shrewd than the people who are investigating him, Willard comes extraordinarily close to Devereux's theorem of the reciprocity of observation as a basic feature which distinguishes research in the humanities from that in the natural sciences.

To what extent did Willard actually implement the programme he had justified in such an extraordinary way? The title of the book, *Tramping with Tramps*, which begins by presenting the above deliberations on method in its first chapter, serves in fact to underline its method: participant observation.[7] Nevertheless, *Tramping with Tramps* is not a monograph in the strict sense of the term, but a collection of articles which had already been published. Like Jacob Riis' *How the Other Half Lives*, this is what gives the work its additive character. But unlike Riis, who was at pains to systemise his 'studies' (from the introductory chapter 'Genesis of the Tenement' through to the concluding chapter 'How the Case Stands'), even the structure of Willard's book is influenced by his journalistic origins. The book is divided into three large blocks, corresponding to the newspaper article genres of the day: the 'studies', the 'travel reports' and the 'sketches' that were so popular then. A fourth part is appended, a glossary of tramp slang. It is evident that the 'studies' and parts of the 'travel reports' come closest to what

---

[7] The pattern 'an X among Xs', which is the basis of the title, was to become a model for identifying anthropological field work and guaranteeing its quality for a long time to come. See, as an example of this, Frazier's preface to Malinowski's 'Argonauts of the Western Pacific' (Malinowski 1979).

we might term ethnography, and it is true to say that the titles of the individual sections promise to provide a reconstruction of aspects of tramp subculture: 'The Children of the Road', 'Club Life Among the Outcasts', 'The American Tramp Considered Geographically', 'The City Tramp', 'What the Tramp Eats and Wears', 'The Tramp and the Railroad', etc. As today's term has it, all these individual investigations are 'studies of crime in natural settings', albeit with a touch of sensationalism about them. Whether Willard is reporting on the life of the tramps in their 'hang-outs' or in the railroad 'box-cars', whether he is describing the 'lodging-houses' or the 'stale-beer shops', he always conveys the impression of having an intimate knowledge of the circumstances and life-style of the group he is studying, a knowledge which he has gained from his own experience and participation. This impression is reinforced by the fact that, without fail, he includes slang terms,[8] such as the term 'two-cent dossers' for tramps who doss in 'beer shops'.

The individual studies are similar in terms of formal structure. The object of such a study is either one aspect of the life-style of the tramps or one section of 'tramps' as a social group, for example, vagrant children or city tramps. Willard differentiates and classifies this segment of the overall group 'tramps' by making use of personal statements ('narrative interviews') given by individual members of the group, in order to support his classification and illustrate the way they think and act. This leads to a classification which seems almost over-exact, yet it is one that does reflect his inside knowledge of the tramp phenomenon, one that otherwise appears to the outside world to be homogeneous.

For example, in the 'The City Tramp' chapter, which by today's criteria has to do with homeless people, he makes a distinction between the different kinds of beggars according to whether they beg in the street, at houses, in shops or for old clothes. These beggars are classified according to the places where they beg, as well as according to the begging techniques which are adapted to these places and based on differing abilities. Here, he comes very close to what 'street ethnography' now does. It must be said, however, that in all this detailed presentation of the exotic internal complexity the basic distinction between 'hoboes', 'tramps' and 'bums' gets lost, so that reportage actually results in the ambivalent

---

[8] By allowing jargon to be included, Willard pre-empts the impression management of the sociological field investigator by having something act as an insider signal, both on the inside (to the group being investigated) and to the outside (to the researcher's reference group). See in this context Weinberg and Williams 1973 as well as Gerdes and von Wolffersdorff-Ehlert 1974.

picture that the citizen has of the vagrant: i.e., the picture of a 'happy-go-lucky' social parasite.[9]

Willard satisfies the requirement made of investigators of tramps by another, literary-orientated specialist in tramps, namely Jack London:[10] he gains his credentials by actively participating in the life of the tramps. As a consequence, he is able to explore the finer nuances of the world the tramp lives in. It was not by chance that London dedicated his book *The Road* (1907) – a book which likewise consists of a collection of essays – to Willard, for he considered him to be an authority on tramps.

In an essay first published in 1902, London explains why the sociologist who 'wades'[11] in the milieu must necessarily always remain in ignorance:

> The 'profesh' [professional tramps] do not lend themselves to putting inquisitive 'mugs' wise. They do not lend themselves to putting any one wise save their own 'prushuns'. Nor can the superficial investigator come to know the 'profesh' by merely 'hitting the road'. So far as they are concerned, he will be despised, as a 'gay cat' [amateur tramp], or in more familiar parlance, as a short horn, a tenderfoot, a new chum. He cannot know the 'profesh' until he has hobnobbed with them, and he cannot hobnob with them until he has qualified. And he may be so made that he can never qualify . . . Unless the investigator qualify, as Josiah Flynt qualified ('The Cigarette'), he will never know them. And unless he be able to qualify and to know them, he will be no fit exponent of the Underworld to the Upperworld. (Etulain 1979, pp. 94ff.)

In spite of the fact that he flaunts his insider status, London's remark does represent a plea in favour of participant observation, or to be exact, the rôle of 'participant as observer'. It is doubtful, however, whether Willard actually met the requirement that he be on familiar terms with the 'profesh'. It could not have escaped the notice of the professionals among the tramps that Willard was for a time in the pay of the railway companies, who entertained high hopes that his investigation would provide them with hints on how to combat more efficiently the 'Riders of the Rods and the Blinds', to use Holbrook's term. At any rate, Filler emphasises that several times Willard 'narrowly escaped injury at the hands of vicious tramps who suspected him of not "belonging"' (Filler

---

[9] The 'happy-go-lucky' tramp, 'over his shoulder a stick, on the end of the stick a small bundle, tied like a bag in a red bandana handkerchief' (Holbrook), who corresponds exactly to the stereotype and who is still to be found today in the porcelain departments of hardware (household goods) stores, also decorates the jacket of the first editions of Anderson's *The Hobo*.

[10] See, concerning London as a literary figure in the context of tramps, Feied 1964 and Etulain 1979.

[11] London is probably referring here to Walter A. Wyckoff, whose series 'The Workers', which appeared in 1897–8, he fiercely criticised. Wyckoff is the only one of the early revelation journalists who actually later became a sociologist.

1968, p. 69). This shows where the limits of 'the born actor, Flynt' (Cook) in 'taking the rôle of the other' actually lay.

Willard was also considered in scientific circles to be an authority on tramps. A remarkable example of this is an article which appeared in 1902 in the German specialist magazine *Archiv für Kriminalanthropologie und Kriminalistik*. In this article, Else Conrad reproduces the content of *Tramping with Tramps* over 36 printed pages. Without concealing her admiration for the undertaking, Conrad emphasises, at the beginning of her review, the special nature of the study:

Josiah Flynt has succeeded in carrying out an undertaking over a number of years which seems almost incredible, namely *Tramping with Tramps* ... As such [as a tramp], he crossed all parts of the United States, joined up with those who are now his equals, roamed around with them and accompanied them in begging their way from place to place. In the course of this, he also looked for and found the opportunity to enter into close contact with various down-and-out persons, even attaching himself to criminals in order to acquaint himself with their way of life and above all with their philosophy of life. No place was too dirty, no human being too depraved, to stop him getting to know them intimately. (Conrad 1902, pp. 129ff.)

The almost incredulous astonishment at this 'scientific heroism' ('and perhaps also a small dose of the American thirst for adventure and enterprising spirit') can be read as an indication of the novelty of partic- ipant observation in the area of criminal anthropology. Fascinated as she was by this method, Conrad does little more than reproduce the content of the book. The exhaustiveness of this report (Conrad's paper corre- sponds in its size to a sixth of the original) itself indicates the importance which was attached to this work.

At the end of the article, Conrad draws some conclusions, arising out of Willard's work, for criminological research and criminalist practice:

We believe that the result of this self-sacrificing undertaking is primarily to be seen in the fact that the cultured world has for the first time learnt what an enor- mous mass of down-and-out, good-for-nothing and ingenious tramps it is toler- ating of its own accord, even encouraging these people in an irresponsible way to idleness by thoughtless generosity and gullibility. If the poor man is better off when he is begging than when he is working, what reason is there for not choos- ing the former, when he is not able to appreciate the benefits of a change to a respectable way of life? *Flynt*, through his book, additionally provides an inter- esting insight into the philosophy and opinions of the tramp in general, which could only have been gained in this way. (Conrad 1902, p. 164)

In the United States, Willard's book has found its way into university teaching. In the Park/Burgess Reader, *Tramping with Tramps* is listed as recommended reading as part of 'Materials for the Study of the Person'. More interesting is a reference which provides a direct link to Anderson's *The Hobo*. In his autobiography, *The American Hobo* (1975), Anderson mentions an episode which was not without significance for his future career. In 1912, when he resumed his studies at Brigham Young University, having broken them off six years earlier, he was successful in being able to take part in an 'upper level' course for students beginning college, offered by John C. Swenson of the Department of Economics and Sociology. During this course, Swenson gave Anderson the task of reviewing Willard's book, which Swenson thought highly of as a report. Anderson came up with an unfavourable appraisal, primarily because Willard had not included the large group of itinerant workers, the genuine hoboes, in his investigation. Swenson himself was of the opinion that the term 'tramp', as described by Willard, included all types of homeless people, a conclusion fuelled by the fact that Willard used the terms 'tramp' and 'hobo' alternately and indiscriminately for one and the same type. In any case, Swenson was not convinced by Anderson's criticism and his appearance in the seminar turned into a fiasco: 'the other students grinned, marking me a wise guy who thinks he knows more than the author of the book. That rebuke smarted long after' (Anderson 1975, p. 128). Yet Anderson had every reason to consider himself a knowledgeable person. His father, Nels Anderson Sr, after emigrating to the United States in 1882, had lived for five years as a hobo and, amongst other things, had worked as a coal miner, lumberjack and bricklayer. Even after his marriage he remained a restless spirit, and only settled down to become a farmer in 1903 at the request of his wife. Nels Anderson Jr, like most of his brothers and sisters, followed the example set by their father. Only two of the nine children became farmers, as their father had wished them to:

Four of the boys became migratory workers before settling on other careers. My three sisters also left home and did some moving about before settling. *But none of my family became a drunkard, gambler, or loafer.* All became self-supporting in some occupation above common labor. In that solid sense my parents did not fail. (Anderson 1967 [1923], p. vii; my italics)

It is exceedingly clear from this passage, what it was about Willard's portrayal that upset and possibly even insulted Anderson, namely, the insinuation that the career of a migratory worker necessarily ended in his becoming a drunkard and a loafer. This explains why Anderson does not tire of emphasising that the hobo is above all else a special category of worker, someone who was historically indispensable when it came to tapping natural resources. With a clear sideways glance at Willard, Anderson states that although he had never been a drunkard, he had sometimes been penniless and forced to beg (see Anderson 1967 [1923], p. ix). In his autobiography, this need to justify himself leads to a portrayal of the hobo life which makes it appear joyless. The emphasis is on looking for work, contracting for work and itinerant journeys from one workplace to the next. In this way, the stress is rightly placed on the prime importance of the domain of work, which is hardly touched upon as a topic in Willard's book. At the same time, the fascination associated with this form of migratory work gets almost completely lost: the fascination of an unfettered form of work, which drove Anderson's father and brother 'out on the road' again and again. Instead of this, in his autobiography, Anderson paints the picture of a puritanical existence, one he led for six long years, from 1906 from 1912, working amongst other things as a navvy, casual crop-picker and carpenter.

In 1921, Nels Anderson took up his study of sociology at the University of Chicago. One of the reasons which led Albion Small to accept the candidate for study, despite the obvious gaps in his previous knowledge and the lack of any documentation on previous studies, was the fact that Anderson had reached Chicago by travelling hobo-style aboard a freight train. Right at the beginning of the course, this went to show how correct Swenson was when he persuaded Anderson not to study law, as he was about to, and recommended sociology instead: '"My background", he said, "would be useful in law, but valuable in sociology" ... Swenson had suggested that the most alive place then to study sociology would be at the University of Chicago' (1975, p. 157). In his first quarter, Anderson took a course in social problems, given by Burgess. There he became acquainted with a social worker who recommended him a lecture by Ben L. Reitman, a doctor who had a practice in the hobo district:

It would be useful at this point to reconstruct in detail the influence which Reitman, a representative of the marginal intelligentsia with a charismatic image, had on students of the sociology department. Bulmer, who speaks of Reitman as 'a fabulous kind of person' [Lofland 1980, p. 262] and enthusiastically recollects Saturday afternoons in his office, gives us a sense of this; according to Bulmer, both Alfred Lindesmith's study on drug addicts as well as Edwin Sutherland's *The Professional Thief* originated in Reitman's office; it was here they met their informants. Reitman was an ambivalent character in the milieu, being at the same time symptomatic of its change of direction towards *Hobohemia*. A former hobo, self-styled 'Hobo King', a bohemian, and someone not without vanity who occasionally dressed up in the style of Aristide Bruant, a 'Main Stem Dandy' with anarchist tendencies, the lover of Emma Goldman and for a time something like her informal secretary, he headed up the 'Hobo College', as well as carrying on his practice. The Hobo College was a sort of meeting place for hoboes, where they not only received tips on where to stay the night and where to obtain free meals, as well as exchanging experiences, but they could also recite poems and listen to lectures – on philosophy, history and literature as well as on legislation and public health – and give lectures, such as the ones 'Professor' Ohio Skip gave on geography, i.e., places which were recommended for hoboes and places they would do well to avoid [Bruns 1987]. What makes the Hobo College interesting in the context of the history of the Chicago sociology department is the fact that both sociologists and sociological students gave lectures there [Bulmer states, in his conversation with Hughes, that he was named Dean of the Hobo College on the strength of a lecture he gave], also that the college became an informal place of contact and meeting place for a number of sociology students. In 1923, the Hobo College, in the tradition of the inter-university debating teams, was the scene of a memorable philosophical debate between a group of hoboes, all of them dyed-in-the-wool soap-box speakers, and a team of students from the sociology department, at which the hoboes by all accounts carried the day, as a result of their ready wit, eloquence and mastery of excuses.

During the said lecture, given by Reitman to a group of social workers, Anderson attracted his attention by his contributions to the discussion. In a subsequent conversation, Reitman suggested he carry out an investigation into homeless men in Chicago. Reitman was successful in obtaining a small stipend for this from William Evans, the former head of the Public Health Department which was administered under the trusteeship of United Charities. Ernest W. Burgess, to whom the idea of the project was submitted, in his capacity as scholarly director, suggested setting up a committee, something which would give the scheme more prestige. This suggestion characterises Burgess very well. Himself a member of various organisations such as the Juvenile Protection Association, he made consistent efforts to strengthen the confidence of both political and welfare organisations in sociological expertise, as well opening up opportunities for research (see Bulmer 1984, pp. 117ff.; James T. Carey 1975, pp. 121ff.). The membership list of the fourteen-man Committee on Homeless Men, set up exclusively for Anderson's project under the chairmanship of Burgess, thus reads like a Chicago 'Who's Who' of social and charitable organisations. Seen in the context of the actual study, his committee had more of an ornamental function. Admittedly, some of the concrete problem areas were included owing to the particular interest of certain organisations (possibly as a concession to them). However, seen in retrospect, the influence of the committee and its sponsors made itself felt primarily in the actual way in which the results of the research were selectively turned into recommendations (see Anderson 1967 [1923], pp. 263ff.; James T. Carey 1975, pp. 143, 148 n 10).

With regard to the actual research project, Burgess had no advice to give, as Anderson somewhat arrogantly expressed it: 'which perhaps I should have known' (1975, p. 164). This is where Anderson's inclination to stress the cultural gulf which marked him off from his academic surroundings and his fellow students, by dint of his origins, comes through. It was, in fact, his knowledge both of the milieu being investigated and the people who were at home there which facilitated access and guided him in his conversations:

Wisely or not, I began with informal interviews, sitting with a man on the curb, sitting in the lobby of a hotel or flop house, going with someone for a cup of coffee with doughnuts or rolls . . . I was at home in that area. As a boy of ten and eleven I sold papers in that area, and it had not changed greatly since, and, as the autobiographical parts of this account bear witness, I was equally at home among the inhabitants of the area. I did not need to be self-conscious in conversation with different types of men. I could talk without uneasiness about having come from one place or other in the West, of having done one kind of work or another. It was an advantage to be able to talk about the types of work men in that society do, and work talk turned out to be a productive inducer to general conversation. (Anderson 1975, p. 165)

Anderson rented lodgings in his area of study, something which had the additional (and for him apparently most important) effect of providing him with a cheap place to stay. He drew up various maps so as to locate bars, doss-houses, cheap hotels, eating-houses, brothels, etc.; one of these found its way into *The Hobo* (1967 [1923], p. 15). In *The Hobo*, Anderson first of all draws a picture of 'Hobohemia' (pp. 3–15) and the 'jungles', hobo camps alongside the railway lines (pp. 16–26). In these passages it becomes clear that linking ecology and ethnography and studying space and culture is particularly fruitful. Anderson begins his treatise by saying that every big city has a district which forms the focus for homeless people, hoboes, vagrants and city tramps. What makes Chicago's 'Hobohemia' different from other foci, such as New York's 'Bowery', is the position of the city as a railway traffic hub, something which makes it the natural destination for hoboes and tramps, who usually travelled illegally on freight trains. Whereas the Bowery is primarily characterised by city tramps, Hobohemia offers employment, entertainment and winter quarters for itinerant workers and vagrants. It is this concentration of people in a similar social situation which makes Hobohemia into an isolated cultural domain with its characteristic establishments. In an especially impressive way, Anderson acquaints the reader with the culture of the hoboes in his description of the 'jungles'. Here, in the temporary or permanent hobo camps which Anderson aptly terms 'social centers', the hoboes show solidarity in their dealings with each other; each centre has a modest material culture of its own (pots, pans, kettles, jugs for general use) as well as its own system of rules and standards, 'a code of etiquette', to which each of the temporary inhabitants must conform. In one splendid ethnographic document, there is a description of a typical day in such a camp from the point of view of an insider (pp. 21–5). The 'jungles' not only have their own code, they also form a self-contained cultural domain, where the hobo tradition is passed on and where novices are initiated into the practices, customs, language, stories and songs of the hobo culture.

The interpretation of the 'jungle' culture is of peripheral importance in the overall context of the study; the primary subject is, of course, the ecology and culture of Hobohemia. Anderson follows on from his 'jungle' interlude by providing a description of the characteristic establishments of this 'natural area': the boarding houses and the doss-houses (with a report of a night in 'Hogan's Flop', based on his own participant observation), the restaurants and cheap eating-houses, the clothing shops, the second-hand-goods shops and the pawn-brokers, the bars, the cinemas and the burlesque theatres (pp. 27–39). In chapter 4 (pp. 40–77), Anderson outlines the techniques for 'getting by', and it is this chapter, with its references to casual jobs, small-time rogueries and swindles, as well its description of various begging techniques, that shows the greatest similarity to Willard's ethnography in his chapter 'The City Tramp'.

In the second part of his work, Anderson draws up a typology of homeless people. In differentiating between 'hoboes', 'tramps' and 'bums', he draws on statements made by experts, but the definitions given by Ben L. Reitman, John Tucker and Nicholas Klein (see pp. 87ff.) mostly correspond to the distinctions made by the homeless people themselves: 'The hobo, the saying went, was a migratory worker, the tramp a migratory nonworker, and the bum a nonmigratory nonworker' (Bruns 1987, p. 44). Of greater sociological importance than this differentiation is his analysis of the causes which drive people on to the streets. In the relevant chapter (pp. 61–86), he comes very close to Marx's analysis of the various forms of existence of relative overpopulation (Marx 1969, pp. 670–7). Anderson considers seasonal work and unemployment, followed by 'industrial inadequacy', to be the prime factors which provoke migratory work, vagrancy and homelessness. He subdivides the economic causes, which are summarised under point 1, into (a) seasonal work, (b) local changes in industry, (c) seasonal and cyclic fluctuations in the demand for wage-labour and (d) unemployment.

'Industrial inadequacy' is due to (a) physical disabilities caused by accidents, occupational and other sorts of illnesses, (b) alcohol and drug dependency, and (c) the age of the person looking for work. Both these groups of causes cover the population groups which Marx analysed as an industrial reserve army and its 'pauperised section'. In Anderson's scheme of things, these weigh more heavily than those factors triggering industrial inadequacy which were emphasised in the literature of the time, namely: psychic defects and wanderlust, crises in the life of the person concerned (marriage, family conflicts), as well as discrimination on the basis of race or nationality.

Let us compare the results which Willard (Flynt) and Anderson arrived at in their respective studies:

Flynt, *How Men Become Tramps* (1895/6, p. 945)	Anderson, *Why Do Men Leave Home?* (1967 [1923], p. 61)
I The love of liquor	(a) Seasonal work and unemployment
II Wanderlust	(b) Industrial inadequacy
III The county jail (contagion hypothesis)	(c) Defects of personality
IV The tough and rough element in villages and towns	(d) Crises in the life of the person
V The comparatively innocent but misguided pupils of the reform school	(e) Wanderlust

What is the reason for these differences? Do they reflect the differences between journalism and sociology? Firstly, in the face of the conventional patterns of explanation, which are riddled with prejudices, it must once again be stressed that Willard's studies were taken very seriously by the sociology and criminology of the day. It was not by chance that Bruns labelled Flynt the leading nineteenth-century author on the life of tramps, and described Anderson's *The Hobo* as the most detailed investigation of Hobohemia ever conducted (Bruns 1987, pp. 20, 210).

This comparative assessment, which we can trace up until the early 1930s, does admittedly relate to ethnography. If we compare Willard with Anderson in this respect, then Willard was actually closer to the image of the participant observer, who 'descends into a pit, assumes a rôle and later ascends to brush off the dust' (Anderson 1967 [1923], p. xiii), than was Anderson. In the places where Willard's report is based on his own observations and where he comes close to providing an ethnography of the vagrant way of life, it is plausible and often shows an impressive exactitude of detail. But in the places where he starts to speak about the causes of the vagrant way of life, he relies on the ideas (and prejudices) of the reformers of the day. Willard adapts his conclusions to fit a strategy for change which had already been formulated by the reformers, namely prohibition (factor I), prison reform and legislation for the protection of young people (factor III) together with reform of the system of education for young people in care (factor V).

The personal dilemma of Willard emerges in this discrepancy between ethnography and interpretation. Willard does not conform to the bourgeois way of life himself, but is at the same time unable to free himself from conventional social mores. The risk, which lies in providing a sympathetic report from the world of those who in the eyes of the average citizen are 'good for nothing' and 'parasites', can only be taken at the price of making a concession to the stereotype of the 'explanation pattern' which, as it were, administers the absolution for this transgression.

In comparison, the greater analytical and perceptual content of Anderson's investigation is derived less from a better scientific conceptualisation of the object of study (it is doubtful whether Anderson knew Marx's *Capital*), than from the simple fact that Anderson had himself worked for six years as a hobo, navvy, crop-picker and carpenter. It was these experiences which instructed him in his study, without he himself having had the benefit of study.[12] Seen like this, Anderson's *Hobo*, as he himself notes, was not only his answer to Flynt, but also to his fellow students:

When Thrasher, for example, talked about his study of boy gangs, or Reckless talked about vice areas it seemed to me that much which was discussed as sociological wisdom was, after all, but common sense knowledge. But if I spoke of the hobo or other men in my sector of Chicago, their ways of life and work, it was all remote from their understanding. They would respond with some sort of

[12] Anderson had only been studying for six months when he obtained the commission for the investigation.

weary willie humor, which reminded me over and over of a sort of cultural gap between my colleagues and me. It seemed wise to talk as little as possible about my study among my middle-class fellows; their values and outlook were so different from mine. (Anderson 1975, pp. 164ff.)

In a certain sense, at the time he made the study, he resembled a 'cultural hybrid' (Park): half hobo, half sociologist. It was this hybrid existence which we have to thank, above all, for the insights which the sociology of homeless people provides. The fact that some local colour becomes lost in the process is purely a side effect of this hybrid situation: Anderson, as he writes in the introduction to the 1967 Phoenix Edition, was 'in the process of moving out of the hobo world'.

For many reasons, *The Hobo* was a stroke of luck for Park. First of all, this work was pragmatically speaking an 'asset' for Park, as he had entertained the idea for a series of research monographs about Chicago for as long as four years. The study came just at the right time: as Anderson emphasised, it served as an illustration for the planned series, a trailer, as it were, which would attract funding for further research projects. This may explain the haste with which Park pressed on with publication. But this pragmatic aspect alone does not do justice to the ideal-typical character of the study. Even if Anderson as a person tended to be atypical, his study did represent the Chicago line, in both its themes and its method. It showed in an exemplary way what was meant by regarding Chicago as a social laboratory and using it as a sociological laboratory.

As can be seen from the correspondence with the publishing house, the title originally planned was *Hobohemia* (UCP 24:6). This was dropped for legal reasons, because Sinclair Lewis had already published a short story with the same name, which was a key text for the understanding of the New York bohemian world (Sinclair Lewis 1917), if ironic in tone. It can be assumed that the proposed title came from Park, who suggested the name 'Hobohemia' to Anderson, instead of the more usual – and more accurate – 'Main Stem', to describe the West Madison area. This translation of concepts into metaphors owes itself not only to the social-economic concept of habitat; it is also a reference to the fascination which urban life exerted on Chicago sociology. 'Hobohemia' is a good example of this, because the term accentuates that aspect of the hobo existence which Anderson relatively speaking neglected, i.e., its relationship with the world of the bohemian (see, in general, Kreuzer 1968, pp. 226–38). In his essay 'The Mind of the Hobo', Park characterises the hobo as 'the bohemian in the ranks of common labor. He has the artistic temperament' (1925b, p. 160). But the view represented by Park has been shifted quite a way, from the marginal intelligentsia on to the phenomenon itself; it is not by chance that in the essay being discussed here, he cites Walt Whitman as the most important of all hobo poets. The itinerant worker as a social type is, first and foremost, the result of the economic and social conditions which Anderson recorded. Only in the course of adapting to these conditions do those things develop which can rightly be regarded as the culture of the modern nomads, i.e., their way of life, their language, their songs and their legends. However, to the extent that the migratory worker comes up against the limits of the economic basis of his way of life, as a result of the opening up of the continent, it is not incorrect to characterise the hobo as a bohemian, a person who always manages to muddle through. In this context, the cultural elements, removed from their social basis, take on a life of their own. The hobo as migratory worker is joined by the hobo as bohemian, who swears 'that when work becomes an art and a joy, he will take off his coat and go to work'. The person who says this, the 'Hobo King' Dan O'Brien, is himself a symptom of the new age. Choosing a King of the Hoboes (and this title was hotly disputed in the 1920s and 1930s, because of its being lucrative) only makes sense, of course, if it is a prize for the pureness of life-style. Only by placing the emphasis on voluntary exile do we arrive at the division into 'genuine', i.e., freely chosen, and 'forced', or 'parasitic', vagrancy, into 'profis' and 'fakirs', this division being one which can be found as a formal principle in subcultures to the present day. At this stage, what is primarily important is the non-conformist life-*style* and no longer the vagrant *way* of life.

The relationship between vagrancy and bohemian society is the result of a contact between two cultures, namely, the mutual rapprochement and cross-fertilisation of marginal intelligentsia and marginal itinerant workers. This cultural contact, which gives birth to a new form of publicity,[13] brings about a change in the image of the hobo. A way of life bound to economic conditions evolves into a condition of quasi-professional outsiders (a new kind of 'getting by'), which stresses the bohemian features of the hobo existence ('love of individual freedom', 'deviation from conventions', 'absent time budget') above and beyond their real significance and then condenses them into a life-style.

The neologism 'Hobohemia' expresses the result of a blend between people who exist as vagrants and those who live in the eccentric circles of

[13] Ben Benson, who was twice chosen as 'Hobo King' in Britt – a folkloric campaign of the town's – used to sell a photograph of himself with the inscription 'Hobo Benson is at liberty for talks, radio and movies' (Benson 1942, p. 95).

the marginal intelligentsia. As Albert Parry tells us in his history of the bohemian in the United States, a new character of tramp started to appear in Greenwich Village around 1910:

A new colorful word, Hobohemia, was the result. Floyd Dell wrote a story devoted to the new type in the village, exclaiming in the title 'Hallelujah, I'm a Bum!' He said of his tramp-hero: 'He had discovered in Greenwich Village a kind of tramp he had never known before – the artist kind. These painters, poets, story-writers, were old friends in a new guise. He and they understood one another perfectly.' The bum took to modelling in clay and to free love with artist-girls; also to studio parties where he taught the villagers to sing the wobbly songs. (Parry 1960, p. 288)

The use of the title 'Hallelujah, I'm a Bum' can be taken as an indication of the changes that were happening. Originally the title of a propaganda song by the Industrial Workers of the World (IWW, known as the Wobblies), which so successfully parodied the hymns of the evangelists that they lost their taste for the word 'Hallelujah' (Anderson 1989, p. 87), it became used in the course of the bohemianisation of the hobo existence to glorify the marginal way of life. In his short story 'Hobohemia', Sinclair Lewis gives us an ironic insight into the manners and customs at the studio parties in Greenwich Village, at which 'scarcely any other topics were discussed' 'except the war, sex, Zuprushin, Mr. Pincus' paintings, birth control, eugenics, psychoanalyses, the Hobohemian Players, biological research, Nona Barnes' [possibly Djuna Barnes] new hair style, sex, H. G. Wells, the lowness of popular magazines, Zuprushin, Mr. Pincus' poetry and a few new aspects of sex' (Sinclair Lewis 1917, p. 121).

Hobohemia in Chicago was not the West Madison area but the Near North Side (the Greenwich Village of Chicago), with Bughouse (Newberry) Square as its centre. Here, writes Anderson, who devotes two pages to this area: 'a class of transients have drifted together, forming a group unlike any in either of the other areas of Hobohemia. This is the region of the hobo intellectuals. This area may be described as the rendezvous of the thinker, the dreamer and the chronic agitator' (Anderson 1967 [1923], p. 8). The poet and essayist Kenneth Rexroth, who later became a critical accompanist of the 'beat generation', described Chicago's Hobohemia as 'ragamuffin bohemia', a place where university professors met up with popular orators, would-be writers with publishers, and veterans of the worker's movement with representatives of the underworld (Rexroth 1966, pp. 135ff.).

The area around Bughouse Square is consequently not so much a 'natural area' for the hoboes as rather an island of the marginal intelligentsia – an 'Outcast Island', which has broken free from the 'Land of Respect', to borrow those territorial descriptions Ben Reitman used to describe the location of Greenwich Village.

DECLINE AND CAREER: ON THE BIOGRAPHICAL METHOD

A great story-teller was I.   Stanley (*The Jack-Roller*)

The importance Park attached to the 'life history' method is, strangely enough, not known to many. This may be due to the fact that he spoke about this mostly in out-of-the-way places, in letters, lectures and research project proposals. It is Burgess who is considered to be the real protagonist of this method; it was also he who supervised the monographs by Clifford R. Shaw that were based on the biographical method. But Burgess' championing of the 'life history' method is more narrow and more functionally intended than Park's; a clear indication of this was that throughout his life he preferred the terms used in social work, 'case study' or 'case history', to 'life history'. Burgess, as we will see, is much more entrenched than Park in the tradition of William Healy, the first American court psychologist, who had been collecting case material on juvenile criminals since 1908. The works by Shaw, as will be shown, make this clear. Compared with that of Burgess, Park's work is much closer to what we understand today as biographical research; at the same time he is in the philosophical tradition of Wilhelm Dilthey, who sees in autobiography 'the highest and most instructive form in which we encounter a *verstehen* of life' (Dilthey 1968, p. 199).

Like Dilthey's forms of 'higher *verstehen*' which are based on empathy and which 'via an inductive conclusion make it possible to understand the context in its entirety' (Dilthey 1968, p. 212), Park sees 'insight'[14] as being the objective phase of empathy, which 'involves an awareness of the circumstances and the situation under which different types of behavior arise in oneself and others' (Park, *Human Nature as Elemental Communication*, unpublished paper, p. 4; REPA 5:9). Thus it should come as no surprise that Park, like William I. Thomas, places particular importance on letters and diaries as source material and, moreover, that he also advocates a study of autobiographies such as Lewissohn's

---

[14] The term 'insight', which precedes that of 'understanding', itself based on Max Weber's category *verstehen*, points to the philosophical tradition as well as the significant influence of Charles H. Cooley, who speaks of 'sympathetic insight' (Cooley 1926, 1966 [1918]; see concerning the influence of Cooley and Weber: Platt 1985).

Upstream, one of his favourite books, or M. E. Ravage's *An American in the Making*, a book which Park reviewed in the *American Journal of Sociology* in 1918. In an undated talk, apparently given in connection with the Race Relations Survey,[15] Park states that such books 'are interesting to us, not only for their form but because they put us in touch with forms of life that are strange and unfamiliar, because they tend to humanize people whom we have known before only externally and whom we thought were strange and different merely because they were strange and different in outward appearance. It is literature of this sort that improves race relations and human relations generally' (undated speech, pp. 31ff.; REPA 6:2).

There is an obvious correlation with trains of thought such as those which Mead developed in 1926, in his essay on the nature of the aesthetic experience. It is also obvious that the model of the 'human interest story' continues to have an influence here, serving as it does, as Carroll D. Clark points out in a paper for Park's 'News' seminar, 'to develop and maintain a widely shared fund of common sense meanings, definitions of situations, derivations and collective representations' (Clark, 'The Concept of the "News"', 30 October 1928, p. 20; REPA 1:15). Just as Park's sociological researcher becomes a reporter-in-depth, so too the 'life history', as Park understands it, can be described as a 'human interest story' which goes into greater detail.

To Park's mind, biographical material, as we have just seen, is not only of scientific value, but serves directly to fulfil what was the main aim of Park's sociology, namely, to develop the ability to put oneself in the position of other people, in order to know and understand other people better and thus bring about mutual understanding (*verstehen*), a common universe of discourse.

William I. Thomas and Florian Znaniecki

The literature on methodology proves to be in rare agreement on dating the beginning of biographical methods in sociology back to Thomas and Znaniecki's monumental work *The Polish Peasant in Europe and America* (1974 [1918–20]) and understanding the biographical method itself as providing a counterpoise to quantifying methods. Admittedly, the recent recourse to Thomas and Znaniecki stems not only from the content of

---

[15] The aim of the Survey of Race Relations, of which Park was scientific director, was an investigation of the relations between Americans and Japanese immigrants on the Pacific Coast. The survey had to be broken off in 1925 because of financial difficulties.

their work, but also and above all from reasons of strategy. Thomas and Znaniecki serve as forefathers of an honourable tradition, while at the same time acting as witnesses for the defence in the dispute with the faction who favour quantification. Thomas and Znaniecki have themselves made a decisive contribution to this assessment, stating as they do, in one of the most frequently quoted passages from their work, that life records represent the perfect type of sociological material, while in contrast, statements on mass phenomena obtained by statistical means can at best furnish only a provisional basis for sociological hypotheses (Thomas and Znaniecki 1974 [1920], vol. II, pp. 1832–3).

In singing the praises of Thomas, however, the present-day protagonists of the biographical method usually fail to see the partial change of mind which he underwent later.[16] *The Child in America* (1928), which he wrote jointly with his future wife Dorothy Swaine, contains a plea for a combination of biographical and statistical methods, or – and here the argument goes much further – a statistical verification of the hypotheses which result from studies of individual cases.[17] Irrespective of whether this plea, as is frequently stated, reflects the influence of Dorothy Swaine (at all events she was one of the most prominent representatives of the 'hard-core' data faction), whether it reflects the argument on methodology between biographical and statistical procedures or whether it shows the open-mindedness of Thomas toward new developments, as is emphasised by Janowitz, the fact is that the phase of pure biographical research, which dissociates itself from statistical methods, lasts only for a short period of time, from *The Polish Peasant* via *Old World Traits Transplanted* (1921) to *The Unadjusted Girl* (1923).

Nevertheless, the fact remains that the publication of *The Polish Peasant* marked the birth of the biographical method in sociology. What are later called 'human documents' were included by Thomas as scholarly source material under the heading of 'unplanned documents' in his research plan on 'Racial Psychology with Particular Reference to the Immigrant and the Negro'. This exposé indicates that Thomas' original research plan went much further, i.e., that it actually went on to compare the European peasants (immigrants) with the black population in the United

---

[16] The 'confessional' way in which the argument with the 'quantifiers' was conducted, is shown by Daniel Bertaux's 'Story of My Conversion', which begins with the sentence 'Once I was a positivist' and shows traces of a life-changing experience (Bertaux 1981).

[17] It goes much further, because his original position – that the statistical method forms the basis for sociological hypotheses which have to be clarified by life histories – is turned on its head. From now on, qualitative investigations serve as explorative pre-studies.

States.[18] In this exposé, Thomas differentiates planned and specific documents, as used by historiography, ethnology and folklore, from unplanned or 'undesigned' documents, i.e., ones which had not been produced with a scholarly purpose in mind. In a letter written in German, which he drew up in Berlin in the summer of 1912 and which he addressed to other scholars with a request for cooperation, Thomas states that he was particularly concerned with 'procuring such material as I described in §20 of my treatise on the psychology of race as "unde-signed records", i.e., unintentional, unedited and unretouched documents, such as letters, newspaper notices, reports on court proceedings, sermons, pamphlets from the clergy and political parties, minutes of meetings and annual reports from the agricultural associations of the peasantry, etc.' (SNH 1:16).

As is well known, Thomas attached particular importance to family letters as sources, these having the advantage of spontaneity when compared with the autobiography. In *The Polish Peasant*, 50 series containing a total of 764 letters are put to use; beside these, Thomas and Znaniecki also have recourse to readers' letters, newspaper articles, church chronicles, association minutes and reports of court proceedings, as well as case reports written by charitable organisations.

Although Thomas places particular emphasis on the importance of letters as material, owing to the assumed high degree of authenticity, to his mind, it is the life story which provides the ideal and, with respect to *The Polish Peasant*, the most representative sociological material. That the life story *must* play such a dominant rôle, both methodically as well as methodologically, becomes clear when we look at Thomas and Znaniecki's methodological ideas and the insights they believed social sciences could yield. Taking as their starting-point the 'fundamental methodological principle' that the cause of a social and individual phenomenon can never be another single social or individual phenomenon by itself, but only the combination of a social and an individual phenomenon, Thomas and Znaniecki advocated analysing reciprocal relationships between social organisation and social personality. Given that the world which influences the subject and on which he has an impact, is

---

[18] Whether Thomas was influenced by Park in this more far-reaching concept is something which would need to be investigated in more detail; at any rate, we should remember that it was just this comparison which was both the impetus for and the theme of Washington and Park's *The Man Farthest Down*. His correspondence with Park in April–May 1912, and with university president Samuel N. Harper in June of the same year, shows that, as far as Thomas was concerned, the significance of the negro question only came into proper focus after he had had his meeting with Park.

always *his* world and not the objective world of science, it is the task of the social sciences to identify how the subject in question sees his world.

A science which endeavours to see the world of the subject as it is seen by him (and not how the scientist sees it) is dependent on documents which give access to the inner side of social processes. The life story, which should be as complete as possible, gives an explanation as to how a subject perceives, experiences and processes the circumstances in which he or she is placed, on the basis of his or her temperament and character development. It provides more than this, however. By bringing these processes of experience and assimilation in the course of a life to the attention of the scientist, the life story simultaneously allows him to participate in the developmental process of the social personality. This is something, as Thomas and Znaniecki emphasise, that never manifests itself as a whole at any one particular point during the life in question, but only within its continuous development.

In other words, the life story provides the researchers with two things: it gives an insight into the inner world of the subject who is involved in action, and it makes available information on the development of the social personality, something which can only be conceived of as dynamic, i.e., changing and subject to change. No other survey method takes into account the process character of social and individual phenomena more than do life reports.

The insistence that life records be as complete as possible not only underlines this analytical claim, it has also to be understood as a reference to the inadequacy of the forms of biographical reconstruction previously used in practice. Thomas was familiar with the work done by the psychologist William Healy.[19] Healy, in his capacity as director of the Juvenile Psychopathic Institute (which later became the Institute for Juvenile Research), had been collecting case material on juvenile criminals, in order to ascertain the reasons for their delinquent behaviour, and in 1912 he published his *Case Studies of Mentally and Morally Abnormal Types*. In this work, Healy brought out the first life record of a delinquent girl, which he described as her 'own story' (his inverted commas), thereby alluding to what was considered to be the novelty of a report written in the first person singular. In this way, the 'own story' distanced itself from the 'case study', such as was already customary in welfare and social counselling circles. However, even during the later period, Healy's 'own stories' not only lagged behind the more predominant 'case studies' in

---

[19] Thomas used the material of Healy and his colleague Bronner on several occasions. See, e.g., *The Unadjusted Girl* (1923).

number, they also remained trapped within their narrow anamnestic perspective of delinquent behaviour.

Thomas and Znaniecki's sociological innovation is perhaps to be seen nowhere more clearly than in their reference to the limitations of a type of investigation geared toward immediately practical aims, the coordinates of which are the desirable and the undesired. In as *complete* a form as possible, the life record makes it possible to avoid selective accounts, the sort of accounts which Allport groups together under the heading of 'topical autobiographies'. These latter types of account constantly run the danger of shifting the focus away from the life of the subject on to things which the researcher is interested in.

Clifford R. Shaw

Alongside Thomas and Znaniecki, it is Clifford R. Shaw who is considered to be the pioneer of the biographical method in sociology. Shaw's background is rather more typical of the first generation of sociology in Chicago, although it was not unusual in the 1920s either (Snodgrass 1976). He grew up, as the son of a farmer, in a small peasant community in Indiana; he initially studied to become a clergyman, but then, after completing military service, he turned in 1918 to sociology. In Chicago, where he took up his sociology studies, he lived in a settlement called 'The House of Happiness'; this fact, again, is rather more typical of the first generation. Shaw, who never went on to obtain his doctorate (an indication of his primarily practical orientation), worked from 1921 to 1923 as a part-time assistant at the Illinois State Training School with prisoners who had been released on probation, and then, from 1924 to 1926, as a probation officer at the Cook County Juvenile Court. In 1926, on the recommendation of Burgess, he became director of the sociological research department at the Institute for Juvenile Research, the former Juvenile Psychopathic Institute, which was under the management of William Healy.

This background has to be borne in mind if we are to understand the particular accent of his investigations: *The Jack-Roller* (1966 [1930]), *The Natural History of a Delinquent Career* (1931) and *Brothers in Crime* (1938), all of which are based on the biographical method. Shaw was indebted to Healy not only for the term 'own story', to describe the biographical document, but also for the protagonist of *The Jack-Roller*, a former 'case' from Healy's practice whom he introduced into sociological literature under the pseudonym 'Stanley'. In his attempt to link scientific and practical interests,[20] he also adopted the anamnestic perspective of delinquent behaviour.

Shaw became acquainted with Stanley when he was his probation officer. Even though this position may have led to a special relationship of trust (Stanley went to visit Shaw after he had been released from prison), it was far from being neutral. This is also true of the place where the data was gathered: Shaw's office in the Institute for Juvenile Research. I shall return to the possible distorting and/or conversation-orientated effects of this situation later, one of the important factors in this context being the long contact that Stanley had with scientists (Healy, Bronner, Shaw). At any rate, Shaw, because of his position, was not lacking in subjects for investigation. Whether this should be considered only an advantage is a matter of opinion; what is interesting, however, is the fact that Shaw, in spite of having collected hundreds of biographies, always drew on only a very limited number of these (especially characteristic ones?) in order to illustrate his points.

What does Shaw hope the life records of his clients will offer? In *Delinquency Areas*, Shaw writes that an analysis of the revelations provided by a life history is the best way of investigating the 'inner world' of a person (Shaw *et al.* 1929, p. 9). Of course, it would be too simplistic to see in this position solely an adoption of Thomas and Znaniecki's approach ('His View of His World'). Shaw, being application-orientated in his perspective and pragmatic in the way he deals with theoretical findings – his theory of the 'life history method' comprises an unreflected mixture of fragments from Healy, Thomas and Burgess – is primarily concerned with a type of research which aims at providing new parameters for teaching.

According to Shaw (1966 [1930], p. 3), the life record fulfils three functions. Firstly, it serves as an aid to in(tro)spection; it uncovers the individual attitudes, feelings and interests of the person supplying the record and shows how he interprets the situation in which he lives. Secondly, the 'own story' makes it possible to obtain an impression of the traditions, normative contours and moral standards which predominate in his family, neighbourhood and peer group and which mould the behaviour

---

[20] According to Bennett (1981, p. 200), the life histories which Shaw collected also served to persuade the public in favour of a certain programme of action, the Chicago Area Project, of which Shaw was the director. Snodgrass writes about this project, which was aimed at the prevention of delinquency: 'The Chicago Area Project was first and foremost a disciplinary force, designed to inculcate values, socialise behaviour and to achieve an accommodation of slum residents to the conventional order' (1976, p. 17).

of the child. Thirdly, such a first-hand report, as a life record, makes it possible to interpret the individual's actions in the light of his or her past experiences.

An aspect that is particularly brought out in the scholarly reception of *The Jack-Roller* and that is emphasised in the introduction by Shaw himself, is the progress in methodology which this study represents. Shaw first of all develops a sort of interview guideline, so as to focus the 'own story' in terms of the issues addressed. From preliminary conversations with Stanley and using official documents to help him, Shaw reconstructs the chronological sequence of the delinquent career which Stanley then had to fill with 'life', i.e., with descriptions of the events and the experiences he had made. This initially results in an abbreviated version (entitled 'Why and How I Became a Criminal', pp. 200–5), which Stanley, interviewed by Shaw after his release from prison, then expands into his actual 'own story' – almost twenty times the original size and with remarkable changes in tone. Moreover, Shaw – no doubt given the nascent debate on methodology – is very conscious of the necessity of checking the validity and reliability of the report. Consequently, he is not content with just having the autobiographical material; rather, he understands Stanley's 'own story' as forming an integral part of a 'complete case history', something which leaves no loopholes – even in the sense of Stanley 'deviating' from the narrative course prescribed. Here, methodological control takes the form of a control over the individual, since even lies and exaggerations, if they are to have any scientific value, must be recognised as being lies and exaggerations. In order to make it possible to examine the validity and reliability of Stanley's 'own story', but also so as to be able to add to it, Shaw states beyond contradiction that every case study should

include, along with the life history document, the usual family history, the medical, psychiatric, and psychological findings, the official record of arrest, offenses, and commitments, the description of the play-group relationships, and any other verifiable material which may throw light upon the personality and actual experiences of the delinquent in question. (Shaw 1966 [1930], p. 2)

The nature of this data alone indicates a step backwards compared with the approach of Thomas and Znaniecki. This retrogressive step is already indicated in the functional narrowing of what is understood by 'inner world'. Stanley's 'own story' ranks among the tradition of narratives of people's own 'fall', such as were first established by the two prison chaplains, John Clay in England and Johannes Jaeger in Germany.[21]

This perspective is predetermined by the guidelines Shaw drew up for the interview, which is actually nothing more that a list of Stanley's misdemeanours, and it is assumed by Stanley himself with the heading to the first chapter of his 'own story': 'Starting Down Grade'. Stanley's life record is nothing more than the story of a delinquent career, from which almost everything which has nothing to do with this career has been occluded. All those experiences in closed institutions which do not conform to the model of 'correction' are excluded. For instance, Stanley's remark that he made Shaw and his friend (possibly McKay) laugh by relating his funny experiences in prison ('I got a great kick keeping them laughing about the funny experiences I had in prison'), is not mentioned in the actual report, as though funny experiences are not reconcilable with the perspective of degeneracy (see Bennett 1981, pp. 196ff.). The chapter heading is also interesting for another reason, reflecting as it does the literary influence. Titles such as 'Starting Down Grade', 'The Baby Bandhouse' and 'The Lure of the Underworld' seem to correspond directly to the conventions of the pulp magazines that were extremely popular in the 1920s. It may have been these headings which led William Stott to the fatal conclusion that *The Jack-Roller* and *The Natural History of a Delinquent Career* resembled the 'pulp confessions' of the day (Stott 1973, p. 199). Even if borrowings from trivial literature ('The birds were singing, but not for me') cannot be ignored, by and large

---

[21] In 1839, the year in which the single-cell system was introduced into Preston Prison on his initiative, the prison chaplain John Clay began to collect 'short narratives of their lives' from the inmates, aptly described by Clay's son Walter Lowe as 'cell confessionals'. These narratives were meant not only to serve as 'therapy' (absurdly enough, the fact of relating their life histories was supposed to alleviate the suffering associated with solitary confinement, the technical precondition for an individual narrative), but also provided information about those things which up until then people were in the dark about: 'the actual social and moral state of our poor fellow-subjects' (see concerning Clay: Bennett 1981, pp. 65–88). The confessions of offenders collected by the German prison chaplain Johannes Jaeger appeared in volumes 19ff. (1905ff.) in the German *Archiv für Kriminalanthropologie und Kriminalistik*. As the criminologist Hans Gross writes in his 'introduction', the 'emanations of offenders' are supposed to help improve knowledge relating to the psyche of criminals (Jaeger 1905, p. 1). Starting from the assumption that the inner world of a human being is more important that his external side, Jaeger introduces the material he had collected as proof that the idea of the criminal as a typical variety of the *genus humanum* is false. The status and profession of these collectors of information illustrates very clearly that religious confession is the historical model for modern self-confession. Bennett (1981, p. 68) writes that: 'in Clay, it [oral history] is a religious act used for secular reform'. The first life histories are narrations of the person's own 'fall', or 'fall from grace', with the 'delinquent' appearing as the secular version of the 'sinner'.

The Jack-Roller resembles less a product of 'confessional' literature than a scholarly study carried out by a criminologist.

It should be remembered that Shaw saw the unique aspect of the 'own story' in the fact that it is written in the first person singular, i.e., in the actual words of the person concerned and not in the language of the person investigating the case. If we compare such stories with the case reports written by welfare workers and court psychologists, which serve as a foil here, then this assessment is understandable. Unlike the case reports, which always have something of the official document about them – including all the accompanying formal and structural connotations – each 'own story' provides a high degree of authenticity, not least because of its narrative character. In a naive way, seen from today's point of view, the 'own story' is assumed to be the truth, simply because it is written in the first person singular – and thereby avoids all those distortions that come about when something is translated by a third person, whose values and ideas, points of view and interpretations all then permeate the description of the case. What is missing, however, is the complementary insight, not only that a subject's report can be distorted by a third party translating it, but also that the subject is capable of assuming the rôle of the researcher and, thus, his or her definitions.

In his brief survey on biographical research, Fuchs (1984) notes that in places in his report Stanley sounds like a criminologist. It must be assumed that Stanley, who is described by Shaw as someone who knew how to express himself convincingly and how to put himself in the position of other people (it was for precisely this reason that Shaw arranged for Stanley to be employed as a salesman), had learned a great deal from his long contact with Healy and Shaw.[22] We find in his 'own story' the Broken Home thesis (p. 47), the Bad Companion thesis (p. 51) and the Bad Neighbourhood thesis (p. 171) cited as causal factors of delinquent behaviour, as well as assumptions deriving from social Darwinistic psychological theory and sexual pathology. Moreover, Stanley assiduously adopts the language of the welfare worker and reformer, particularly when assessing his fellow sufferers ('The population of the House of Correction is composed of the lowest kinds of human derelicts and wrecks').

---

[22] In a letter to the University of Chicago Press dated 22 January 1971, Michael P. Majer (Stanley) states: 'Mr. Shaw, from the years dating from 1921, until the day of his death, became not only my very close friend, I might add also that he was more like a father, whom I lost in 1920' (UCP B 406, F.1.). With this assertion, Majer sets himself up, so to speak, as his heir, the subject of the letter being of course the royalties for the new edition.

Assuming the causal factors quoted are not actually a case of translations by third parties (something which according to Shaw we can exclude), then Stanley is deploying scientific patterns of explanation in order to explain himself. Shaw emphasises that the value of the personal document is not exclusively dependent on the amount of truth it contains; on the contrary, he asserts that rationalisations, made-up stories and exaggerations, precisely because they are subjective interpretations, have just as much value as knowledge. However, after arriving at this perception, he stops, without, of all things, going on to appraise the scholarly value of the 'own story'. Again, long passages of this story appear to be documenting a self-fulfilling prophecy.

If we compare the findings concerning the causes of delinquent behaviour, summarised by Burgess in the appendix, with the 'causative factors' which William Healy cites on the basis of his clinical research (see Shaw 1966 [1930], appendix 1, p. 199), then the gain in new perceptions from including the 'own story' is relatively small. Admittedly, Bennett is right when he says that Shaw lends force to the fact that sociological investigations are needed, simply because he is not capable of recognising physiological abnormalities. Essentially, however, Shaw's findings boil down to sociological 'translations' of psychological prejudices. The 'bad influences' of family, neighbourhood and peer group, as quoted by Healy, are now supplanted by the 'cultural patterns' of family, neighbourhood and peer group, which determine the attitudes and wishes of those concerned. The moral category of the 'bad influence' is replaced by the scientific category of cultural patterns which have a 'bad' effect in a moral sense.

This is not to contest the scientific value of documents such as the 'own story' in any way, as far as their providing knowledge goes, but it does imply a definite shift of emphasis. We cannot, of course, exclude that the factors quoted (family, neighbourhood, peer group) do indeed play an important part in the creation of delinquent behaviour, though this must be seen against the background of the disastrous neglect of economic and social circumstances. However, what are more important are the insights which the 'own story' provides into the processual character of social phenomena and into the subjective side to institutional processes. Above all, personal stories are an example of the research context itself as an interactive situation, one which contributes to the self-definition of a subject who has a highly developed ability to take on other rôles. Shaw, who relies very heavily but at the same time very superficially on Thomas' situation theorem, neglects to apply this same theorem to the situation being investigated. If 'attitudes and values are modified to correspond to the requirements of a given situation' (William I. Thomas 1965, p. 88), then this assumption must also be valid for the situation being investigated. The change in situation (from the status of delinquent object to the status of subject who is sought after and questioned) goes hand in hand with a change in behaviour. In this regard, we must agree with Stott when he writes that *The Jack-Roller* and *The Natural History of a Delinquent Career* seem to be based less on self-experiences than on performances (Stott 1973, p. 199). The Thomas theorem ('If men define situations as real, they are real in their consequences') finds itself confirmed here as a scholarly self-fulfilling prophecy.

Hutchins Hapgood

Kohli (1981a, 1981b) states that he expects the biographical method to provide methodological access to social life which, firstly, is as comprehensive as possible; secondly, stresses the self-perspective of the subject being dealt with; and thirdly, pays attention to the dimension of history. Taking Kohli's assumptions as a basis then, the autobiography of a thief published by Hutchins Hapgood can rightly be considered as documenting this method. Just as Willard was described as monopolising the vagrancy theme in the journalism of the day, so too Hapgood can be considered the leading representative of the 'own story' genre of journalism. Besides *The Autobiography of a Thief* (1903), Hapgood published *The Spirit of Labor* (1907) and *An Anarchist Woman* (1909), the latter being a book which was supposed to show 'under what conditions, in connection with what personal qualities, the anarchist habit of mind arises' (preface). Hapgood personally saw the thematic shift, from thief to radical, as involving a development. Soon after the publication of *The Autobiography of a Thief*, he pronounced his judgement that the world of crime, in comparison to the radical workers' movement, was socially meaningless (Hutchins Hapgood 1939, p. 172).

Hapgood's documentary works are marked by an interest in characters who turn their backs on conventional society, an interest in the human characteristics which lead to a person joining the radical workers' movement or becoming a thief.

The story of a thief published by Hapgood also follows the story line, familiar from *The Jack-Roller*, of someone being 'led astray' at the beginning of their career through to when, at the end of the record, they express their willingness to better themselves. This story line seems to be intrinsic to the genre, assuming as it does the subject's willingness to go on record. But the story told to us by Hapgood's protagonist, a professional pickpocket, is quite different from that narrated by Stanley. Hapgood became acquainted with his story-teller Jim (Caulfield) through Willard, who was a friend of his. After his release from Sing-Sing, Caulfield had turned to Willard for help; this reminds us of Stanley, who looked up Shaw after being released from detention. Although the initial circumstances may be similar, there is a distinct difference between (on being released) going to see a probation officer and researcher into delinquency and going to look up a journalist who is known and respected in the underworld. This difference may possibly be a reflection of the sort of person the protagonist is; it most certainly should be reflected in the accentuation and perspective of the life history.

Hapgood, who looked after Jim at the request of Willard while the latter was otherwise engaged, was initially not enthusiastic about the task, but he soon became so interested in Jim's character that he suggested he write a book about his life. In an 'editor's note', Hapgood gives us some information about how he went about reconstructing Jim's career:

The method employed in composing the volume was that, practically, of the interview. From the middle of March to the first of July we met nearly every afternoon, and many evenings, at a little German café on the East Side. There, I took voluminous notes, often asking questions, but taking down as literally as possible his story in his own words; to such a degree is this true, that the following narrative is an authentic account of his life, with occasional descriptions and character-sketches of his friends of the Under World. Even without any explicit assurance, the autobiography bears sufficient internal evidence of the fact that, essentially, it is a thief's own story. (p. 12)[23]

There can be no doubt about this being at least a proto-scholarly approach. Moreover, Hapgood's realistic view of his enterprise is borne out by the fact that he describes his method as 'assisted biography', something which in my view applies to the whole of the 'life history' genre. Surprising, for a product of journalism, in comparison to *The Jack-Roller*, was the unspectacular title of the book: *The Autobiography of a*

---

[23] Compare this description with Shaw's explanation of his procedure: 'The technique which we have most frequently employed to secure the delinquent's "own story" is that of the personal interview. The task of securing complete and useful documents by this technique usually necessitates a series of interviews, which in some cases extend over a relatively long period of time. In most of our cases a stenographic record of the interview is made, so that the story is recorded in the exact language of the interviewee. Thus the record of the interview is not only complete, but its objectivity is preserved' (Shaw 1966 [1930], pp. 21ff.).

Thief, a title which in retrospect seems decidedly prosaic, especially when compared with other journalistic and scientific products (I am thinking for instance of *Hustler! The Autobiography of a Thief*, a sociological document published by R. L. Keiser (1966)).

Jim's narrative also contains traces of its initiator and the world in which the latter moved. Jim's emphasis on the world of vaudeville, together with the intimate knowledge of theatres and performers which he reveals, seems to derive from Hapgood. The occasional 'character sketches' of criminals are quite evidently a concession to the expectations of the readers of the day. More importantly, the perspective and focus of Jim's life history are quite different from those of Stanley's. Even if Jim defers, so to speak, to the genre, describing his entry into the delinquent world as the product of having been led astray, his case history is less a history of his case than an inside view of the world and life of professional delinquents. In this way, the story takes on what we call today an ethnographic perspective: we learn from the standpoint of a professional pickpocket what it means to be a pickpocket. Analogous with Willard's participant observation of vagrants, an important rôle is played in Jim's own story by the deliberate inclusion of slang – a trademark, so to speak, of journalistic accounts of the underworld. Thus, amongst other things, we learn that 'fall' means an arrest, 'mouth-piece' a lawyer and 'moll-buzzer' a pickpocket (despised in the criminal hierarchy) who specialises in female victims. But *The Autobiography of a Thief* provides more than fleeting glimpses into the linguistic customs of a criminal subculture. It is the story of the development of a professional thief, including a description of his characteristic attitudes and behaviour, his specific skills and techniques, as well as his milieu and way of life.

Hapgood clearly understands the 'own story' in sociological terms. Burgess, in his discussion of *The Jack-Roller*, points out that the study of a particular person throws light on the activities of a group, since the experiences of an individual reflect the opinions held by his group (Shaw 1966 [1930], p. 186). In like manner, Hapgood stresses that the articulate individual has to be not only interesting in himself but at the same time representative of a 'class': 'If he be thoroughly identified with some social *milieu*, his story cannot be well told without involving that *milieu*. In the process of touching his life, the ideals and habits of his class would be shown' (Hutchins Hapgood 1903, p. 244). In contrast to the 'Jack-Roller', who is always bemoaning fate being against him, it becomes clear from the autobiography of the pickpocket why someone could choose such a career. In this regard, the life history recorded by Hapgood tends to satisfy the demand laid down by Shaw, namely, to provide a picture of the evolution of delinquent behaviour as the result of a process of inter-action, more than does Shaw's *The Jack-Roller*. It seems to be rather less a case of being led astray by 'bad associates' than of admiring the example set by the professional law-breaker – the 'swell guns' (or 'big shots', as they were called in the 1920s) – that encouraged Jim to take up such a career in the immigrant quarter. John Landesco, another of the Chicago sociologists, came up with similar findings in the 'life histories' which he collected (Landesco 1932/3b). To me, this seems to be no coincidence, since Landesco, as the child of Romanian immigrants, himself grew up in an immigrant quarter.[24]

The reports are saturated with references to various rôle models and fields. Whereas Stanley tends to play down the seriousness of his crimes (as well as possibly playing down the crimes themselves), but is otherwise busy portraying his inexorable 'fall', Jim, by contrast, manifests a certain pride in his profession: just as Shaw was interested in a story which pro-vided information about the cause and the unfolding of a delinquent career, it can be supposed that Hapgood had primarily been thinking of an 'insider' report from the criminal milieu, a perspective which took account of the public's taste. In comparison to Stanley's own story, this gives Jim's autobiography a touch of the sensational; by presenting the language of swindlers and giving 'character sketches' of some of the 'crooks', the same appetite for sensations was being appealed to which was otherwise satisfied by the 'slumming tours' of the day.[25] If we bear in mind Howard Becker's view (expressed in his introduction to the new edition of *The Jack-Roller*) that the life story, 'because it is the actor's "own story", is a live and vibrant message from "down there", telling us what it means to be a kind of person we have never met face to face' (Becker 1966, p. xiv), then *The Autobiography of a Thief* satisfies this demand rather

---

[24] Unfortunately, the life history of a professional pickpocket, collected by Landesco and particu-larly suitable for the purpose of comparison, was never actually published, although it is listed in the bibliography of the second revised edition of Thrasher's *The Gang* (1968), under the title *The Pickpocket* (Chicago, 1932). Excerpts from this study into 'Eddie Jackson the Immune' have been published in the *Journal of Criminal Law and Criminology* (vol. 25, 1934/5).

[25] In his autobiography, Hapgood describes how Jim, on the basis of his publication, was asked by a young married woman who belonged to the so-called *fashionable world* to be taken on tour round the Bowery (Hutchins Hapgood 1939, pp. 168ff.). The people of Chicago seemed not to have been entirely able to escape the fascination which the underworld exerted over parts of so-called high society. Faris, in his description of the department's 'tours', which were arranged for visiting guests, mentions that: 'for a time slumming visits were a fashion among young Chicago intellectu-als' (Faris 1970, p. 65).

better than *The Jack-Roller* does. In the final analysis, Jim's life record, with its description of the way of life of a professional thief, its statements about the hierarchy within this group of professionals and its portrayal of a typical day (Hutchins Hapgood 1903, pp. 125ff.), comes much closer to a modern-day study in the context of street ethnography than Stanley's 'own story'. A comparison of Hapgood's document with Inciardi's 1977 field study into professional pickpockets shows a surprising amount of common ground in their findings. Not only does this comparison confirm the story of Jim as seen in retrospect, we are also made aware of how little the professional world of pickpockets has changed in the course of the last 75 years: beginning with the slang (they still talk about 'moll-buzzer' and 'fall'), including the preferred fields of activity (race-courses and sports stadiums; church congregations and services; public transport and railway stations), even as far as the significance of clothing as a tool of the trade.

To sum up then, a comparison of both life histories shows that each is a complete document of a delinquent career, written in the first person singular. Both editors explain in a preface how they went about collecting the data, both use the interview method and both understand the product to be an 'own story'. Moreover, both of them are convinced they are dealing with an authentic account and both emphasise the 'literary' competence of their protagonists. But Shaw's presentation is incomparably more scholarly. Shaw uses supplementary information from other sources to check the validity and reliability of the report; in footnotes to Stanley's story, he provides information and interpretations that go well beyond the descriptions Stanley gives, and he pin-points Stanley's social and cultural background by means of the social-ecological method. However, the methodological procedures seem to be simply tagged on to the study in order to emphasise its scientific nature and make it stand out from the 'confessions' genre of the day. Embedding the 'own story' (it takes up pages 47–163 of the total of 205 pages) in extensive methodological prefaces and postscripts has the effect of a scientific exorcism of journalistic spirits; Bennett rightly speaks of 'life history sandwiches'. Shaw's effort to be different also explains why he deliberately avoids using any popular autobiographies of offenders to supplement the material: Shaw sees the value of such documents as being crucially reduced by the fact they contain no additional material (such as court records or statements made by prison staff) that would enable the authenticity of the life history to be assessed. In this (but not only this) respect, Shaw's study differs strikingly from Sutherland's *The Professional Thief* (1972 [1937]). Sutherland, who is seen as the founder of criminology based on the interaction theory, makes comprehensive use of such material and his most frequently quoted source proves to be Hapgood's *Autobiography of a Thief*.[26] This is not surprising when we consider that Sutherland was concerned to reconstruct theft as a profession with its own codes, traditions, techniques and forms of organisation. Hapgood's study, which gives an insider view of a deviant professional world and way of life, put in the crucial preliminary work to this end.

[26] Whereas Hapgood is quoted 14 times, Sutherland refers to Shaw only three times. Sutherland also makes use of the contemporary autobiographies of offenders, which Shaw did indeed quote but rejected as unreliable.

PART II

When Winifred Raushenbush was still considering what title to give her biography of Park, which was to come out later simply as *Robert E. Park: Biography of a Sociologist* (1979), Edgar T. Thompson, who was likewise a pupil of Park's, proposed the title 'Robert E. Park: Marginal Man'. The title sounds attractive and it is perfectly conceivable that Park himself would have been pleased with it. As far as his involvement in sociology is concerned, Park was undoubtedly a marginal man; it is also beyond doubt that he had an greater impact on American sociology than almost anyone else. The fundamental question is whether it was not this marginality that played the main part in creating an American sociology as such.

Everett C. Hughes has described the combination of curiosity about what is happening in the world coupled with a theoretical interest in explaining it as the outstanding quality of American sociology. Curiosity can also be paraphrased as the wish for new experience; it is this wish which takes centre stage in W. I. Thomas' treatise on the person and its wishes (1923). Thomas and Park both ascribed this desire to themselves in their autobiographical claims as to what had been most important to them: Thomas, 'driven certainly by the desire for new experience', Park who made up his mind 'to go in for experience for its own sake' (Paul J. Baker 1973, pp. 248, 253). This desire is by no means unique to Park and Thomas in their day. The central rôle played by the category of experience in the thinking of a whole generation of intellectuals can only be understood against the background of what they are trying to get away from, namely the moral and cultural strait-jacket of a puritanical milieu which denies authentic experiences. The generation we are dealing with here is a generation in the course of transition from the 'genteel tradition' to the culture of modernity; it is a generation which is no longer characterised by unity, but by variety.

CHAPTER 4

Marginality and experience

MARGINAL MAN

. . . a man on the margin of two cultures and two societies . . .   Robert Ezra Park

The concept of the 'marginal man' is probably Park's most significant contribution to the sociology of culture. It is a concept which proved, and is still proving, to be fruitful for the interpretation of many different socio-cultural phenomena, regardless of whether these are processes of spatial and social mobility, issues connected with emigration, escape and banishment, questions of cultural contact and cultural conflict, the problem of social and cultural change or the analysis of rôle conflict.

The concept is an excellent example of Park's way of thinking, which is characterised by the progressive development from experience to knowledge. As has already been mentioned, in drawing up the concept, Park had a concrete type in mind. In a preliminary sketch of the problem, he summarised his preliminary considerations under the title of 'The Marginal Man; a study of the Mulatto Mind.' In an essay published in 1931 ('The Mentality of Racial Hybrids'), Park returned to the topic of hybrids, but by then he only regarded 'racial hybrids' as one particular case of the *cultural hybrid*, as a prototype of a personality who lives between cultures.

What is it that characterises the marginal man? In general, we are concerned here with a person who finds himself on the margins or in the border area of two cultures, someone who participates in two cultures without really belonging to either. In his essay 'Human Migration and the Marginal Man', written in 1928, Park presents the marginal personality as a product of cultural contact, and attributes the latter to mobility processes of a spatial, social and cultural nature, 'a man on the margin of two cultures and two societies, which never completely interpenetrated and fused' (Park 1928, p. 892). Admittedly, Park is referring

154

here specifically to the figure of the emancipated Jew, but in his view this personage is prototypical, in so far as emancipated Jews heralded modern man in the form of 'the first cosmopolite and citizen of the world'. The marginal personality becomes the key figure in cultural contact, because such contact is transposed into it – indeed, embodies it – by forming the melting pot in which cultural processes take place. Life in limbo, 'afloat between cultures', leads initially to a psychological crisis in which the feeling of deracination and disorientation predominates. But the process of getting over this crisis gives marginal man an opportunity that does not fall quite so easily to anyone with firm roots. 'Inevitably he becomes', Park writes, 'the individual with the wider horizon, the keener intelligence, the more detached and rational viewpoint' (Park 1961, pp. xvii–xviii). It is worthy of note that Park illustrates this idea by referring to the philosopher George Santayana. The latter's novel, *The Last Puritan*, which Santayana maintained was a philosophy in the form of a fable, is understood by Park to be an autobiography in disguise, the leading figures in it, Oliver and Mario, symbolising the two cultures which the author unites within himself and which shape his philosophy.

By virtue of the dual cultures in which he moves, marginal man loses that naive self-confidence which characterises persons with firm roots and strong links to their own culture. Lacking the appropriate cultural techniques, he is at the same time not in a position simply to submerge himself in the new cultural milieu. As a consequence, he is, as Stagl remarks, 'placed in a position of having to reflect on cultural differences and cultural change' (Stagl 1981, p. 67). The person afloat between cultures unites within himself the knowledge and insight of the initiated with the critical attitude of the outsider, something which predestines him for the rôle of mediator and interpreter.

The concept of marginal man can quite rightly be termed an American concept, reflecting as it does the particular social and cultural situation in the United States, especially in the first quarter of this century.[1] To a certain extent, it can be regarded as a social and psychological correlate to the sociological metaphor of the melting pot. In our context, however, one further aspect of this concept is of

---

[1] Just as the concept of 'marginal man' is tailor-made to American circumstances, so some related concepts such as *déclassé* and *deraciné* reflect European and French conditions. Stonequist came across Park's concept via the French terminology which he became acquainted with during a period of study in Paris. When he explained his interest in the theme of the *déraciné*, to Park, the latter answered spontaneously: 'Here we call such individuals "marginal men"' (Stonequist n.d., p. 3).

significance, namely, the implications it contains for a sociology of knowledge.

Mobility of a spatial and social nature, according to Karl Mannheim (1958), creates that distance which makes the attitude of 'dispassionate observer' possible in the first place. Simmel coined the category of 'objective man' to circumscribe the case of someone who is not tied down by any sort of fixed prescription, 'which could prejudice his receptivity, his understanding and his appraisal of given circumstances' (1983 [1908], p. 510). This attitude of objectiveness, which to use Simmel's phrase is a 'particular construction consisting of distance and proximity, indifference and commitment', is to be found in its purest state in the sociological form of the stranger.

Simmel's 'The Stranger', a work which in Levine's view 'had the earliest and perhaps most publicised impact on American social research' (Levine, Carter and Gorman 1981, p. 55), helped decisively in the formulation of the marginal man concept.[2] Marginal man can be regarded as a special case of the stranger, a person who 'can . . . view all things without the bias of the individual who knows only one viewpoint, namely, that of his own culture' (Bowdery 1951, p. 90). This phraseology already points to the differences between the two concepts, differences to which a number of authors have referred, Levine being the most prominent among them (1977; Levine, Carter and Gorman 1981).

It is not without significance that Simmel uses the figure of the trader to exemplify the form of the stranger. The agent of circulation is not only the ideal-typical stranger because he is the epitome of a mobile person, but also because he is the epitome of the indifferent person, someone who regards everything as the same. Levine believes Simmel's stranger can be seen as a metaphor for money (personal communication, 15 May 1987); at any rate, this figure contains modern man in embryo form, a person whose relationships are characterised by a tendency to address only the facts. The starting-points for Park's considerations, by contrast, were concrete empirical facts, i.e., his experiences with ethnic minorities. To point up the differences as sharply as possible, Simmel's stranger is objective *because* he is free, free of all family ties or ties to a location or profession which would prejudice his receptivity and understanding of the given circumstances. In contrast to Park's marginal man, Simmel's stranger does not seek membership of the new group – after

---

[2] The first American translation of Simmel's *Excursus*, which appeared in the Park/Burgess Reader, was by Park.

all, being temporarily or permanently refused such membership is what makes marginal man marginal in the first place. The stranger remains distanced even when close to things; it is precisely this which makes him so suitable for the rôle of what Cressey has called the 'anonymous stranger', someone to whom the most surprising examples of frankness and confessions are offered.

Marginal man's objectivity, which expresses itself in *multiple* viewpoints, is neither the result of indifference (in the sense of having a nonpartisan position) nor is it the result of a critical attitude in itself, which makes him doubt the apparently obvious. The deeper reason for the objectivity of marginal man (and here Park's marginal man is not unlike Schütz's 'stranger' (1944)) lies rather in his recognition of the limits to 'thinking as usual'. He is someone who has become a stranger, someone who, precisely because of (his) socio-cultural alienation, has the chance to see things clearly.

Just like Schütz's stranger, the ideal type of which is the immigrant, Park's marginal man is thrown back on his own resources as a result of his having experienced in practice that his cultural pattern, which had become a natural frame of reference for him, is not suited to enable him to understand his new environment. It is the force of circumstances, not the freedom of the situation, which leads him to question the quasi-natural view of the world which the particular cultural pattern puts forward as a means of simplifying complicated processes.

The cultural pattern of the group, which the stranger as Schütz understands him is trying to get closer to, is, Schütz maintains, 'not a matter of course but a questionable topic of investigation, not an instrument for solving problems but a problematic situation itself and one hard to master' (Schütz 1944, p. 506). The stranger who is interested in action per se is therefore momentarily an 'dispassionate observer', since, as he lacks the ability to make use of the things that are culturally obvious to the new group, he cannot find refuge in comfortable platitudes. The individual who is thrown back on to his own resources becomes conscious of his own self, i.e., he begins to see himself, his attitudes and habits, his cultural impressions and his social inheritance with new eyes. Park stressed this aspect over and over again in the context of providing an adequate assessment of the situation of immigrants and their assimilation: only the Pole in America becomes conscious of himself as a Pole. Park saw in this a necessary, crisis-ridden transitional stage, one which cannot be simply avoided by applying crude voluntarism to the question of Americanisation. Retreat into one's cultural niche,

be it 'Little Poland' or the 'University in Exile', the New School for
Social Research, is an opportunity for cautious acclimatisation to a
foreign cultural milieu; being exposed to this without such protection
would otherwise lead to disorientation. The awareness, which a person
afloat between the cultures gains of himself at the same time, points to
something beyond any form of traditional ties: what actually emerges is
a subjectivity which knows what differences mean.

If, by virtue of his objective situation, an existentially marginal man is
driven into a process of reflection which extends his intellectual horizon
beyond that state of narrow-mindedness to which people with deep
roots in their surroundings are subject, by dint of their having been
placed without question in particular circumstances, then the epistemological question clearly arises whether there is not such a thing as an
experimental marginal man.

Dennison Nash (1963) has applied the model of the stranger to the
ethnologist, seeing in him a sort of professional *Wandervogel*. Indeed, it
would seem that being a stranger in this fundamental sense of the term is
a precondition for any sort of field research, just as the field researcher
himself appears to the object of research as a generalised stranger, as,
e.g., 'the white man'. In a reflection on participant observation,
Frankenberg writes that what all ethnologists have in common, regardless of whether they are carrying out field research in the South Seas,
Africa or in the factories of Manchester, 'is the experience of having sub-
merged themselves for anything from a year to three or four years in a
cultural environment different from their own' (1982, p. 50). Even if the
idea that field research presupposes a journey can no longer be
unquestioningly accepted, given that studies are carried out in a familiar
environment, the *perspective* of the stranger is nevertheless upheld; heuristic artifices such as 'the other person's viewpoint' and 'artificial naiveté'
all point to the necessity of looking at the familiar with different eyes.

The essential reason for adhering to the perspective of the stranger is
that, were we to abandon it, we would simultaneously jettison an epistemological premise, one which Merton, paraphrasing Simmel, summarises as follows: 'it is the stranger, too, who finds what is familiar to the
group significantly unfamiliar and so is prompted to raise questions for
inquiry less apt to be raised by insiders' (Merton 1972, p. 33).

It is immediately obvious that the reason why it is sensible to have
someone from outside observe what is happening is that such people are
able, by contrasting it with their own experiences, to pin-point those spe-

cific things which a person closely involved accepts as self-evident and not worth talking about. Strictly speaking, such a premise is nothing more than a correlation between social existence and style of thinking; it is the objective status of the stranger himself which gives rise to this way of seeing things. Being a stranger is fundamental to participant observation as the paramount path taken by field research. We can conceive participation and observation as the unity of proximity and distance in Simmel's sense. But the objectively given status of being a stranger in the methodology of field research is doubled up on, namely, in the necessary condition of distance. The objectively given status of being a stranger, which is the pre-condition for research, is once again called for in the field in the form of controlled rôle-behaviour. It seems to me that this methodological doubling of the status function, which serves to legitimate the science and its superstructure, is intended not only to protect the researcher from frightening data (Devereux 1976), but also to allow the ethnographic experience to gel into a respectable professional rôle. In the argument over which method should be given scientific recognition, the call for distance has the same status as controlling all factors in experiments in the natural sciences. By keeping his distance, the researcher keeps himself as a factor under control. Just as is already discernible in the turn of phrase 'keeping oneself under control', which can be understood not only technically but also metaphorically (just like 'losing control over oneself'), there is more at stake in the case of this necessary condition. Understood as 'distance' which needs to be preserved, distance is a category, based on 'civilised behaviour', which prescribes the proper way of dealing with people. Here, keeping one's distance from others means, above all, taking up a position of distance *vis-à-vis* oneself, in order to avoid giving in to one's emotions – i.e., being *in* a situation yet still being *above* things. The vehemence used to warn people against 'going native' cannot be explained simply in terms of the wish to ensure scientific rules are adhered to; what is at stake is dignity as a behaviour which commands respect.[3] 'Going native' consequently appears to be a variant of 'letting oneself go', in the sense which relates to civilisation; this is something that is severely reprimanded by the scientific community. Seen thus, it becomes clear that this precept is a reflection of its own age: the verdict 'going native' is a late Victorian category, adapted to ethnological activity in the context of the colonial system. Typically, people are now asking whether there are not actually two

---

[3] Malinowski's field diary is full of examples of struggling to maintain his dignity, and they all have little to do with the problem of scientific objectivity.

types of 'going native', the traditional one and the one on 'this', 'our' side (Tedlock 1985, p. 66).

With reference to the situation of the ethnographer, Stagl (1981) has rightly distinguished the rôle of the 'stranger' from that of the 'marginal man'; the ethnographer is a 'stranger' on the strength of his objective situation, and a 'marginal man' on the strength of his contact with the culture. The fact that the field researcher is a stranger, who combines within himself both proximity and distance in Simmel's understanding of the terms, to the extent that he is physically near and culturally distant, follows from the *conditio sine qua non* of ethnographical research. The researcher always begins by being a stranger, but it is the objective of his research to neutralise this strangeness, even if only in his mind. By focusing on reconstructing the way in which human beings interpret their own world, the researcher must think himself into the world of thought, into what Geertz calls the 'self-spun web of meaning', of the group he is investigating; he must change from being an outsider to being a 'marginal man'.

The researcher in the field is consequently an *experimental marginal man*, and, like the marginal man as a cultural type – on the strength of his dual cultural situation which, although deliberately being sought here, is nevertheless (except at the price of failure) something he cannot escape from – he loses that naive self-certainty which characterises the type of person who is firmly rooted in his culture. It would thus be fundamentally wrong to understand the small field studies, in the introductory courses which Park insisted were given, as being exclusively concerned with teaching research techniques. The primary objective of the introductory course was rather to teach the fundamentals of sociological thought. Whether in the (auto)biography of people existing as marginal men or by means of experimentally placing oneself in strange situations, in both cases the aim is to highlight and break through the limits of 'thinking as usual'. Insistence on going out into the field is not only the same thing as the classic dual initiation of the field researcher into both the strange culture and the scientific community, it also aims at something which can be termed controlled self-alienation. Only when a person leaves his own preconceived ideas behind, only when that person becomes thoroughly acquainted with the way others think and act, is he ready to perceive both sets of circumstances – his own and the stranger's.

The potential of the concept of marginal man for the sociology of knowledge is by no means exhausted with the rôle of the experimental marginal man. The question still remains as to how far marginality goes hand in hand with innovation (see Bargatzky 1981, pp. 155ff.). Park's statement that marginal man is the individual with the broader horizons, the sharper intellect and the unprejudiced standpoint suggests this is the case. Also, his reference to the fact that marginal man comes up against the limits of 'thinking as usual' makes the search for innovative paths and an experimental attitude downright imperative. The criticism that the American approach, unlike the ideas of Simmel and Schütz, is concerned in the final analysis with the question as to how we can make 'them' (the strangers, the immigrants) more like 'us' (Harman 1988, p. 14) clearly falls short with respect to Park's position. In the final analysis, he is concerned with two themes coming under the main theme of 'marginal man', namely, acculturation *and* cultural change. Harman is certainly right when he says that Park draws a contradictory and inconsistent picture of the marginal man ('one who suffers yet is better off'); it is difficult to reconcile the simple Polish immigrant under the same heading as the emancipated European Jew. This inconsistency may be one reason why, in the wake of Park's work, sociologists have accepted the concept only within the context of limited empirical research, whereas Park's main concern, namely, the rôle of marginal man in the cultural process, has to a large extent remained unnoticed (Stonequist 1964, p. 344). In the foreground of sociological research are groups of the population who are struggling for a place in society; even though his work was geared empirically to the situation of the immigrants, Park was interested in more than this. He considers marginal man a new type of personality, which, after being released from its traditional bonds, becomes the agent of cultural change and the embodiment of modern subjectivity (see Makropolous 1988). The experience of crisis in the marginal situation, which leads to the dissolving of habits and customs, the 'cake of custom' (a favourite phrase of Park's which he borrowed from Bagehot), has a liberating effect on the individual who is able to overcome the constraints of conventional ways of thinking; 'one of the results is that he (the marginal man) sees more of life, more of the life of human nature, enters deeper into life, has a wider range of experiences' (lecture manuscript 'The Marginal Man', 4 December 1934; REPA 5:10).

If it is true, such a concept of marginal man has consequences for the sociology of science. Various authors have pointed out that, in scientific research, *pioneering* discoveries and inventions have been made by outsiders, people who were in a marginal position *vis-à-vis* the official institutions and professors with their fixed orientations and ways of looking at

problems. Ben-David (1960) speaks of 'fundamental marginal inventions' and refers to the beginnings of bacteriology and psychoanalysis as
examples: Koch, Pasteur and Freud, at the time of their discoveries, were
in a marginal position, neither fully practitioners nor fully scientists. Ben-
David terms persons of this type 'rôle hybrids', a term reminiscent of
Park's 'cultural hybrids'.

Marginality is also involved, or rather directly involved, when it comes
to thinking about marginality: it appears as if it is primarily the marginal
man who gives serious thought to marginality, strangeness and deracination. In Lewis A. Coser's view, Simmel's originality is bound up closely
with his relatively isolated position at Berlin University, an isolation
which resulted both from the anti-Semitic antipathy toward him as well
as from his unorthodox way of working (which was, no doubt, fostered
by that antipathy). The situation is, moreover, exacerbated by the literary
brilliance of his writings and the fact he tended not to cite evidence or
provide footnotes, a by no means insignificant breach of the academic
rules. Coser sees in Simmel a 'stranger in the Academy', someone who
developed, just as the strangers he analysed did, a type of behaviour
which was marked in equal measure both by proximity and distance *vis-
à-vis* the academic world (Coser 1958, 1965).

Coser (1984) has also arrived at similar conclusions in respect of
Alfred Schütz, who published his essay on the 'stranger' five years after
he had been forced to leave Austria, namely, that he was a 'marginal
stranger in the American academy'. It is surely no coincidence that, for
Schütz, it is the figure of the immigrant who is the example *par excellence*
for the situation of the stranger. It is also no coincidence that Schütz's
analytical studies deal primarily with the limits of 'thinking as usual' in
the new environment.

Even the third person in the group of those who have something to
say about marginality and being a stranger, the now almost forgotten
Ernst Grünfeld, seems to have been forced by his life's destiny to reflect
on marginality. His figure of peripheral man ties up with Simmel's
stranger, 'but it is surely an easy matter to trace the existential preconditions for the things he said, both in his choice of topics as well as in his
individual statements' (René König 1981, p. 120). Characteristically,
Grünfeld, himself a Jew expelled from Germany, differentiates between
strangers and people who have been ostracised (Grünfeld 1939).

These impressive examples of a link between person and concept in
the lives of the above three men lead us to ask to what extent Park can be
described meaningfully rather than metaphorically as a marginal man,

as Edgar Thompson has suggested. If we look at Park's abbreviated biography, then we notice his use of concepts which point to a mobile existence with transitory character. His childhood, which ran along 'wandering trails', the characterisation of his life in the 1890s as 'intellectual vagrancy', his stated wish for an activity which was both romantic and meaningful – all these are pointers to a search, fuelled by inner unrest, for existential possibilities which were at the same time a renunciation of traditional preconceived ideas. Park's remark that the tradition he was brought up in offered neither a justification nor an explanation for his intellectual curiosity about the world makes him appear as a representative of that intermediate generation within the process of cultural change, whose thirst for experience points to anti-puritan motives.

Park's life, at least between the ages of 20 and 40, is characterised by a constant oscillation between the worlds of academia and journalism, though it should be said that Park, at home on the tight-rope between the two, was relatively disappointed by both spheres. He was quite obviously in search of a synthesis that reconciled the wish for experience with the wish for knowledge. Everett C. Hughes, in his notes to Park's biography, never tires of emphasising that Park combines 'the dialectic of the reporter with the philosopher', merging the curiosity of the one with the analytical sharpness of the other. Against this background, when we bear in mind his definition of the marginal man, developed with reference to the figure of the emancipated Jew, as someone 'living and sharing intimately in the cultural life and traditions of two distinct peoples; never quite willing to break, even if he were permitted to do so, with his past and traditions, and not quite accepted, because of racial prejudice, in the new society in which he now sought to find a place' (Park 1928, p. 892), then we cannot help getting the impression that there is more 'intended' here than just the situation of the emancipated Jew. Journalism and philosophy can rightly be described as two cultures, each with its own distinct tradition, system of rules and language, representing different ways of approaching and interpreting the reality of life. If we give the 'two distinct peoples' of the definition concrete form, as journalists, on the one hand, and philosophers, on the other, and if we understand 'racial prejudice' to mean a bias specific to a specialist subject, then the text can also be read as a subliminal message from a person who is balancing on the fine line between journalism and philosophy. The fact that Park thoroughly sympathised with the 'marginal man' theory being extended to include combinations of different academic disciplines is shown by his characterisation of William Lloyd Warner as a 'marginal man' between anthropology and sociology.

'Might there not be,' asks Hughes in his 'Essay on the Marginal Man', 'in the most settled society, persons who are in protest against the rôles assigned them; persons, even, who want to play some rôle for which there is no precedent or defined place in culture?' (Everett C. Hughes 1949, p. 65). With his inner unrest, his self-doubts and his wish for an activity that was both romantic and meaningful, Park shows traits of being such a person, someone searching for something. This culminates in the form of sociology he advocates, a sociology that is a synthesis of two traditions and two perspectives considered irreconcilable, a synthesis which generates American sociology *sui generis*:

Park combined philosophical and theoretical interest with what some are inclined to derogate as journalistic interest. It has been a peculiar cachet of American sociology to combine curiosity about what is going on in the world, with a more theoretical interest. Park, more than any one before or during his time, brought these two interests together. (E. C. Hughes; REPA 9:8)

THE WISH FOR EXPERIENCE

The wish for new experience is found equally in the vagabond and the scientific explorer. William Isaac Thomas

Stagl's remark, that we find 'a certain inconstancy, a constant urge for a change of place . . . in the biographies of many ethnographers' (1981, p. 86), points to the psychological disposition of the researcher's personality. The example of Lévi-Strauss is well known; he ascribed to himself an inconstant 'neolithic intellect': 'Like a bush fire he occasionally sets unexplored territories on fire, which he perhaps fertilises, in order to hastily bring in a few harvests, leaving a barren land behind' (Lévi-Strauss 1978, p. 46). This idiosyncratic way of thinking reminds us of Thomas' 'wish for new experience', to which he gives a prominent place in his treatise on man and his wishes; in the final analysis, it is a treatise about the intrinsic driving forces for social change.

Conceptually speaking, Thomas does not clarify what he means by 'wishes'. In the course of the various explanations he gives, he oscillates between action impulses, motives and value-orientated attitudes.[4] Although the theory of wishes is inspired by the debates on a psychology

---

[4] The first version is to be found in the essay 'The Persistence of Primary-Group Norms in Present-Day Society and Their Influence in the Educational System' (1917); the final version is in *The Unadjusted Girl* (1923).

of human instincts, it cannot be equated with any theory of instinct. In the context of his personality theory, Thomas' 'wishes' have the value of variables which mediate between organic nature and social influences and/or are the product of the mediation between organic nature and social influences. Thomas' personality theory is dynamic in the truest sense of the term. It is typified by concepts which emphasise activity, development and change. The concept of wishes is of decisive importance here, because to a certain extent it relates to the driving force of personal and social development; wishes are 'the forces which urge us into action'.

Thomas reduces the variety of concrete forms which human wishes can take to a basic four, all except one of which remain the same in the various explanations: namely, the wish for new experience; the wish for security; the wish for response (in the first version: for control); and the wish for recognition. The particular constellation within which the wishes relate to each other engenders certain types of personalities: it is the specific weighting of the first two wishes which primarily determines the basic forms of these types, which are the 'philistine', the 'bohemian' and the 'creative person'.

The philistine, whose personality is predominated by a wish for security, gears his actions wholly to the prevailing definitions and norms. He is a limited, self-satisfied person, whose reflexive actions exhibit such a degree of inflexibility that the only possibility for development lies in the gradual changes occasioned by aging. The bohemian is the opposite of the philistine. In the case of the bohemian, the wish for new experience is dominant, but the wish is seldom productive, since the bohemian is a non-conformist on principle. Instead of turning the process of shattering norms into something productive and making it into something of social significance, the rebellious gesture becomes an end in itself. The creative person represents a positive synthesis of both of these. His character is self-contained and -organised, while at the same time including the potential for change and the necessity for development.

From today's viewpoint, the problem with Thomas' personality typology is that we see an expression of its particular period in its representational phraseology. Because his typology was formulated around 1917, it is reasonable to assume that Thomas took Greenwich Village bohemia as the starting point of his considerations, as this was the centre of the prewar revolt against neo-puritanism – i.e., philistinism – and also its failure, due to non-conformist behaviour becoming an end in itself. Yet the personality theory, with its thesis–antithesis–synthesis structure, has had a thoroughly successful sociological career. Kluckhohn and Murray's differentiation between the 'under-socialised' (bohemian), 'over-socialised' (philistine) and 'correctly socialised type' (creative personality) faithfully follows Thomas' model; in addition, Riesman's distinction between 'conformed', 'abnormal' and 'autonomous' is also in this tradition (Kluckhohn and Murray 1948; Riesman, Denney and Glazer 1958).

Philistine, bohemian and creative person are ideal types. Thomas stresses that no one of these forms can ever be perfectly realised by any one person in all of his or her activities. Rather, they represent ideal limits of personal development. Mannheim believed this differentiation of personality types paralleled his own considerations on entrenched as opposed to mobile elements within the intelligentsia (Mannheim 1958, p. 67 n1). The creative person quite clearly corresponds to Mannheim's mobile type, with the difference that the latter sees himself forced by changing environmental circumstances into reflexion, whereas the reflective attitudes of the former show a propensity for change. This difference is obviously connected with the assumption that there is a wish for new experience, a wish to which Thomas gives priority. The wish for new experience

is seen in simple forms in the prowling and meddling activities of the child, and the love of adventure and travel in the boy and the man. It ranges in moral quality from the pursuit of game and the pursuit of pleasure to the pursuit of knowledge and the pursuit of ideals. It is found equally in the vagabond and the scientific explorer . . . In its pure form the wish for new experience implies motion, change, danger, instability, social irresponsibility. The individual dominated by it shows a tendency to disregard prevailing standards and group interests. He may be a complete failure, an account of his instability; or a conspicuous success, if he converts his experience into social values – puts them in the form of a poem, makes of them a contribution to science, etc. (William I. Thomas 1924, p. 489)

In the pure form just described, the wish for new experience contains all the elements of the neolithic intellect, as understood by Lévi-Strauss, which paradoxically enough is characteristic of modernity, namely: movement ('I am not capable of virtuously tilling a field whose harvest I am obliged to gather in year after year'), change ('unexplored regions'), instability ('haste') and social irresponsibility ('leaving a barren land behind'). The imperative of change, the *morale canonique du changement*, which characterises modernity (Gumbrecht 1975), seems to be transposed here into the mode of experience itself, as an urge for new sensations which, reflectively, allows new experience to be gained. This urge is expressed in an elemental way in the lust for adventure, a lust sublimated and rendered productive in ethnographical research (William I. Thomas 1965, p. 227). Such an epistemological model, which incorporates the *contemplatio* part of the *vita activa*, presupposes a specific notion of the underlying patterns of thinking. Using Watson's experiments with animals as a basis, Thomas proposes the hypothesis that the animal's entire psychological mechanism is geared to movement, to hunting (William I. Thomas 1965, p. 153). From this he concludes that the schema of intellect essentially resembles that of the hunt or the pursuit:

> Turning now abruptly from the rat to the creative man, any one who studies the history of a practical invention or a scientific discovery will be impressed with the resemblance between the activities of the human being before his problem and those of the rat before his box or maze. For some years, in fact, I have been in the habit of pointing out that scientific pursuit is precisely of the hunting pattern. The intensity of interest on the part of the discoverer or experimenter, his random and frenzied movements, his following of every scent, his abandonment of false trails, his elation when he has got his result, remind us of the animal in quest of his prey and after he has made his kill. (William I. Thomas 1951, p. 113)

What is immediately striking here are the strong parallels to Ginzburg's paradigm of 'clues'. Ginzburg argues that, toward the end of the nineteenth century, a new epistemological model began to assert itself in the humanities (according to context, called the hunter, prophetic, circumstantial evidence or semiotic paradigm), the roots of which go back a long way in time. Behind the circumstantial evidence paradigm Ginzburg 'senses' 'the perhaps oldest gesture in the history of the human intellect: that of the hunter, squatting in the mud and poring over the spoor traces of his quarry' (Ginzburg 1983, p. 72). This hunter paradigm corresponds to Thomas' 'intellectual schema of the hunt' – even in terms of its anthropological component. Just as Ginzburg illustrates this model by using examples of the way in which the art historian Morelli, the detective Sherlock Holmes and the psychoanalyst Freud all proceeded, Thomas refers to Pasteur's detective-like search for the lost 'racemic acid',[5] this being an example which could equally well have been quoted by Ginzburg (William I. Thomas 1965, pp. 154–5).

[5] Pasteur's investigations have their criminalistic counterpart (and prototype?) in toxicology, which is full of examples of the search for missing substances. In this regard, Uwe Nettelbeck's history of the customs of the police records department (1979) provides a rich source of material.

Ginzburg stresses that those sciences characterised by their reliance on circumstantial evidence are 'to a high degree qualitative sciences which focus on what is unique in cases, situations and documents' (Ginzburg 1983, p. 73). Using the biographical and/or documentary method and by utilising life histories, diaries, letters, etc., Thomas transfers this epistemological model on to sociology, making it into a science of circumstantial evidence in Ginzburg's sense, intending it to provide an explanation as to why, in a given situation, different people react differently.

In this connection, the anecdotes about how Thomas discovered biographical material as sociological source material are of great interest because even they follow the pattern laid down by the science of circumstantial evidence; that is to say, they are told in such a way as to provide circumstantial evidence for the science of circumstantial evidence. In the short description of his life that he prepared for L. L. Bernard, Thomas traces the origin of his interest in documents:

to a long letter picked up on a rainy day in the alley behind my house, a letter from a girl who was taking a training course in a hospital, to her father concerning family relationships and discords. It occurred to me at the time that one would learn a great deal if one had a great many letters of this kind. (Paul J. Baker 1973, p. 250)

A variant of this anecdote would have it that one morning, 'around 1910' (!), Thomas ducked to avoid some rubbish which was being thrown out on to an alley in Chicago's West Side and a bundle of letters fell at his feet: 'In the sequence presented by the letters, he saw a rich and rewarding account and in time he was led to pursue the personal document as a research tool' (quoted from Bennett 1981, p. 123).

It is relatively unimportant as to which version is correct or which at least comes near to the truth; both of them are at any rate well told.[6] In their faithfulness to detail ('on a rainy day'), they illustrate that apparently fateful principle of chance, that only he or she who is aware of this principle 'chances' upon great discoveries. Seen like this, the alley belongs to the letters, just as the crystal deposits at the bottom of a wine bottle belong to Pasteur's racemic acid.[7] The back alley, which appears

---

[6] 'Thomas was a great raconteur. He loved telling stories about himself as well as about others. He didn't tell them always in the same way' (letter from E. C. Hughes to Bennett, Bennett 1981, p. 123).

[7] The following sentence also comes from Pasteur: 'Dans le champ de l'observation, le hasard ne favorise que les esprits préparés' [In the field of observation, chance only favours those minds prepared for it] (quoted from Cannon n.d. [1945], p. 79).

just as out-of-the-way and unconventional a place for generating data ('out of the way' in both senses of the term), as does the sociologist who is hanging around there, becomes (like the rubbish bin which is emptied over the sociologist's head) a metaphor for a type of sociology which uses deviant methods, a sociology which concerns itself with deviant phenomena. Both versions are based on what Merton calls the serendipity component of research, i.e., discovery 'by chance or sagacity' of data that is not actually being looked for (Merton 1968, pp. 157–8).[8]

The serendipity pattern belongs to those imponderable elements which play a part in all sciences of circumstantial evidence, namely: keen hearing, sharp sight and sensitivity, combined with an unerring, almost instinctive feeling for the opportune moment (see Gerhard König 1986). In this context, it is important to emphasise that according to the serendipity pattern, findings cannot be brought about by design; serendipity cannot be intended. Serendipity, as Norbert Miller (1986, p. 139) puts it, consists in 'attentiveness for the moment', as the anecdotes from and about Thomas show us so impressively.

Moreover, the coincidence between scientific procedure ('chance discoveries') and scientific theorem ('wish for new experience') should make us prick up our ears, with the wish appearing to be the precondition for the procedure. In fact, Thomas' statement that the wish for new experience has 'enterprising' (meaning: mobile and adventurous) features, is mirrored in what Cannon has to say about serendipity, where he emphasises that a 'non-enterprising [set in its ways] intelligentsia' finds perfect security in received opinions: 'There is no adventure in the world of ideas for people who live according to a pattern' (Cannon n.d. [1945], p. 81).

Miller has described the serendipity pattern as being a composite mixture of the art of being on the trail, such as detectives and scouts are capable of, and the attitude of the oriental caliph who goes out into the nocturnal labyrinth of strange destinies, strange streets and strange adventures (Miller 1986, pp. 137ff.). Both hold true for Thomas the sociologist: from amongst the rubbish – the useless residue – he is able to pick out and read the tracks which provide him – and this is a methodological innovation compared with the empirical sociologist who devotes himself to the inner world – with a glimpse into the labyrinth of strange destinies.

---

[8] Horace Walpole coined the term 'serendipity', borrowing from the fairy tale of the 'Three Princes of Serendipp', in a letter to Horace Mann on 1 January 1754. Merton, who first discussed the term in 1945 (although, be it chance or not, the physiologist Walter B. Cannon used the term in the same year in a treatise about 'The Way of an Investigator' to describe chance discoveries), made a significant contribution to its spread in the social sciences.

Thomas was anything but the sober and reserved professor who dominated the alma mater scene in his day. On the contrary, his life-style actually offended some of the *bien pensants* (Coser 1977). Thomas was described as a *bon viveur*, dressing in a distinguished manner, a great one for eating and drinking, society and conversation, while proving himself to be a 'fantastic gossip and a great raconteur' (E. C. Hughes; REPA 6:3). A particularly informative description is provided by Hutchins Hapgood, who had been introduced to Thomas by Robert Morss Lovett:

Thomas is a scientist, a sociologist well-known among the interested; he held a position as Professor of Sociology for many years at Chicago, but his impulse to dig deep into sociological groups of people naturally separated him from the academic life, and for years he has made his living by being employed to make investigations in this country and in Europe, ascertaining the manner of living in large groups, approaching the work with no prejudice . . . In his little apartment in New York, he did his own washing, much of his own cooking, and, during Prohibition at any rate, made his own drinks; as a pastime he invented what he thought was a new type of golf-ball, but I don't think he was ever able to put it on the market. In fact, he was just as clear as any working man of personal relations with capitalistic graft; for, in fact, he is a working man; also a man of extraordinary life-desire, a sense of sex and of mental amusement in the midst of moderate drink. During Prohibition days, many a time Lovett and I dined at his apartment. At these parties Will [Thomas] would do the cooking, and he cooked beautifully, concoct the drinks, and genially analyze the human animal, temperamentally and sociologically. As I have had frequent opportunity to observe, the scholar may have a permeating geniality peculiarly marked. Then Lovett would often take us to one of his delightful speak-easies, run by some Italian; or we would go to see dear old Luke O'Connor.[9] (Hutchins Hapgood 1939, p. 542)

A scientist who goes to speak-easies during Prohibition, who is just as much at ease in 'high society' as in the *demi-monde*, at scientific conferences as in literary circles, is, as Coser describes, certainly an ambivalent enough character to provoke animosity on the part of the staider members of the faculty club. But he is also the sort of person who knows how to appreciate both personal experience and personal documents, and he draws up a personality theory which revolves around three ideal-typical figures: the philistine, the bohemian and the creative person. The mere fact that Thomas asserted that the wish for new experience was to be found preponderantly just as much among tramps, adventurers and

---

[9] Luke O'Connor was a well-known bohemian landlord in Greenwich Village, whose bar was jokingly called the 'Working Girls' Club' or 'Working Girls' Home'.

vagrants as among inventors and scientists must have been a bone of contention for the *bien pensants*. For the statement, if it is read against the grain, contains the supposition that every scientist, especially the empirical one, has something of the tramp, adventurer and vagrant within him. In Thomas' view, the scientist is indeed an improper person; he has to be, since, after all, in his opinion, the high cultural level of the Western world derives from the tendency to shatter norms. What marks off the scientist from the tramp, however, is not the wish in itself, not even the strength of it, but the capacity to sublimate this wish, as is evidenced in creative people, whether they be poets or scientists: 'a Thomistic autobiographical distinction surely', comments Bennett drily (1981, p. 139).

'On the whole, with reference to my sociological history, I feel that my dominant interest has been new experience of concrete types' (Paul J. Baker 1973, p. 250). It is striking how much this is in agreement with various things Park had to say. In the description he gives of his life, he emphasises that books had indeed been of help to him in his thinking, 'but the majority of the aspects of life which interest me derive from my personal experience' (Paul J. Baker 1973, p. 258). Thomas' wish for new experience finds its counterpart in Park's romantic interest in life; this, according to Park himself, is inevitably orientated toward the strange, the far-away and the unusual (Park 1950c [1934], p. 134). The sociological researcher appears in this context as a social type who makes his romantic interest in life into his profession.

Alvin Gouldner sees the romantic point of view as being an emancipatory point of view, to the extent that it expresses a form of resistance against what is historically out-of-date, against unnecessary rules and restrictions: 'It [the romantic point of view] provides a starting-point for the great breakthrough to a modernity of sensitive *subject* experience, which stands in contrast to the *objectivist* concept of modernity as enlightenment' (Gouldner 1984, p. 175). This is precisely what constitutes the fundamental difference between Simmel's 'stranger' and Park's 'marginal man': marginal man is objective because of his experience of subjectivity, not because he is gifted with rationality and has a matter-of-fact view of things.

In his essay on 'Deep Structures in the Social Sciences', Gouldner differentiates between classical and romantic thinking in the social sciences (in Gouldner 1984). Whereas classical thought stresses the universal applicability of standards, norms and values, romantic thinking emphasises their relativity. Seen thus, romantic thinking inherently possesses a tendency to shatter norms. Although, in Gouldner's view, romantic thinking is to be found in the discipline of cultural anthropology, while classical thinking manifests itself as a discipline in sociology, he nevertheless maintains that romantic ideas are to be found in their most unadulterated form in Chicago School of sociology:

> This Chicago standpoint embodies a species of naturalistic Romanticism; it prefers the offbeat, i.e., the extreme case, to the familiar or average case; the evocative ethnographic detail to the dispassionate and dull taxonomy; the sensuously expressive to dry, formal analysis; informal, naturalistic observation to formal questionnaires and rigorous laboratory experiments; the standpoint of the hip outsider to that of the square insider. In short, and as the nineteenth-century Romantics might have said, they prefer the standpoint of bohemians to that of philistines. (Gouldner 1984, p. 192)

Gouldner attributes this state of affairs to the fact that the founders of the Chicago School were most closely linked to the German tradition. But there are actually important factors arising out of their own cultural tradition which helped to promote the formation of a romantic attitude as a motivation for protest.

In this context, it is of particular significance that, in the romantic view, variety is in itself of value; the romantic attitude is in essence pluralistic. It not only directs attention toward hitherto neglected areas of social life, thereby leading to some extent to a 'democratisation' of the concept of data. But also, within this attitude, there is included an implicit criticism of the conventional view of the world which divides reality up into 'refined' and 'exemplary' areas, and, deviating from these, 'lower' areas, those which can be neglected or at best left to moral judgement (Gouldner 1984, p. 197). In the final analysis, what is being criticised is the curtailment of experience. Walt Whitman is generally considered the spiritual founding father of the romantic interest in human diversity, which was at the same time based on an underlying democratic impetus. In George Santayana's view, he was the only American poet of the nineteenth century who succeeded in breaking away completely from the genteel tradition. For the young generation at the end of the nineteenth century, who were rebelling against moral and cultural confinement, Whitman was the guiding light of cultural dissent; at the turn of the century, coming out in support of Whitman meant declaring oneself a cultural dissident.

Park also came out in support of Whitman during this period. In a speech entitled 'Walt Whitman', which he gave in 1930 to the Chicago branch of the Walt Whitman Fellowship, he revealed his enthusiasm for

Whitman, an enthusiasm which was primarily inspired by his hope for a break with tradition:

My remarks are likely to assume something of the character of a confession . . . As a young man I was thrilled by the note of insurgency in the 'Song of Myself' and in 'The Children of Adam'. I looked forward with confidence to when thought and literature in America should be free, untrammeled by the traditional forms and the inherited conventions . . . As a matter of fact, when I was young – and when I first began to read Whitman, though I was rebellious – I was what the Quakers call a seeker – I had not found my vocation. I was unsettled, unmarried, and without a program. In *Leaves of Grass* I encountered a new type of man; a man who had broken with tradition but had found, nevertheless, a new vocation and a new faith . . . When I first encountered Whitman I was, as I have said, disturbed and unsettled, but I had my moments of ecstasy also. I was a newspaper man then, as Whitman had been. A newspaper man, more than most people, I suspect, knows, and feels, and is thrilled by the vast, anonymous and impersonal life of the city. Walking on upper Broadway or down to the Battery on a bright afternoon, or watching the oncoming and outgoing human tide as it poured morning and evening over Brooklyn Bridge, was always for me an enthralling spectacle. I remember writing, not a poem, but an article for the Sunday paper, on that theme. It was for that reason, no doubt, that I began to read with a certain amount of enthusiasm Whitman's musings on the city's surging life. Crossing Brooklyn Ferry, you remember, inspired Whitman to reflections upon life and death and I felt, as he did, that there was something inspiring, majestic – in the spectacle of the manifold and multitudinous life of the city. (Freedman 1970, p. 103)

Park's enthusiasm for Whitman is characteristic of many of the young intellectuals of his generation, who, seeking what Whitman termed 'something yet unfound', broke with tradition. For them, the metropolis becomes a domain of experience, which leaves behind all that is provincial and narrow; it is a place characterised by heterogeneity of opinions, life-styles and cultures, which permits subjectivity and an experience of oneself.

In her commentary on the Whitman speech, Florence Freedman states that Park found in Whitman's poems an artistic expression of his own interest in the diversity of people, their forms of interaction and their life in the big cities: 'Like Whitman, he continued in his later work to have the journalist's eye for the present, for the event, while probing and expressing its deeper significance through philosophy and sociology as Whitman did through poetry' (Freedman 1970, p. 99).

Whitman and Park seem in an almost ideal-typical way to correspond to the type of person governed by the wish for new experience, a person who is successful because he manages to turn his experiences into social values, in the form of a poem or as a contribution to science. 'Freedom to loaf, to look and to see; that is enough' – to me, no sentence from Park's speech seems to be more characteristic in describing the intellectual tramp and marginal man that was Park. In his description of his life, Park mentions that after completing his studies with Dewey (and under his influence), he drew up a life plan which only had as its objective the contemplation and knowledge of the world, without any practical intentions: 'My program was to see and to know what we call "Life"' (Paul J. Baker 1973, pp. 253ff.).

CHAPTER 5

'To see life': the cultural undercurrent

'TO SEE LIFE'

The newspaper is, like art to the artist, less a career than a form of excitement and a way of life.

Robert Ezra Park

'To see and to know "life"', a turn of phrase which seems almost tailor-made as a characterisation of empirical sociology à la Chicago: this phrase was in circulation toward the end of the nineteenth century as a justification for people turning to journalism as a profession. Park, as well, reconstructs his move to journalism with the help of these words. In a 'Class Room Plan' for the seminar entitled 'The Newspaper' in 1921, where he applies to himself his demand that his students make sure of their motives by reflecting on themselves, he begins his biography with the statement: 'Motives for entering the profession: To see life' (REP 2:8).

In the 1890s, encouraged by magazine journalism, a new type of journalist became established. Whereas the old reporter was a hack, 'uneducated and proud of his ignorance . . . regularly drunk and proud of his alcoholism', the new type was 'younger, more naive, more energetic and ambitious, college-educated, and usually sober' (Schudson 1978, p. 69).

In his autobiography, Steffens writes that, in his capacity as publisher of the *Commercial Advertiser*, which he took over in 1897, he was on the lookout for young and enthusiastic authors 'who would see and make others see the life of the city' (Steffens 1931, p. 313). He found them in the universities of Princeton, Yale and, above all, Harvard, probably not only because he met a particularly understanding member of the faculty there, the literary scholar Charles T. Copeland, but also because Harvard in the 1890s was considered to be an especially attractive university from the intellectual point of view, with a pronounced 'anti-philistine sentiment'. It was certainly no coincidence that it was a Harvard professor, the philosopher George Santayana, who attempted to answer the question of what a philistine was (1967c [1892]). The answer, that a significant feature of the philistine was his conventionality, may itself appear conventional today, but it does throw light on the spirit of Harvard, which Santayana likewise made the theme of an essay (1967b [1894]). The Hapgood brothers, who studied in Harvard from 1886 to 1894, enjoyed not only the freedom of learning guaranteed by the elective system and, as a by-product of this, the diversity and flexibility of the courses, but also, which was just as important, the electrifying intellectual atmosphere that expressed itself in the attitude of questioning and doubting everything. This is precisely the 'moral' which is contained in Santayana's analysis of philistines, a doctrine which we best understand if we read it in the context of Santayana's thoughts on the spirit and the ideals of Harvard. The thing which marked the American philistine off from the English Tory, who after all still had his preferences and prejudices, was his shallow rigidity. In the final analysis, because the philistine internalises conventional maxims which, acting as a filter, colour his perception, existence as a philistine means that experiencing things only at second hand. This blindness on the part of the philistine, who protects himself against doubts by exercising rigid self-control, is contrasted by Santayana, in his thoughts about Harvard, with that industry in doubt which captures the spirit of Harvard. What was special about Harvard was that it nurtured doubt, it invited people to experiment and explore and it developed a notion of work worthy of an academic, characterised above all by being done in an unconstrained way. The elective system was both symbol and medium of such an understanding of what being an academic was all about.

Among those who found their way from Harvard to the *Commercial Advertiser* were Robert Dunn, Carl Hovey, Humphrey T. Nichols and Hutchins Hapgood, all of whom made a lasting name for themselves in journalism. John Reed, a graduate of Harvard and a student of Copeland,[1] also turned to journalism. We have him to thank for one of the most impressive portrayals of the fascination which the big city, at the beginning of the century, exerted on those who knew how to observe it.

To Reed, New York was an enchanted city. He spent hours wandering its streets, marvelling at everything:

The soaring imperial towers of downtown, the East River docks smelling of spices and the clipper ships of the past, the swarming East Side – alien towns

---

[1] Reed wrote a portrait of Charles Townsend Copeland for the 'Interesting People' column of *American Magazine* (Reed 1911).

within towns – where the smoky flare of miles of clamorous pushcarts made a splendor of shabby streets . . . I know Chinatown, and Little Italy, and the quarter of the Syrians; the marionette theatre, Sharkey's and McSorley's saloons, the Bowery lodging houses and the places where the tramps gather in winter; the Haymarket, the German Village, and all the dives of the Tenderloin.

He found wonderful obscure restaurants where he could try the foods of all the nations. He knew where to procure drugs, where to go to hire a man to kill an enemy, how to get into gambling rooms and secret dance halls. He was well acquainted 'with the parks, the upper-crust quarters, the theatres and hotels, with the ugly growth of the city, which spread like a disease, with the poor quarters, in which life ebbed away, and the squares and streets where an old, marvellously comfortable way of life was being drowned in the ever louder din of the slums':

I came to know Washington Square with its artists and writers, its bohemians and radicals. I attended a gangsters' ball at Tammany Hall, took part in an excursion of the Tim Sullivan Association, joined the surging crowds at Coney Island. *Within a block of my house was all the adventure in the world; within a mile was every foreign country.* (Reed 1977; my italics)[2]

The compressed, sequential enumeration of the individual zones of observation gives a vivid impression of the restlessness which is ascribed to the reporter in numerous descriptions of the day. This restlessness functions like the psychosomatic expression of a thirst for experience which gradually becomes a motor function. The reporter appears here as someone with an inborn restless nature, driven on by curiosity. Understood as an instinctual drive, this characteristic becomes transformed, with the gradual emergence of journalism as a profession, into a requisite of journalism, which was considered desirable if not actually indispensable: 'an insatiable curiosity, a flexible and social personality and a nature to be satisfied by a variety of experience' reads a guidebook to the qualities which the person turning to journalism as a profession should possess (Johnson and Harriss 1948, p. 4). This psychogram of the reporter appears to be almost a blueprint for the type of personality that is characterised by the wish for new experience.

In a sketch entitled 'The New Reporter', the latter's motives are described in an illustrative and informative way:

[Reporting] was so much better than dreamily drinking beer in Germany and telling himself that he was a sociologist. It had been a pleasant, contemplative

---

[2] See also Reed, unpublished autobiographical essay; Gelb 1973, pp. 48 and 49; Hicks and Reed 1968, pp. 71 and 72.

existence for a while, and he had heard some interesting theories, but he had been doing the student thing too long . . . He decided that he was sick of the ease and inexactness of the scholar, sick too, of having someone else pay his bills, sick of leisurely reading theories about man as a unit. He wanted to see something of men as warm beings with their passions and pursuits, their motives and their ways of looking at things. He could not have chosen a better field for it. (Williams 1898, pp. 573–4)

Even if, as was customary at the time, reference in this passage is being made to a definite person,[3] we can still accept it as a sort of key text for the understanding of journalism both as a field and as a sphere of experience (and not just a profession). The young reporter's thirst for experience, as he turns his back on the academic world, can only be understood against the backdrop of the contemplative existence of the scholar. The restless spirit is the opposite of the leisurely scholar who, as characterised by Williams, 'reads in big books, by a comfortable study-table, with a pipe in [his] mouth'. Toward the end of the nineteenth century, the constantly recurring tension between erudition and originality, identified by Merton (1981) as an important component in the history of science, assumes the form of an antithesis between 'mere' book-learning and 'real' experience. The students who take up a career in journalism are exchanging book learning for knowledge gained from experience, exchanging the alma mater for the big city as the place where real life is lived. It is the street, not the lecture room or the library, which now becomes the place of study: 'The professors were tough city editors, the classrooms were docks, jails, morgues and hospitals, and the dormitories were the cheap rooming-houses which were all that salaries of five to fifteen dollars a week could command' (Weisberger 1961, p. 158).

Against the background of the tension between erudition and originality, between book knowledge and experience, it seems appropriate for us to reconsider the relationship between journalism and empirical sociology, to look at it in a new light. Characteristically, the debate about the differences and common interests of journalism and the social sciences is accentuated by viewpoints relating to both theoretical knowledge and methodology. The journalistic and sociological enterprises have been investigated as ideal types (Jacobs 1970); a study has been made of objectivity and partiality in both social sciences and journalism (Fabris 1981); the understanding of reality as seen by journalism and empirical science

---

[3] The time and place of publication (New York, 1898) as well as the references in the text make it seem not out of place for us to suppose that Williams is referring here to Hutchins Hapgood.

has been examined (Rühl 1981). In this way, a constellation that is the product of history is projected back on to previous history; it is assumed that these two paths of approach to reality always co-existed. This becomes particularly clear in the light of the considerations of Harriet Jacobs, who used to be a journalist and then became a sociologist. Not only does she, with the characteristic zeal of a convert, exaggerate the differences which undoubtedly exist between journalism and sociology (in referring to a mistake in her first sociological papers – writing 'reporter' instead of 'fieldworker' – she ironically confirms the relationship between them), she also neglects to take account of the fact that the methodological procedures which distinguish sociology from journalism result not only from attempts to demarcate the discipline away from competing directions and related disciplines, but also, via this discussion, away from journalism. What Lepenies (1981) has to say on the attempts to justify a discipline in the context of related, competing, exemplary or subsidiary disciplines also holds true in the case of empirical sociology in its relation to journalism. It is a matter of emphasising the uniqueness of the orientations and research tools and at the same time laying a claim to seniority; Park's references to Charles Booth, whom he actually did not follow, can be understood in this sense. The criticism made of early empirical sociology, that it was carrying out 'journalistic sociology', is both part of and an expression of these discussions. At the same time, however, it blocks access to an unprejudiced account of the roots of empirical sociology. Saying that a certain type of empirical sociology grew out of journalism can only be construed as a reproach if we are inclined to conceive the emergence of new disciplines and directions as being a process of (scientific) parthenogenesis.

If we turn our attention to the generation of journalists under consideration here, we could be quite justified, with a view to their work, in speaking of it as a sort of hidden sociology. The contemporary appraisal that this or that reporter was a 'realist sociologist' was an indication of this. Reporters such as Jacob A. Riis and Hutchins Hapgood, Ray Stannard Baker and Lincoln Steffens, Alfred Hodder, Josiah Flynt Willard, Walter A. Wyckoff and very many others can all be considered as surrogate sociologists without strong academic roots. Wyckoff did in fact later lecture on (industrial) sociology, in his capacity as assistant professor of political economy in Princeton; interestingly enough, his study 'The Workers', which was based on participant observation and which actually qualified him for sociology, appeared in *Scribner's Magazine*.

All the above-mentioned journalists, with the exception of Riis who occupies a special status for several reasons,[4] were university graduates, usually in literature or philosophy. Of these, Hutchins Hapgood is especially noteworthy because both his social background and academic career show remarkable parallels to those of Park. Both of them, Park (born in 1864) and Hapgood (born in 1869), grew up in small towns on the banks of the Mississippi; both were (as indeed were most of the new generation of reporters) the offspring of old New England families; both came from well-off middle-class families; and both refer to their fathers as puritans, even though they ultimately displayed an amazing understanding for their sons' careers, departing as they did from the family tradition, and gave their sons financial support.

Hapgood's studies began at the University of Michigan, where Park obtained his BA; in 1889 he moved to Harvard, where he studied under William James, Josiah Royce and George Santayana, amongst others, and graduated as BA in 1892. Once again, the special atmosphere in Harvard is emphasised in Hapgood's report on his student days: the flexible curriculum which avoided rote learning, the intellectual and moral freedom, combined with an attitude of questioning, doubting and probing, and above all, the 'Harvard indifference', an attitude which had something of the aristocratic *réserve* as well as the modern 'coolness' about it. An almost farcical expression of this attitude was the Laodicean Club (with Norman and Hutchins Hapgood as members and Santayana as chairman) which dissolved itself after its second meeting, since one of its rules was that it ceased *ipso facto* to exist if a quorum of members was present. This gesture of indifference, which has to be seen against the background of neo-puritan involvement, heralds the attitude of the observer who does not interfere, but takes note.

After a further year at graduate school, Hapgood went to Europe in 1893, and from 1893-4 he studied under, amongst others, Simmel in Berlin and Windelband in Strasbourg; this, too, parallels Park's career. We do not learn much about his studies in Germany (more about the pleasure of drinking German beer and the customs of the *Corps* students); it is open to question as to how seriously he took his studies. But it is certainly not without significance that in Berlin Hapgood made the acquaintance of Arthur F. Bentley and Celestin Bouglé. He later visited Bouglé in Paris, when the latter already held a professorship at the

---

[4] Amongst those quoted, Riis not only was the sole immigrant, but he also belonged to another generation (born in 1849), something which is not without significance. All these factors contributed to Riis being the only reformer out of those quoted, someone who was concerned with the 'betterment' of the lower classes.

Sorbonne: the description of the dinner in Bouglé's house, where his mother, 'obviously considered the First in the family', 'held court' at the head of the table, is most enlightening (Hutchins Hapgood 1939, p. 98).

After a trip around the world, Hapgood returned to Harvard, where he obtained an MA and was appointed assistant professor of English literature. He looked set for an academic career, especially as he was offered a lectureship by the Harvard president, Eliot. But Hapgood declined the offer, in order to turn his attention to his career as a journalist (which was poorly paid and received no social recognition). He was not alone in so doing: Alfred Hodder (born in 1866), who was a close friend of both Hapgood and Willard, likewise preferred journalism to an academic career. Hodder was considered as an up-and-coming philosopher. Josiah Royce, his academic teacher, said of him that he had been the most brilliant student he had ever had, while at the same time voicing the fear that Hodder would allow himself to be diverted from philosophy because of his 'romantic temperament' (Hutchins Hapgood 1939, p. 164).[5] Hodder, too, sounds as though he was fed up with studying books. In an obituary for Josiah Flynt Willard, he wrote:

I had chosen a passably dreary seminary course in Harvard in which all the literature of criminology had been got up and reported. I myself had looked into some of the books – too many – some is too many. Five minutes of Flynt's talk turned my books into a heap of rubbish. Five hours' stroll with him made me forget that the rubbish heap existed. (Hodder 1908, p. 347)

The fact that some leading representatives of the new generation of reporters had studied under James and Dewey would suggest that pragmatism (see Joas 1988) formed a sort of 'background philosophy' for the profession, as it did for the Chicago School. However, this should not be understood in the sense of pragmatism offering theoretical potential but rather as an attitude of orientation. Pragmatism provides not only the justification for an experimental attitude (as expressed by stepping into journalism), it actually fosters it. 'Really' knowing something means stepping into 'reality' and, without any immediate intention of taking action, gathering 'experiences' in order to open up new possibilities for taking action. This accommodated those who, dissatisfied with their merely second-hand knowledge, namely, what Wyckoff calls their 'slender book-learned lore', turned to journalism as a field of experience. Against this background, however, the question still has to be answered as to why

---

[5] William James had highly praised Hodder's doctoral thesis 'The Adversaries of the Sceptic or the Specious Present' and mentioned it at various times in his writings.

these *sociologues manqués* did not actually become sociologists, given that at the turn of the century the thrust of American sociology was still to a considerable extent empirical. If we bear in mind the intellectual scene at the end of the nineteenth century, the answer is obvious: the empirical sociology of the time presented no alternative to those who turned to journalism, for the simple reason that it was directly linked to a social gospel; in other words, it was geared toward imposing norms.

In the first two decades after the American Civil War, a social interpretation of the gospel gradually came to be accepted; it has gone down in the history of theology under the name of 'social gospel' (see Hopkins 1940). A Christian moral doctrine takes the place of the preoccupation with salvation of the individual and life in the world to come and orientates itself to the conditions of modern life, characterised by industrialisation and urbanisation. This re-orientation became necessary in order for the Church to uphold its claim to provide leadership in matters to do with the outer world. The preachers of social Christianity called for an attitude which the Reverend J. H. W. Stuckenberg, in his treatise *Christian Sociology* (1880) – a treatise which formed the basis for the social gospel – termed 'Christian realism'. Realism here means giving the Church a secular twist, which includes borrowing scientific methods, emphasising the Church's social rôle and providing a definitive programme of education aimed at forming character.

The close link between theology and sociology is also expressed in the educational background of those who represent sociology in the teaching profession: more than a third of all the professors who devoted themselves to sociology before 1900 were trained theologians.[6]

Morgan (1969) has shown convincingly that the extremely rapid spread of academic sociology in the United States was due to its having been geared toward the social gospel. This link ensured the interests of both parties were protected: the Church obtained a foothold in the modern world, while in the 1890s, sociology received rapid recognition as a teaching subject. The fact that this link was based on a sort of 'gentlemen's agreement' emerges precisely at the juncture where we clearly detect a certain distance between the two. In his editorial to the first year's issue of the *American Journal of Sociology*, Small answers the anticipated 'possible' question as to the relation of the *Journal* toward Christian sociology in the following words: 'The answer is, in a word,

---

[6] This is also true for the Chicago Department of Sociology. Small, Henderson and Zueblin had trained as priests; moreover, Henderson, the principal representative of the social gospel line in Chicago, was also the university chaplain.

toward Christian sociology sincerely deferential, toward alleged "Christian sociologists" surely suspicious' (Small 1895, p. 15).

A type of sociology committed to the social gospel was necessarily a practical discipline geared toward social problems, one which tackled the issue of what was to be done: 'Big C' sociology (Charity, Crime, Correction), as it was called at the time. Characteristic of such a sociology were courses such as 'Charities and Corrections', 'Charities and Penology' and 'Charities and Crime'. It is clear from Tolman's 1902 overview of the study of sociology in colleges in the United States that most of the courses, if we discount those devoted to general sociology, were in the areas of 'Sociology of the Industrial Group; Social Economics' (60 courses in total); 'Social Reform, Practical Sociology; Social Problems' (57); and 'Sociology of the Dependent Classes; Charities' (40).

Up until the First World War, American sociology was primarily a discipline devoted to improving things, closely bound up with charity organisations whose work was based on the feeling that Christians were duty-bound to show practical brotherly love. The public image of the sociologist, according to Lapiere, was 'that of a blue-nosed (i.e., Puritan) reformer, ever ready to pronounce moral judgements, and against all pleasurable forms of social conduct' (quoted in Harvey 1987a, p. 24). 'Real life', approached empirically by a type of sociology which allied itself with the social gospel, was perceived through the filter of moral assumptions. The things that were noticed and/or concentrated on were the 'Many Ds' (drink, drugs, disease, desertion, delinquency, disorganisation). Within the Chicago department, it was primarily Charles Henderson, director and president of the United Charities of Chicago, president of the Chicago Society of Social Hygiene and a member of numerous charity organisations, who represented the viewpoint that the rôle of sociology was to improve things. In his *Introduction to the Study of the Dependent, Defective and Delinquent Classes*, a standard work of practical sociology, he was searching for 'the ethical basis of charity, the ideals of philanthropy, and the social mechanisms for attaining in larger measure what ought to be' (Henderson 1906 [1893], p. vii).

In an environment geared toward the moral salvation and betterment of the dependent classes and foreign ethnic groups, there could of course be no place for a 'romantic temperament', stimulated by the way of life of the 'other half'. Moreover, such stimulation could only be had, if, on the one hand, researchers distanced themselves from such efforts made to improve things, and on the other, strove to eliminate the distance between themselves and the 'other half'. Thus, it is not surprising that the young intellectuals who turned to journalism as a domain in which to gain experience did not remain on the defensive. Works of literary journalism, such as Hapgood's *Spirit of the Ghetto* (1967 [1902]), were directed expressly against the improvement perspective:

The Jewish quarter of New York is generally supposed to be a place of poverty, dirt, ignorance and immorality – the seat of the sweat-shop, the tenement house, where 'red-lights' sparkle at night, where the people are queer and repulsive. Well-to-do persons visit the 'Ghetto' merely from motives of curiosity or philanthropy; writers treat of it 'sociologically', as a place in crying need of improvement. That the Ghetto has an unpleasant aspect is as true as it is trite. But the unpleasant aspect is not the subject of the following sketches. I was led to spend much time in certain poor resorts of Yiddish New York not through motives either philanthropic or sociological, but simply by virtue of the charm I felt in men and things there. (Hutchins Hapgood 1967 [1902], p. 5)

This genuinely 'aesthetic' interest in another way of life, which the journalist did not wish to be repelled by but instead whose charm he wanted to enjoy, is an expression of the yearning to experience real life without having to see it through some moral filter. The metaphor 'real life' expresses an interest in reality as it is; it is a romantic interest to the extent that people's own yearning to escape from convention is projected on to the object of contemplation. What the young journalists were searching for were forms of life which were authentic in themselves (authentic in Lévi-Strauss' understanding of the term), forms of relationship and views of the world which were more vivid and more immediate, but also more human and more emotional than those to be found in their own culture. 'Romantic temperament' and 'real life' converge in the *yearning for authenticity*: in the final analysis, the romantic interest in real life is a reaction to enlightened neo-puritanism, the academic representative of which was evangelical sociology.

The figures of the 'reformer', on the one hand, and the 'reporter', on the other, can be considered as the symbolic representatives of these opposing positions; their differing agenda when approaching social reality is already inscribed in the terms used to describe them. The pronounced anti-reform stance taken by the reporters cannot be understood if we do not take account of their symbolic significance. The cynical posture of the turn-of-the-century reporter, who was against everything and believed in nothing, was just as much a component of this controversy as were the symbolic boundary transgressions, which aimed at praising everything that appeared 'base', 'common' and 'depraved' in the eyes of the 'do-gooders'. In contrast to a sociology which saw the saloon as a place 'where the tone and topics of conversation are frequently suggestive of antisocial conduct' (Henderson 1906 [1893], p. 251) – this being a view of a sociologist who was proud of never having entered a saloon in his life – the reporters were malicious enough to stress the social importance of saloons, their attitude deriving not least from their antagonism to efforts to improve things:

The poor man looks upon the saloon as his club, partly because he knows full well that there is no philanthropy in it. Even if he likes coffee as much as beer, he will avoid the coffee saloons which have been established as beer antidotes, for he feels that they are not 'on the level', that in some way their promoters are trying to help his soul, and the poor man desires strongly to look after his own moral welfare. (Hutchins Hapgood 1910, p. 26)

Against this background, we can understand the irony contained in the description of Luke O'Connor's bohemian saloon as the 'Working Girls' Home' – a mocking reference to the 'Working Girls' Clubs' set up by charitable organisations, which were supposed to offer young working girls and serving girls a cheap, morally irreproachable place for get-togethers, conversation and education.

The posture of 'shocking' middle-class standards, so important to the journalists' view of themselves, was expressed in an eccentric way in the Whitechapel Club, set up by Chicago journalists in 1889. The name 'Whitechapel' refers to the part of London where Jack the Ripper committed his crimes in 1888 and is in itself an infringement against the precept of piety. We would not be doing justice to the parody contained in the founding of this club if we were to fail to see the club as a genuine establishment of the East Coast gentry, with its own criteria as to which prospective members were fit to join the club ('clubability') and a club code that gave meetings, which were supposed as much as anything to bring together the intellectual and financial elite, a relaxed and refined air (Persons 1973, pp. 103ff.).

The Whitechapel Club was surprisingly like the Cannibal Club set up by the anthropologists' faction of the Royal Anthropological Institute (see Stocking 1971). In ways which from today's perspective seem puerile (the room was decorated with genuine murder weapons, ropes used to carry out executions and a collection of skulls from dead bodies, donated by a doctor from a mental institution), it aimed its shock effects against the established standards of the elite. As Tobin (1973) remarks, the fact that the club was more a place for drinking bouts than for literary conversation may be considered an exaggerated expression of deliberate disregard for the genteel code. As a club for press men, it was a place where literary self- and group criticism took place, contrasting with the aesthetic debates of the Literary Club of the Chicago upper crust. The main emphasis was on debating realistic journalism, where the themes had to be contemporary and urban, where the style had to be true to life. In this way, they went beyond a critique of the genteel tradition in literature and turned to criticising this tradition in general. As far as politics were concerned, the club was radical – 'the more conservative favoured a redistribution of property, while the radicals believed in the free use of dynamite' (Duncan 1948, p. 164) – and its members were united in their rejection of the 'do-gooders', in their fight against the 'blue noses' with their 'anti-vice crusades' and in their hostility toward the intolerance of those whom they described as 'silk stocking' puritans. All descriptions of the club atmosphere are unanimous on one point: 'This is the hatred of cant, sham, hypocrisy, in short, of the urban type now known as the stuffed shirt' (Duncan 1948, p. 167).

This abhorrence, which Park shared[7] and which we can generalise as having existed far beyond the narrow circle of the Whitechapel Club, is an indication of the fact that as far as this new generation of intellectuals is concerned, we are dealing with *cultural dissidents*, whose predilection for social outsiders and marginal people was directly related to their alienation from their own Anglo-Saxon Protestant culture. Steffens' 'discovery' that he likes crooks better than reformers (because in their own way the former are more honest, and at all events are closer to real life), the anecdote that Park's favourite reformer was an ex-crook (who knew from experience what needed to be reformed), Hapgood's stylisation of the 'Bowery tough' into a 'character', i.e., a real personality rather than a mere character mask – all these are part of the logic of the cultural dissent expressed in gestures intended to turn the reformers' world 'upside down'.

'Bored by what they felt was the vicarious nature of middle-class life', writes Skotheim in his introduction to Hapgood's autobiography, 'the young intellectuals were attracted to that which their families and their society were not' (Skotheim 1972, p. xix). To paraphrase Lévi-Strauss' words, which he applied to ethnography: the fascination that journalism has as a profession which reconciles character and life can be compared to the power of attraction which primitive cultures exercised on those researchers who were repelled by their own culture (see Stagl 1981, pp. 77ff.). The degree of concordance with the attitude of the ethnographer as analysed by Lévi-Strauss is striking: in both cases, the ethnographer as

---

[7] Everett C. Hughes: 'He hated cant and hypocrisy' (REPA 7:7).

well as the turn-of-the-century journalist, the value attached to exotic or home-grown exotic cultures seems to be 'a function of his disdain for, and, occasionally, hostility toward the customs prevailing in his native setting' (Lévi-Strauss 1978, p. 377).

The 'wish for new experience', both as a pattern for action and a theoretical concept, represents a transformation of 'suffering the experience of experiencing nothing', as Karl-Heinz Kohl (1979) diagnosed in the case of Lévi-Strauss. However, the suffering which we have to analyse here is less the result of a deformation of modern perceptual ability, which only permits experiences to be garnered as sensations, than a reflex of a type of habitualising socialisation which appears no longer to permit actual authentic experience. It expresses itself in the feeling characteristic of the generation of cultural dissidents, a feeling of being cut off from reality, while second-hand experience, the 'slender book-learned lore', figures as its substitute.

As a lever of transformation, this wish is at the same time symptomatic of a cultural change which brings forth a new type of personality. This is condensed in Thomas' typology of personalities. In terms of a sociology of culture, we could interpret 'philistine', on the one hand, and 'creative person', on the other, as labels for modal types which embody certain variants of the current prevailing ethic. What Thomas describes as the attitude of the philistine corresponds in large measure to the 'character' ideal of the nineteenth century, with its emphasis on self-control, self-mastery and the strict moral code on which these are based. Henry L. Mencken summed this up from the viewpoint of the rebellious generation with his memorable remark that philistinism is only another word for puritanism.

By contrast, the notion of the 'creative person' conveys a sense of that modal type of 'personality' which corresponds to the culture of the twentieth century, and here quite different labels are used to characterise this personality: reputation, morals and duty are supplanted by creativity, sensitivity and power of persuasion (see Susman 1984).

The generation born around 1865, which had still been brought up in the puritan spirit, was an intermediate generation within the process of cultural change and its representatives were quite conscious of this: Hapgood gave concise expression to this generation-specific tension when choosing the title of his autobiography: *A Victorian in the Modern World* (1939).

It was this generation that developed an interest in personal peculiarities, idiosyncrasies and temperaments, as well as looking into problems to do with the development of ego identity and personality in the context of a given culture. Park (born in 1864) and Thomas (born in 1863) as well as Hapgood (born in 1869) and Steffens (born in 1866) all belong to this generation. Hapgood's predilection for 'characters' – i.e., people who, in the authenticity of self-presentation, in the genuine manner of their way of thought and in the way they express themselves in words, actually stand out from the standardised 'character' ideal of puritanism – corresponds at the literary level to Thomas' preference for the creative person. Both positions reflect a development in the course of which the value assigned to personality development aimed at *self-expression* takes the place of the concern about character formation aimed at *self-control.*

Mead's model of 'I', 'me' and 'self', which is based around a dialogue of instinctual impulses and social expectations for the purpose of generating a unified image of the self that is at the same time capable of change and open toward the future, provides an analytical concept for this transformation (see Joas 1980, pp. 91–119). It is because of the concretist phraseology used in Thomas' theory of personality that its structural affinity with Mead's model and also the similarities in the genesis of the two theories are overlooked. Yet at the level of social characters (bohemian/philistine), Thomas deals with the subject no differently than does Mead in his depiction of the dialogue of instinctual impulses and social expectations. The creative person, the person who reconciles his wish for new experience with society's wish for stability by interpreting situations in a new way and creating new norms of higher social value, is the successful synthesis, the 'self'.

The transition from character forming to personality development as the ideal of socialisation takes place against the background of a social caesura which destroys the educated person's natural enracination in the social system, while still not providing a safe haven for the new type of intellectual who defines his relation to society according to his purported ability of being able to speak about society with greater objectivity than those who are directly involved in the practical business of production and politics (Lasch 1965, p. ix). Personality development is thus, above all, a problem which confronts the new generation of the intelligentsia which, as the avant-garde of dissent spawned by its own culture, still has to find its place in a changing society.

Journalism provides those who have broken with tradition, without having found their true calling in the existential sense, with a social moratorium and a field for personal and social experiment. It is its experimental character which gives this field some of the features of a counter-cultural milieu. What is important to the journalist, indeed potentially more important than what he writes about, is the knowledge he acquires in this experimental field. Lincoln Steffens put this discrepancy into words by saying that what the reporter knows about, but does not report on, becomes either literature or sociology. Access to journalism, as far as the marginal intelligentsia of the intermediate generation is concerned and as Lévi-Strauss phrased it with regard to ethnography, becomes a *technique de dépaysement* (a technique for dislocation). In hindsight, Steffens interpreted this phase of life as a 'life of unlearning', in which disillusionment can be equated with a sort of re-education.

The disillusioned stance which is regarded as central to the generation of reporters around the turn of the century and which can so easily be misunderstood as mere posturing, is the necessary precondition for the formation of a detached attitude, which makes another way of looking at social reality possible in the first place.

Although evangelical sociology uses empirical procedures (thereby showing itself to be part of enlightened puritanism), it does so only half-heartedly (at arm's length, as it were) out of a Christian duty to alleviate suffering and convey a sense of decency. The cultural dissident, by contrast, insists on an experience that is not impregnated with conventional moral opinions. Just as the ethnologist lives in the hope of still encountering ways of life that are as far as possible uncontaminated by contact with other cultures, the dissident searches for the local colour of ethnic enclaves before it is erased in the process of Americanisation. It is not by chance that the image of the child is invoked as an analogy for the unprejudiced absorption of the different and the new; to the over-socialised late Victorian, the child appears to be receptive to new experience as a matter of principle. For this reason, as in the writing of Dewey and Thomas, it can also be taken as a model for scholarly thought: the child is still curious and wears no blinkers to dictate his or her field of view. This theme is already discernible in the talk 'The Student as Child', which Hapgood gave in 1892 on the occasion of his academic valedictory at Harvard. In this speech, which conjures up the 'naive quality of the child' as an ideal for the student to aspire to, Hapgood compares the child with the artist:

They both stand expectant, with their mental pores open, eager for impressions, and beyond those impressions, they do not care to go; they do not care for moral significance, for practical value. They do not care for future ends, for present experience is so entrancing, that it is an end in itself. (quoted from Marcaccio 1977, p. 28)

This aesthetic interest, which rejects both the moralistic perception of phenomena and the utilitarist thinking about them, builds the bridges for an empirical method which approaches its object in an unprejudiced way. It is precisely the disinterested interest in phenomena, 'the unprejudiced quality of the child', which distinguishes the journalists who are interested in people from the humanitarian-minded sociologists. Contemporary reviews of *The Spirit of the Ghetto* make this difference clear, emphasising that the author is abandoning the standpoint of the politician and churchman and even divesting himself of the more comprehensive ideals of the sociologist, in order to give the public a picture of the ghetto as it is and not as the opinion of earlier researchers said it should be (Colbron 1903). At the same time, it is certainly the case that even the new generation of reporters only shows what it wants to show. Yet, because this way of looking at things is combined with an alienation from the culture they had grown up in, they show the 'other half' as something actually different and not as something dependent, defective or delinquent. In a nutshell, this shift indicates the transition from a preventative to an understanding perspective. This shift in perspective is also to be found in the vocabulary: the 'dependants, defectives and delinquents' of Henderson are replaced by Hapgood's 'the low and dispossessed, the disinherited, the rebellious and the semi-criminal'. This perspective does not actually denature the object of contemplation from the outset, but does run another risk: that of romanticising a social group which stands as a living negation of all that is detested in the parents' culture.

SHIFT IN PERSPECTIVE

We are mainly indebted to writers of fiction for our more intimate knowledge of contemporary urban life.   Robert Ezra Park

Newspapers, as Larzer Ziff (1966) remarks, were just as much cemeteries of talent as schools of talent, and every local editor's office had its living dead. Those who did not manage to get out in time, either into the higher echelons of the newspaper business or into another profession, were left, if the worse came to the worst, on reaching forty, with either the East River or with that sense of bitterness which, not by accident, characterises those bohemians who are getting on in years. But journalism was not seen by the new generation as a job for life, either. 'To see life', as a reason for going into journalism, indicates the transitory nature of this occupation, even if many people did stay on in the profession. As we have seen, it is true to say that in the context of the big city press at the end of the nineteenth century the most frequently made remark refers to the newspaper as a school, with a teaching schedule that is unequalled as regards variety and closeness to life. Most of the reporters who had turned their backs on an academic milieu understood their time with a newspaper as a period of study, both as an empirical phase in which they gained experience of real life, and as a training ground for their literary ambitions. There can be no doubt that the newspaper offered an opportunity for literary five-finger exercises as well as being helpful in the development of a personal style and opening up new areas of language. David Graham Phillips, the journalist and Naturalist author, was not wrong when he compared the significance of the newspaper for the future author with that of the hospital for the student of medicine.

But the first and most important lesson which the big city press provided, in its rôle as an academy for the 'freshman', was in the art of seeing. The newspaper office was, above all else, an 'eye-opener', in the sense that it taught people that even if they had their eyes open they would see nothing if they went through life wearing blinkers. Nothing should be taken at 'face value', especially not in the big city, which is the ideal setting for every type of 'front'. Learning to see means looking behind the curtain of preconceived opinions (ideas of virtuousness just as well as of depravity), looking behind the public backdrop and the private façades. Hence the close link between the attitude of disillusionment and the ability to preserve distance, in the sense of maintaining detachment.

Such a perspective, one which calls into question things that are taken for granted, also pays off when observing everyday situations and uncovering paradoxes. One of Park's favourite anecdotes is about a trainee reporter who is supposed to do a report on a trapeze act. He comes back empty-handed, since the artist could not appear, having broken his leg when falling out of bed. Such anecdotes are part of contemporary journalistic folklore (see also Williams 1898). They are thoroughly didactic in character. The situation always involves a trainee reporter whom the editor has to teach the art of seeing: what is the particular feature of the situation, what is the 'funny side' of the story? In this way, the newspaper practice develops a sense for seeing the social world from an unusual perspective; it is for this reason that the reporter is able to coin successfully such apparently paradoxical turns of phrase as the 'honest crook' and the 'dishonest do-gooder'.

Learning to observe also means developing an eye for differences and details in order to be able to gain any sort of perspective in the first place and to be able to place different phenomena in relation to each other. This applies not only to the flagrant differences, e.g., between the 'Gold Coast' and the 'slum', between 'Wall Street' and 'the Bowery', but also to the fine nuances such as the description of the differences between 36th Street and 37th Street, the latter being a test which Steffens set cub reporters.

Against this background, newspaper practice appears to function like an introductory course into the ways of seeing of Naturalist sociology, as set out by Gouldner and Matza. Within this practice there are undoubtedly moments of perspective shift ('perspective by incongruity'), overlap and irony. Furthermore, investigative journalism, which is all about demonstrating the links between the 'upper' and the 'under' world, is really based on expounding and relativising problems to do with 'good' and 'evil' (which Matza considers fundamental to the Naturalist way of seeing things).

The prevention perspective, which emphasised the bad consequences of evil, 'obscured the possibility of evil arising from things deemed good and good from things deemed evil' (Matza 1973, p. 29). Shift in perspective, as Gouldner demonstrates using the example of Goffman, helps to destroy the simple image of the world as a closed hierarchy. Matza writes: 'Since being in the world is rather complicated, fidelity requires a rendition maintaining that complexity'; he sees this rendition being redeemed in the Naturalistic tradition of sociology that is receptive to 'overlaps' and 'irony' (Matza 1973, p. 94).

Yet, is there not something more than a grain of truth in the disillusioned reporter's conclusion that reality is really the opposite of what people have been taught to believe? ' "Good people" were really bad people, because their illusions did more harm than the intelligent crimes of the "big bad men" ' is how Lasch summarises Steffens' credo (Lasch 1965, pp. 262 ff.). This exemplary instance of perspective by incongruity surely resembles Park's verdict that it was the reformers and not the corrupt politicians who had done the most damage to Chicago (REPA 7:2). It is criticism of the *gentility* and its self-satisfied social status which sharpens the eye for apparent paradoxes; it is journalistic practice which teaches people to see ambiguities and overlaps.

Even if some of the works of literary journalism were classified by contemporary reviewers as being sociological, the reporters' ambitions as regards applying their insights and experiences in journalistic practice were not in fact directed toward sociology; what many, if not most, of them were aiming for was a literary career.

Even Park cherished this ambition for a while. As Raushenbush mentions in a letter, he had at first wanted to be a writer and apparently he had tried his hand at writing plays (REPA 7:2). Around 1892, together with his long-standing friend and colleague Hartley Davis, he had planned a book for which apparently they had concluded something like a preliminary contract with a publishing house. Furthermore, a fragment or rather – to judge from what was accessible to me – the sketch of an idea for a novel exists, with the working title 'Island of Enchantment'. The novel was to be set in New York and was to begin with a description of Washington Square, the heart of Greenwich Village. The place of the action and the theme of the book – the relationship between three people – Prudence, a young emancipated woman, Simon, a newspaper reporter, and Caleb – indicate that the novel was planned entirely in line with the model, sketched out by Duncan (1948), of the sort of Chicago literature developed by journalists, with heroes of big city calibre (amongst possible protagonists, Duncan quotes the reporter and the 'new woman' type), who explore scenes of an urban nature. One heading in Park's plot says, characteristically: 'They go slumming'.

The fact that journalists' literary ambitions were no idle fancy is shown by an article by Norman Hapgood from 1897, on 'The Reporter and Literature', in which he points out that an attentive observer of the literary scene cannot but help notice that newspaper reporters occupy a prominent position in the literary world year after year. They owe this position, above all, to their familiarity with the subject, a familiarity which the author who comes from a newspaper background makes thoroughly good use of in his battle with the genteel literary tradition. Details are portrayed with meticulous precision, details such as could only have been gained from personal observation; special slang and dialects are presented and no opportunity is missed to show that the author has an insider perspective.

It is impossible to conceive of American Naturalism without the influence of journalism. It is difficult to think of even one major Naturalist author who was not a journalist for a greater or lesser period of time. It is true that social Darwinist assumptions play an important part as an aid in enhancing drama, especially as far as the early Naturalists are concerned. Nonetheless, the journalistic experience is reflected in the detailed description of the big city, in the feeling for genuine urban forms of life and mentalities and in the recourse to a milieu-specific language:

For if the novelist was analogous to the sociologist [in the sense of basic social Darwinist assumptions], so he was to the journalist, the hard-boiled city room reporter or the crusading investigator of social facts, the man who walked in the city, observed, explored, exposed, *the man who had been there, in the place of experience* – the ghetto, the stockyard, the apartment block, the battlefield, the social jungle. (Bradbury 1983, p. 8; my italics)

This bipolarity leads to the Naturalist novel as 'analytical sociology' merely imitating science, while, as 'descriptive sociology', making reality substantively accessible. Such a bipolarity is not without its pitfalls. The use of scientific fragments as a organising principle leads all too easily to the devaluing of details, the presentation of which is the actual strength of the story. Norris' *Octopus*, for example, a novel which from the point of view of realistic content is first-rate, ultimately becomes a second-rate work, in Ziff's view, precisely because of its popular Darwinist setting (Ziff 1966, p. 269).

If we speak of the Naturalist novel as having a sociological edge to it, then we must differentiate clearly between something being given scientific overtones and something having a scientific content. As a rule, the Naturalist novel is both a deterministic novel (in the sense of assumptions based on social Darwinism) and a big city novel rolled into one. In its guise as a deterministic novel, it transfers a scholarly method on to literature, whereas as big city literature it fills holes which sociology had up until then left unfilled. The one has merely been read about, whilst the other is based on experience.

Dreiser's *Sister Carrie*, for example, not only portrays the inexorable downfall of Hurstwood (with occasionally penetrating insertions of fragments of Spencer's thought), but the reader additionally learns something of the big city from the naive view of the newcomer. The Naturalist novel, like sociology at a later date, used the big city as a laboratory in order to depict the interplay of person, environment and society. In the introductory passages, Dreiser offers a splendid panorama of the big city as it must probably have appeared to any newcomer. With the help of descriptions of persons and situations, he draws a picture of the contrast between rich and poor; he gives an insight into life in hotels, apartment houses and shelters for the homeless; in his portrayal of the behaviour of his protagonists, he provides an insight into the meaning of 'front', bluff and indifference as types of behaviour specific to the big city. At all events, he uses the experience he gained in newspaper practice – what he called the 'careful investigation of the most important streets, shops, hotels and residential districts' – in order to draw a true-to-life picture.

It is this trueness to life which makes the Naturalist novel a thoroughly remarkable source for a sociology interested in making reality accessible. When Park recommended that his students read Dreiser, Lewis and other Naturalists, then it was because, among other things, he was well aware that these authors knew their subject first-hand. On the occasion of a visit to Park's house, Werner Cahnmann expressed his astonishment that there were more travel books, journalistic articles and novels in Park's library than treatises to do with the social sciences. Park explained his preference with these words: 'Of course, these books are not sociology, but those who wrote them have one advantage over sociologists – they knew people' (REPA 6:7). What strikes us about this explanation is that in 1940 Park was still expressing his position using the tone of a journalist with a natural antipathy toward academics who have no idea of real life.[8] In conversation with Carey, Cottrell, a student of Park's, remarks that his father, a journalist, was prejudiced against academics 'who tried to write about problems they really didn't know about', but he revised his judgement when he learnt that Park was a former journalist: 'He [Cottrell Sr] thought that was a good idea. Maybe he'd be able to teach us something' (JTC 1:6). Park's greatest service as an academic teacher lies in the fact that he made it possible for scholars to make disinterested interest in social worlds sociologically productive.

At the same time, given his opinion that 'Big D' sociology as it was still being taught in the 1920s in the colleges was really not sociology at all (REPA 9:2), Park was concerned to draw people's attention to the distortions to which a short-winded sociology closely bound up with charitable service must necessarily be subject. The first thing to do was to open the eyes of those students who were contemplating the idea of 'service'; literary works and autobiographies could make a not inconsiderable contribution toward doing this.

The close affiliation with contemporary literature expressed in the titles of the classic monographs should not be misunderstood as mere plagiarism of big city literature (although the hope that they would be taken up by the public at large did certainly play a part). More than anything, it documents the unity of a Naturalist approach. Park was well aware 'that the social scientist and the writer are often labouring in the same vineyard' (Borenstein 1978, p. 170), but also that they were doing

---

[8] Even today, we can describe the controversy between journalism and sociology, as ways of approaching reality, in terms of 'acquaintance with' versus 'knowledge about'. Whereas journalists reproach sociologists for not being acquainted with their subject ('no idea'), sociologists criticise journalists for their inadequate knowledge of their subject ('imprecise and superficial').

this from different points of view and with different aims. Park himself explained these differences by saying that the psychological or sociological novel ceases to have a function once an individual case has been described, whereas sociology goes beyond this to the extent that it attempts to reach generalisations (Park and Burgess 1924 [1921], p. 146). Literature was indispensable, in Park's view, because it was able to provide an 'insight', an understanding of what was going on behind the veneer of human habits and social proprieties. Providing this was also the task of sociology, a task which could only be fulfilled if scholarly analysis went hand in hand with interest in human nature. The fact that a reviewer, as in the case of Zorbaugh's study, could be of the opinion that such and such a work was really a sociological study, one which was equally persuasive both on account of its scientific methodology and its 'human interest', does not, in Park's eyes, detract from its value. On the contrary, it means that special praise is being given to a type of sociological research which has as its aim both to understand and provide a better understanding of people in the world in which they live. In this respect, Park was completely unlike Ogburn. In a scholarly polemic, which was probably also targeted at Park, Ogburn saw the thrust of social sciences as having evolved in connection with the then current practice of attempting to turn scientific results into literature: 'The audience for these [scientific] articles will be the Scientific Guild, and no attempt will be made to make these articles readable for shop girls or for the high-school youth' (Ogburn 1930b, p. 301). However, this rejection of the mixing of scientific and literary styles means, as a consequence, abandoning an important and, in Park's view, characteristic element of the scientific ethos. For Park, whose understanding of science was imbued with Dewey's ideal of 'shared experience', sociology had not least an important communicative function, which extended far beyond the Scientific Guild:

Time and again he [Park] insisted that it was not enough merely to learn about human beings and their ways of life, but that one's knowledge must also be communicated clearly to other interested persons. 'Just tell the story of what happened or of what you have found to be true', he would say, 'and tell it in such a way that anyone with a reasonable amount of intelligence can understand it.' (Pierson to Matthews, REPA 7:3)

CHAPTER 6

Uncle Sam and Young Sammy: sociology between reform and report

> He's not Uncle Sam, the father, that prim, pompous, honest man,
> Yankee, or Virginian, rather: Sammy's an American.
> George Santayana, *Young Sammy's First Wild Oats*

However impressive the correlation may be between journalistic reporting and sociological field study as regards themes and methods, we would be missing the fundamental component of the influence of journalism on Chicago sociology were we to restrict ourselves to this one aspect. Such a restriction all too easily conjures up the ultimately futile debate which revolves around superficiality vs depth, description vs analysis, as the *differentia specifica* of the two intellectual enterprises. It has, in this respect, been all too easy to criticise empirical sociology for being 'merely descriptive' and thus journalistic, but this also goes for that rejoinder which, with a view to taking the wind out of the sails of such criticism, points to the 'more systematic' and thus scientific character of sociology. Saying that the Chicago sociologists understood themselves as scientists (and not as journalists, commentators or literary people) (Bulmer 1984, p. 97) is tantamount to a pleonasm; how else should they have understood themselves, other, that is, than as sociologists?

The influence of journalism on empirical sociology, an influence which is due to a large extent to Park as a person, can only be reconstructed if we ask ourselves why it was that he was able to exert this influence at all. What was it that made journalism, as it were, into a model discipline, whose focus, problem statements and research tools were worth developing further? The central thing here is the value of journalism not only as a profession but as a *milieu*. The significant impact of this milieu is undoubtedly the fact that it engenders a different attitude toward the social world, one which is closer to the scientific attitude than to the attitude of a practical sociology which makes a pact with the social gospel. This attitude is first of all, in a direct and literal sense, of an ideological nature. It is based on the wish for new experience, an experience not filtered through moral assumptions. This attitude is part of a reaction to the given state of things, where our own interest in cutting ourselves loose from a way of gaining experience shielded by conventions goes hand in hand with an unprejudiced and undisguised interest in the 'Other' and the 'strange'. This means that the Other subjectively takes on the quality of a corrective to our own selves; the power of attraction of what is called 'real life' is a function of the 'unreality' of our own life, which feeds on the feeling that we experience life in all its dimensions only at second hand.

Journalism at the turn of the century was a reservoir for cultural dissidents, who protested above all at the narrowness and sterility, the nice pretence and vain self-satisfaction of what George Santayana (1967a [1911]) termed the 'genteel tradition'. It was a tradition that was, as Sinclair Lewis said in his Nobel prize acceptance speech, an example of the separation of intellectual life from all authentic standards of reality. The journalistic domain thus takes on a sense of the counter-cultural milieu, which not only opens up new experiences, but also permits an experimental way of living. For the most part, those who turned to the metropolitan press as a field for experience were white Anglo-Saxon Protestants (WASPs), protesting against their own culture. In so doing, they also proved themselves to be heirs to this culture to the extent that they understood themselves not only as 'rebels' but also as 'seekers' in the metaphysical sense. This personal search movement is part of a cultural upheaval, in the course of which provincial puritanism is replaced by cosmopolitan liberalism. The fact that this upheaval radiates out from the big cities, the laboratories of cosmopolitanism, should not surprise us, and the fact that its avant-garde should gather together in the sphere of journalism even less: after all, the turn-of-the-century journalists are prototypes of the modern, urban person.

What emerges here is a new understanding of the social rôle of the intelligentsia, which has its basis in the new communication technologies and publication media. Park's conception of sociology as a medium for enlightening public opinion reflects this new understanding: impartial and without regard to anyone's politics or programme, being simply the public's champion.

In *Abweichendes Verhalten* [Becoming deviant] (1973), Matza described the idea of variety as the antithesis to the presumption of pathology. If the former stands for a perspective grounded in understanding, the latter represents the prevention perspective. Inasmuch as these two perspectives seem not to be reconcilable into *one* view, Matza sees the Chicago School as having been caught in the dilemma of describing *cultural variety* while diagnosing *social pathology*. He consequently puts the question as to how we can describe factual variety in the cities of America while at the same time maintaining the pathology thesis (Matza 1973, p. 54). His answer is that the concept of pathology must be transposed from the personal to the social level: the conception of social disorganisation takes the place of individual pathology. This still does not answer the question as to how we actually got caught on the horns of the dilemma in the first place, since the relationship between the prevention perspective and the understanding perspective surely presents itself to us today as an either–or.

Hans Joas (1988, p. 437), without explicitly addressing the dilemma, has described the situation of the Chicago School, with particular regard to the erroneous assessment of their alleged character as dyed-in-the-wool social reformers, as an intermediate position in the history of science between absence of professionalism and complete professionalism. Certainly, the Chicago School could only show its qualifications *vis-à-vis* mere reformers by improving its research into the problem areas, not by giving up any mandate for areas outside the domain of science. But I believe that as far as explaining the dilemma is concerned, we have still to get to the bottom of the position of the school in the history of the social sciences, a position which to a certain extent is itself a symptom of the change in the cultural conception of self.

We can and indeed must talk of two cultural roots in relation to the empirical sociology which distinguishes the 'Golden Age' of the Chicago School (1918–33). In order to understand its own particular hybrid form, it is necessary to see it as a transitory phenomenon, or, in its own terminology, as a 'zone in transition', in the process of change from a 'culture of character' and character formation to a 'culture of personality', a culture of modern subjectivity (see Susman 1984). Chicago sociology exhibits this tension: it is still asking what is to be done ('prevention') and it is already asking what people actually do ('understanding').

The dilemma, describing cultural variety while diagnosing social pathology, results from the fact that the Chicago sociology of the 1920s forms a point of intersection between two different cultural currents, the archetypes of which are the *reformer*, on the one hand, and the *reporter*, on the other. These archetypes correspond to different world views which go hand in hand with different views of reality. This difference is enshrined in their very names. The reformer devotes himself to social reality from the perspective of improving things. As far as he is concerned, other and strange worlds of life are not just other and strange but, measured by moral and civilised standards, at the same time somehow deficient. The reporter, on the other hand, gives a report on other and strange worlds of life. He refers to differences as differences, without at the same time wanting to get rid of them.

Against this background, it becomes clear, from a historical perspective, how short-sighted (and superficial) the objection is that such and such a representation is 'merely descriptive'. What so easily looks like 'mere' description, in a period when people are concerned with purifying their perception of moral preconceptions, proves in fact to be an extremely difficult undertaking. 'Description' for its own sake means getting involved with the subject, instead of altering its character from the outset by means of the normative filters and cultural platitudes of the observer's own culture.

The differences between reformer and reporter, in the field of urban worlds of life, correspond strikingly to those between missionary and ethnologist in the field of 'primitive' cultures. In Malinowski's view, the missionary is someone who explains the white man's way of looking at things to the native (who explains the WASP's way of looking at things to the immigrant), whereas the job of the ethnologist is to translate the native's way of looking at things to the European (the immigrant's way of looking at things to the WASP) (Malinowski 1935, vol. II, p. xxi). This correspondence also includes the subjective aversion that the reporters/ethnologists have toward the reformers/missionaries: the latter are emissaries of a culture the former are trying to escape from (see also Stipe 1980). Both Harvey (1987a) and Joas (1988) are correct in their assessment when they say that the Chicago sociologists are not primarily reform-minded but are concerned instead with the development of sociology as an objective science. In particular, the studies inspired by Park are characterised by their attempt to explore social worlds and social action in an unprejudiced way, in order thus to tap a rich seam of sociological knowledge, which replaces a knowledge gained as a result of practical aims.

Nevertheless, we must record a certain ambivalence, which appears both phase-specific (first vs second phase of Chicago sociology) as well as person-specific (Henderson and Burgess vs Thomas and Park), as well as referring to the intermediate position that Joas has mentioned. If we ignore the contributions devoted to general sociology, an examination of the volumes of the *American Journal of Sociology* prior to the First World War reveals in large part an image of a sociology that understood itself as a science auxiliary to charitable endeavours. Such involvement had its price: in spite of all its efforts at getting close to life, empirical sociology finished up at the end of the day by setting up a programme for improving things. The leading exponent of this orientation in the first phase was Charles Henderson, but this perspective did not completely disappear with Henderson's death in 1915; Burgess, as Hughes remarks, was Henderson's successor in more than one respect. Without a doubt, Burgess was concerned with developing sociology as a science; consequently, it would be wrong to construe him as a contrast to Park in this respect. Nevertheless, Burgess, to a certain degree, remained faithful to the prevention perspective; not only do his contacts with the School of Social Service Administration and his participation in various prevention programmes testify to this, but so does the sociological focus of his research and teaching. With his seminars such as 'Social Pathology', 'Crime and Its Social Treatment', as well as 'Causes and Prevention of Poverty', Burgess is clearly following in Henderson's footsteps. His main research interests (community research with a particular accent on neighbourhood work, family sociology and research into delinquency), characterised by their closeness to social work, serve only to reinforce this impression. It was Burgess who set up the contacts to the charitable organisations and foundations, who obtained research funds and stipends and who set up committees made up of influential personalities and representatives of charitable and social organisations, all with the aim of enhancing the reputation of the sociology committee. It was these committees which were responsible for the ritual of the 'recommendations', a residuum of the prevention perspective which the classical studies always led into, sometimes in a very irritating way. Nels Anderson's *The Hobo* can be regarded as a paramount example of this. We only have to compare the introductory remarks of the committee, of which Burgess was the chairman, with the introduction of the publisher, who was Robert Park, to become aware of the influencing factors which determined the intermediate position of Chicago sociology in its 'golden years' in the history of the social sciences. In the former's remarks, the study appears as an undertaking which supplies facts to the social organisations, on the basis of which they would then be able to deal with the problem of the itinerant worker in an informed way. Park, however, regards it as a contribution to the sociology of urban life, which endeavours to seek out the object of its investigations, the hobo, in the world in which he lives, in order to learn how to better understand the way he acts.

As far as contacts with social organisations were concerned, Park played a careful hand. We could also say that he left it to Burgess to do the donkey work of acquiring research funds, while he got on with the brain-storming. Reckless sees Burgess as the administrator, the person who organised the drawing up of base maps, who set up contacts to the social organisations and got the money, while Park appears as the ideas man, the person who made suggestions: 'But Park nevertheless was, because of his newspaper experience, a field man, he wanted to get out into the field and look what's going on . . . And this was Park's idea, get your feet wet . . . Get down in the streets and get out there and learn things about life' (Reckless, JTC 1:21).

'Get your feet wet': this turn of phrase contains a programme for an approach to social reality, an approach which is concerned with stepping out into unfamiliar zones, as a means of catharsis just as much as a way of collecting data. Learning things about life means not only gaining experience which can be turned into knowledge, but also shedding ill-considered preconceptions which stand in the way of scientific knowledge.

The unprejudiced and yet passionate interest in 'real life', the phrase used to justify the turn to journalism around the turn of the century, is in essence the model for a form of sociological field research carried out for its own sake. This disinterested interest, which turns its attention to the Other in order to understand it and not in order to alter it, is, it must be said, not unselfish. The self-interest lies concealed precisely in the ostentatiously expressed disinterest (in condescension, interference, acting on someone's behalf): the rejection of the traditional way of looking at things is at the same time an act of self-liberation.

The avoidance of a patronising attitude, the search for the 'authentic', the 'genuine' and the 'real', conceals a striving for subjectivity which is free from the restrictions of convention. The reversal of perspective this brings with it, the contemplation of respectable society from the standpoint of a person living outside (or beyond the pale) of respectable society, is, if we follow Gouldner's distinction, of a genuinely romantic nature, including the 'usual professional risk of the romantic', that of being able to tolerate every other custom or habit but his own. As emotional refugees from their own culture, such romantics turn the usual order of things on its head: the opportunity to revive American culture appears to lie precisely in the different nature of immigrant cultures.

This sympathy with the foreign culture in their own country, which arises out of the rejection of their own culture, is something which very much calls to mind the motives of many who turn to ethnology. It has a decisive effect: the knowledge of other ways of life, independent of any moral valuation, appears rewarding.

Thus, the romantic attitude toward social worlds is very much closer to modern ideas on scientific objectivity than the instrumental ideas of a politically orientated or applied sociology are (Gouldner 1984, p. 198). Here, objectivity – and this is only a paradox on the face of it – emerges from the striving for subjectivity.

The extent to which romantic thought is present in the literary journalism of the day is shown by an essay of Hutchins Hapgood on 'Literature in Low Life':

Comfortable people, as a rule, do not like to read about anything they deem 'unpleasant'. If they pay attention at all to 'low' things, it is for charitable purposes. They do it to relieve distress or their own consciences. They do it as outsiders who force their sympathy, not as human beings moved by spontaneous interest in the lives of their kind. Again, many respectable people think that there is something perverted or immoral merely in paying attention, unless the object for doing so is reform, to the 'low' forms of human life . . . And yet is not only the literary interest of such a disinterested attitude unquestionable, but also it is true that without such genuine interest and sympathy, the real facts, without which no reform is possible, cannot be ascertained. (Hutchins Hapgood 1910, pp. 13ff.)

In this statement, which can certainly also be read as a justification for his preoccupation with deviant groups, Hapgood draws a portrait of the 'genteel tradition' in the shape of 'respectable people'. He elucidates the different views of reality by looking at the subject of investigation and he makes us see the contradictions which an interest in the 'Other', the 'stranger' and the 'low' has to cope with if it is not motivated by a desire to change or improve. The belief that only a method which has no pretensions to being orientated toward practice can be of practical benefit in its application was one of the sociological credos of William Isaac Thomas and Robert Ezra Park. In this respect, Hapgood's literary programme is at the same time a programme for an empirical sociology which overcomes any tendency to perceive phenomena from a moralistic angle.

In his notes on the origin of the Society for Social Research, Park attributes the beginnings of a sociology freeing itself from any immediate practical orientation to Thomas:

Thomas' interest was always, it seems, *that of a poet* (although he never, so far as I know, wrote poetry) *and of a literary man in the reportorial sense*, and not that of a politician or of a practical man. He wanted to see, to know, and to report, disinterestedly and without respect to anyone's policies or programmes, the world of men and things as he experienced it. (Park 1982 [1939], p. 337; my italics)

The image of the sociologist as a poet, someone who is concerned about atmospheric content and, as a literary person, someone who is concerned about reporting and not with putting things right, is one further indication of the shift in the view of reality which opposes the distortion of reality by normative preconceptions. The mention of 'poets' in this context is no accident. In a culture distorted by norms, it is the empathy, intuition and sensitivity of the poetic person which can successfully break through the ossified shells of conventional thought. After all, the Greek *poietes* was the creative man per se.

Bibliography

Ade, George. 1931. *The Old-Time Saloon*. New York.

Agar, Michael H. 1980. *The Professional Stranger: An Informal Introduction to Ethnography*. New York.

Alger, George W. 1905. 'The Literature of Exposure', in *Atlantic Monthly*, vol. 96, pp. 210–13.

Algren, Nelson. 1951. *Chicago: City on the Make*. New York.

Allsop, Kenneth. 1967. *Hard Travellin': The Hobo and His History*. New York.

1968. *The Bootleggers: The Story of Chicago's Prohibition Era*. Geneva.

Ames, Edward S., E. C. Hughes, J. H. Nef, L. Wirth and C. S. Johnson. 1944. *Robert E. Park, 1864–1944*. Chicago (privately printed).

Anderson, Nels. 1967. *The Hobo: The Sociology of the Homeless Man*. Chicago and London [1923].

1975. *The American Hobo: An Autobiography*. Leiden.

1983. 'A Stranger at the Gate: Reflections on the Chicago School of Sociology', in *Urban Life*, vol. 11, pp. 396–406.

1989. 'The Poet and the Rebel Press', in *Jahrbuch für Volksliedforschung* [Folksong research yearbook], vol. 34, pp. 83–91.

Angell, Robert. 1923/30. 'Cooley's Heritage to Social Research', in *Social Forces*, vol. 8, pp. 340–7.

1945. 'A Critical Review of the Development of the Personal Document Method in Sociology, 1920–1940', in Gottschalk *et al.* 1945, pp. 175–232.

Anonymous. 1937. 'Hobo Hegemony', in *Literary Digest*, vol. 123, April 10.

Antonovsky, Aaron. 1956. 'Towards a Refinement of the "Marginal Man" Concept', in *Social Forces*, vol. 35, pp. 57–62.

Baker, Paul J. 1973. 'The Life Histories of W. I. Thomas and Robert E. Park', in *American Journal of Sociology*, vol. 79, pp. 243–60; published in German in Lepenies 1981, vol. I, pp. 244–70.

Baker, Ray Stannard. 1911. 'Jacob S. Coxey', in *American Magazine*, vol. 72, pp. 660–4.

1911–12. 'Human Nature in Hawaii', in *American Magazine*, vols. 73–5 (three-part series).

1964. *Following the Color Line*. New York [1908].

Ballowe, James (ed.). 1967. *George Santayana's America*. Chicago and London.

Bargatzky, Thomas. 1981. 'Das 'Marginal Man'-Konzept: Ein Überblick'

[The 'Marginal Man' concept: an overview], in *Sociologus*, vol. 31, pp. 141–65.

Barth, Gunther. 1980. *City People: The Rise of Modern City Culture in Nineteenth-Century America*. New York and Oxford.

Beck, Hanno. 1983. *Große Geographen* [Great geographers]. Berlin.

Becker, Howard S. 1966. 'Introduction', in Shaw 1966 [1930], pp. v–xviii.

1970. 'Dialogue with Howard S. Becker: An Interview Conducted and Prepared for Issues in Criminology by Julius Debro', in *Issues in Criminology*, vol. 5, pp. 159–79.

Bell, Colin and Howard Newby. 1971. *Community Studies*. London.

Belman, Lary S. 1977. 'John Dewey's Concept of Communication', in *Journal of Communication*, vol. 27, pp. 29–37.

Ben-David, Joseph. 1960. 'Rôles and Innovations in Medicine', in *American Journal of Sociology*, vol. 65, pp. 557–68.

Benjamin, Walter. 1974. *Angelus Novus*. Frankfurt on Main.

1983. *Das Passagenwerk* [The passage work], 2 vols. Frankfurt on Main.

Bennett, James. 1981. *Oral History and Delinquency*. Chicago and London.

Benson, Ben. 1942. *Hoboes of America*. No place.

Berger, Morris Isaiah. 1980. *The Settlement, the Immigrant, and the Public School*. New York.

Berger, Morroe. 1977. *Real and Imagined Worlds: The Novel and Social Science*. Cambridge, Mass. and London.

Bergmann, Herbert. 1971. 'Walt Whitman as a Journalist', in *Journalism Quarterly*, vol. 48, pp. 195–204, 431–7.

Bertaux, Daniel. 1981. 'From the Life History Approach to the Transformation of Sociological Practice', in Bertaux (ed.), *Biography and Society: The Life History Approach in the Social Sciences*, Beverly Hills and London, pp. 29–45.

Berthoff, Warner. 1965. *The Ferment of Realism: American Literature, 1884–1919*. New York.

Bigelow, Donald N. 1957. 'Introduction', in Riis 1957 [1890].

Bleyer, Willard G. 1923. *Newspaper Writing and Editing*. Boston [1913].

1927. *Main Currents in the History of American Journalism*. Boston.

Booth, Charles. 1902–3. *Life and Labour of the People in London*, 17 vols. London.

1967. *On the City: Physical Pattern and Social Structure*, ed. and introduced by Harold W. Pfautz. Chicago and London.

Booth, William. 1890. *In Darkest England and the Way Out*. New York.

Borenstein, Audrey. 1978. *Redeeming the Sin: Social Science and Literature*. New York.

Bowdery, Barbara Klose. 1951. *The Sociology of Robert E. Park*. Ph.D dissertation, Columbia University.

Boyce, Neith. 1901. 'The "News" Element in Modern Fiction', in *The Bookman*, vol. 12, pp. 149–50.

Bradbury, Malcolm. 1983. *The Modern American Novel*. Oxford and New York.

Braude, Lee. 1970. 'Park and Burgess: An Appreciation', in *American Journal of Sociology*, vol. 76, pp. 1–10.

Breckinridge, Sophonisba P. and Edith Abbott. 1910. 'Chicago's Housing

Problem: Families in Furnished Rooms', in *American Journal of Sociology*, vol. 16, pp. 289–308.

Bremner, Robert H. 1956. *From the Depths: The Discovery of Poverty in the United States*. New York.

Brown, Lea Ann. 1984. 'Elizabeth Cochrane (Nellie Bly)', in *Dictionary of Literary Biography*, vol. xxv, *American Newspaper Journalists, 1901–1925*, Detroit, pp. 58–64.

Brunner, Henry C. 1894. 'The Bowery and Bohemia', in *Scribner's*, vol. 15, pp. 452–60.

1896. *Jersey Street and Jersey Lane: Urban and Suburban Sketches*. New York.

Bruns, Roger A. 1986/7. 'King of the Hoboes', in *Chicago History*, vol. 15, pp. 4–19.

1987. *The Damndest Radical*. Urbana and Chicago.

Bücher, Karl. 1906. *Die Entstehung der Volkswirtschaft* [The origin of political economics]. Tübingen.

Bulmer, Martin. 1981. 'Quantification and Chicago Social Science in the 1920s: A Neglected Tradition', in *Journal of the History of the Behavioral Sciences*, vol. 17, pp. 312–31.

1983a. 'Chicago School and the Society for Social Research: A Comment', in *Journal of the History of the Behavioral Sciences*, vol. 19, pp. 353–7.

1983b. 'The Methodology of the Taxi-Dance Hall', in *Urban Life*, vol. 12, pp. 95–101.

1983c. 'The Society for Social Research', in *Urban Life*, vol. 11, pp. 421–39.

1984. *The Chicago School of Sociology: Institutionalization, Diversity, and the Rise of Sociological Research*. Chicago and London.

1985. 'The Chicago School of Sociology: What Made It a "School"?', in *History of Sociology*, vol. 5, pp. 61–77.

Burgess, Ernest W. 1916. 'The Social Survey: A Field for Constructive Service by Departments of Sociology', in *American Journal of Sociology*, vol. 21, pp. 493–500.

1925. 'The Growth of the City: An Introduction to a Research Project', in Park, Burgess and McKenzie 1925, pp. 47–62.

1926 (ed.). *The Urban Community*. Chicago.

1927. 'Statistics and Case Studies as Methods of Sociological Research', in *Sociology and Social Research*, vol. 12, pp. 103–20.

1973. *On Community, Family, and Delinquency*. Chicago and London.

Burgess, Ernest W. and Donald J. Bogue (eds.). 1964. *Contributions to Urban Sociology*. Chicago and London.

Burgess, Robert G. 1982 (ed.). *Field Research: A Source Book and Field Manual*. London.

1984. *In the Field: An Introduction to Field Research*. London.

Burton, David H. 1982. *Progressive Masks: Letters of Oliver Wendell Holmes, Jr. and Franklin Ford*. Newark, London and Toronto.

Bushnell, Charles J. 1901/2. 'Some Social Aspects of the Chicago Stock Yards', in *American Journal of Sociology*, vol. 7, pp. 145–70, 289–330, 433–74, 687–702.

Byrnes, Thomas. 1969. *Professional Criminals of America.* New York [1886].

Cannon, Walter Bradford. No date. *Der Weg eines Forschers* [The way of an investigator]. Munich [1945].

Cantwell, Robert. 1968. 'Journalism – The Magazines', in Shapiro 1968, pp. 21–3.

Carey, James T. 1975. *Sociology and Public Affairs: The Chicago School.* Beverly Hills and London.

Carey, James W. 1969. 'The Communications Revolution and the Professional Communicator', in Paul Halmos (ed.), *The Sociology of Mass-Media Communicators* (The Sociological Review Monograph 13), Keele.

Cavan, Ruth Shonle. 1983. 'The Chicago School of Sociology, 1918–1933', in *Urban Life*, vol. 11, pp. 407–20.

Chalmers, David Mark. 1974. *The Muckrake Years.* New York.

Chombart de Lauwe, Paul-Henry. 1965. *Paris: Essais de Sociologie, 1952–1964* [Paris: Sociology essays, 1952–1964]. Paris.

Chombart de Lauwe, Paul-Henry (with collaborators). 1952. *Paris et l'Agglomération Parisienne* [Paris and the Paris conurbation], 2 vols. Paris.

Cipriani, Roberto. 1985. 'Quantité et qualité dans l'analyse sociologique: faux dilemme ou débat ideologique dans la connaissance scientifique?' [Quantity and quality in sociological analysis: false dilemma or ideological debate in the scientific consciousness?], in *Revue de l'Institut de Sociologie*, no. 1/2, pp. 181–90.

Clements, Frederic Edward. 1905. *Research Methods in Ecology.* Lincoln, Nebr.

Colbron, Grace Isabel. 1903. Review of 'The Spirit of the Ghetto', by Hutchins Hapgood, in *The Bookman*, vol. 17, pp. 97ff.

Conrad, Else. 1902. 'Vagabundieren mit Vagabunden' [Tramping with tramps], in *Archiv für Kriminalanthropologie und Kriminalstatistik* [Archive for criminal anthropology and criminal statistics], vol. 8, pp. 129–65.

Cook, Fred J. 1972. *The Muckrakers: Crusading Journalists Who Changed America.* Garden City, N. Y.

Cooley, Charles Horton. 1926. 'The Roots of Social Knowledge', in *American Journal of Sociology*, vol. 32, pp. 59–79.

1966. *Social Process.* Carbondale, Ill. and Edwardsville, Ill. [1918].

Coser, Lewis A. 1958. 'Simmel's Style of Work: A Contribution to the Sociology of the Sociologist', in *American Journal of Sociology*, vol. 63, pp. 635–41.

1965. *Georg Simmel.* Englewood Cliffs, N. J.

1977. *Masters of Sociological Thought.* New York.

1984. *Refugee Scholars in America.* New Haven, Conn. and London.

Coughlan, Neil. 1975. *Young John Dewey.* Chicago and London.

Cressey, Paul Goalby. 1932. *The Taxi-Dance Hall.* Chicago.

1983. 'A Comparison of the Roles of the "Sociological Stranger" and the "Anonymous Stranger" in Field Research', in *Urban Life*, vol. 12, pp. 102–20.

Czitrom, Daniel J. 1982. *Media and the American Mind.* Chapel Hill, N. C.

Dahme, Heinz-Jürgen and Otthein Rammstedt (eds.). 1984. *Georg Simmel und die Moderne* [Georg Simmel and modernity]. Frankfurt on Main.

Dannenbaum, Jack. 1981. 'The Origins of Temperance Activism and Militancy Among American Women', in *Journal of Social History*, vol. 15, pp. 235–52.

Darnell, Regna. 1986. 'Personality and Culture: The Fate of the Sapirian Alternative', in Stocking 1971, pp. 156–83.

Darnton, Robert. 1975. 'Writing News and Telling Stories', in *Daedalus*, vol. 104, pp. 175–93.

Deegan, Mary Jo. 1988. *Jane Addams and the Men of the Chicago School, 1892–1918*. New Brunswick and Oxford.

Deegan, Mary Jo and John S. Burger. 1981. 'W. I. Thomas and Social Reform: His Work and Writings', in *Journal of the History of the Behavioral Sciences*, vol. 17, pp. 114–25.

Devereux, George. 1976. *Angst und Methode in den Verhaltenswissenschaften* [From anxiety to method in the behavioural sciences]. Munich.

Dewey, John. 1926. *Experience and Nature*. Chicago and London.

1927. *The Public and Its Problems*. New York.

1929. *Characters and Events*. New York.

Dilthey, Wilhelm. 1968. *Der Aufbau der geschichtlichen Welt in den Geisteswissenschaften* [The structure of the historical world in the humanities], *Ges. Schriften* [Collected writings], vol. VII. Stuttgart and Göttingen.

Diner, Steven J. 1975. 'Department and Discipline: The Department of Sociology at the University of Chicago, 1892–1920', in *Minerva*, vol. 13, pp. 514–53.

Dollard, John. 1938. 'The Life History in Community Studies', in *American Sociological Review*, vol. 3, pp. 724–37.

Donovan, Frances R. 1929. *The Saleslady*. Chicago.

Douglas, Jack D. (ed.). 1970. *Observations of Deviance*. New York.

Dovifat, Emil. 1927. *Der amerikanische Journalismus* [American journalism]. Berlin and Leipzig.

Downes, David and Paul Rock. 1982. *Understanding Deviance*. Oxford.

Dreiser, Theodore. 1922. *A Book About Myself*. New York.

1923. *The Color of a Great City*. New York.

1924. *The Color of a Great City*, reprint. New York.

Dubin, Steven C. 1983. 'The Moral Continuum of Deviancy Research: Chicago Sociologists and the Dance Hall', in *Urban Life*, vol. 12, pp. 75–94.

Duncan, Hugh Dalziel. 1948. 'Chicago as a Literary Center: Social Factors Influencing Chicago Literary Institutions from 1885 to 1920', Ph.D dissertation, University of Chicago.

1959. 'Simmel's Image of Society', in Wolff 1959, pp. 100–18.

1965. *Culture and Democracy*. Totowa, N.J.

Earhart, Mary. 1944. *Frances Willard: From Prayers to Politics*. Chicago.

Easthope, Gary. 1974. *A History of Social Research Methods*. London.

Ellwood, Charles A. 1909. Review of 'Following the Color Line', by Ray Stannard Baker, in *American Journal of Sociology*, vol. 15, pp. 119–20.

Emerson, Robert E. 1981. 'Observational Field Work', in *Annual Review of Sociology*, vol. 7, pp. 351–78.

Etulain, Richard W. (ed.). 1979. *Jack London on the Road: The Tramp Diary and the Hobo Writings*. Logan, Utah.

Evans-Pritchard, Edward E. 1973. 'Some Reminiscences and Reflections on Fieldwork', in *Journal of the Anthropological Society of Oxford*, vol. 4, pp. 1–12.

Everett, George. 1983. 'Jacob Riis', in *Dictionary of Literary Biography*, vol. XXIII, *American Newspaper Journalists, 1873–1900*, Detroit, pp. 306–13.

Fabris, Hans Heinz. 1981. 'Objektivität und Parteilichkeit in den Sozialwissenschaften und im Journalismus' [Objectivity and partiality in the social sciences and journalism], in *Publizistik* [Journalism], vol. 26, pp. 16–24.

Faris, Robert E. L. 1939. *An Ecological Study of Insanity in the City*. Chicago [1931].

   1970. *Chicago Sociology, 1920–1932*. Chicago and London.

Faris, Robert E. L. (with H. Warren Funham). 1939. *Mental Disorders in Urban Areas*. Chicago.

Fei Hsiao-tung. 1980a. *China's Gentry: Essays in Rural–Urban Relations*. Revised and selected by Margaret Park Redfield. Chicago and London [1953].

   1980b. *Peasant Life in China*. London [1939].

   1981. *Towards a People's Anthropology*. Beijing.

   1983. *Chinese Village Close-Up*. Beijing.

Feied, Frederick. 1964. *No Pie In The Sky: The Hobo as American Cultural Hero in the Works of Jack London, John Dos Passos, and Jack Kerouac*. New York.

Feuer, Lewis F. 1959. 'John Dewey and the Back to the People Movement in American Thought', in *Journal of the History of Ideas*, vol. 20, pp. 545–68.

Filler, Louis. 1968. *The Muckrakers: Crusaders for American Liberalism*. Chicago.

   1978. *Voice of the Democracy: A Critical Biography of David Graham Phillips, Journalist, Novelist, Progressive*. University Park, Pa. and London.

Fine, David M. 1977. *The City, the Immigrant and American Fiction, 1880–1920*. Metuchen, N. J. and London.

Fish, Virginia Kemp. 1985. 'Hull-House: Pioneer in Urban Research During Its Creative Years', in *History of Sociology*, vol. 6.

Fishbein, Leslie. 1982. *Rebels in Bohemia*. Chapel Hill, N. C.

Fisher, Philip. 1975. 'City Matters: City Minds', in Jerome H. Buckley (ed.), *The Worlds of Victorian Fiction*, Cambridge, Mass. and London, pp. 371–89.

Flynt (Willard), Josiah. 1895/6. 'How Men Become Tramps', in *Century Magazine*, vol. 50, pp. 941–5.

   1900. *Notes of an Itinerant Policeman*. Boston.

   1901. 'In the World of Graft', in *McClure's*, vol. 16/17.

   1908. *My Life*. New York.

   1967. *Tramping with Tramps*. London [1899].

   1968. *The Little Brother: A Story of Tramp Life*. Upper Saddle River, N. J.

Flynt (Willard), Josiah with Francis Walton (Alfred Hodder). 1900/1. 'True Stories from the Underworld', in *McClure's*, vol. 15/16.

Ford, Franklin. No date. *Draft of Action*. No place [1892].

Ford, James L. 1894. *The Literary Shop and Other Tales*. New York.

Frankenberg, Ronald. 1982. 'Participant Observers', in Robert G. Burgess 1982, pp. 50–2.

Frazier, P. Jean and Cecile Gaziano. 1979. *Robert Ezra Park's Theory of News, Public Opinion and Social Control* (Journalism Monographs No. 64), pp. 1–47. Austin, Tex.

Freedman, Florence B. 1970. 'A Sociologist Views a Poet: Robert Ezra Park on Walt Whitman', in *Walt Whitman Review*, vol. 16, pp. 99–104.

Frentzel-Beyme, Rainer. 1985. *Einführung in die Epidemiologie* [Introduction to epidemiology]. Darmstadt.

Friedrichs, Jürgen. 1973 (ed.). *Teilnehmende Beobachtung abweichenden Verhaltens* [Participant observation of deviant behaviour]. Stuttgart.

 1977. *Stadtanalyse. Soziale und räumliche Organisation der Gesellschaft* [Urban analysis. Social and spatial organisation of society]. Reinbek bei Hamburg.

Frisby, David P. 1984. *Georg Simmels Theorie der Moderne* [Georg Simmel's theory of modernity], in Dahme and Rammstedt 1984, pp. 9–79.

Fuchs, Werner. 1984. *Biographische Forschung* [Biographical research]. Opladen.

Gee, Wilson (ed.). 1929. *Research in the Social Sciences: Its Fundamental Methods and Objectives*. New York.

Gelb, Barbara. 1973. *So Short A Time: A Biography of John Reed and Louise Bryant*. New York.

Gelfant, Blanche Housman. 1954. *The American City Novel*. Norman, Okla.

Georges, Robert A. and Michael O. Jones. 1980. *People Studying People: The Human Element in Fieldwork*. Berkeley, Los Angeles and London.

Gerdes, Klaus and Christian von Wolffersdorff-Ehlert. 1974. *Drogenszene: Suche nach Gegenwart. Ergebnisse teilnehmender Beobachtung in der jugendlichen Drogensubkultur* [The drug scene: Search for the present. Results of participant observation in the youth drug sub-culture]. Stuttgart.

Gerth, Hans and Saul Landau. 1959. 'The Relevance of History to the Sociology Ethos', in *Studies on the Left*, vol. 1, pp. 7–14.

Gilbert, James Burkhart. 1968. *Writers and Partisans: A History of Literary Radicalism in America*. New York.

Ginzburg, Carlo. 1983. *Spurensicherungen* [Morelli, Freud and Sherlock Holmes: clues and scientific method]. Berlin.

Girtler, Roland. 1979. *Kulturanthropologie* [Cultural anthropology]. Munich.
 1980. *Vagabunden in der Großstadt* [Vagrants in the big city]. Stuttgart.
 1984. *Methoden der qualitativen Sozialforschung. Anleitung zur Feldarbeit* [Methods of qualitative social research. Introduction to fieldwork]. Vienna, Cologne and Graz.

Glazer, Nathan. 1973. 'The Rise of Social Research in Europe', in Daniel Lerner (ed.), *The Human Meaning of the Social Sciences*, Gloucester, Mass., pp. 43–72.

Goffman, Erving. 1961. *Asylums*. New York.

Goist, Park Dixon. 1971. 'City and "Community": The Urban Theory of Robert Park', in *American Quarterly*, vol. 23, pp. 46–59.

Gollomb, Joseph. 1912. 'Abraham Cahan', in *American Magazine*, vol. 74, pp. 672–4.

Gottschalk, Louis *et al.* 1945. *The Use of Personal Documents in History, Anthropology and Sociology.* New York.

Gouldner, Alvin W. 1968. 'The Sociologist as Partisan: Sociology and the Welfare State', in *American Sociologist*, vol. 3, pp. 103–16.

1973. *For Sociology: Renewal and Critique in Sociology Today.* London.

1974. *Die westliche Soziologie in der Krise* [The coming crisis of Western sociology], 2 vols. Reinbek bei Hamburg.

1984. *Reziprozität und Autonomie* [Reciprocity and autonomy]. Frankfurt on Main.

Greene, Theodore P. 1970. *America's Heroes: The Changing Models of Success in American Magazines.* New York.

Grünfeld, Ernst. 1939. *Die Peripheren. Ein Kapitel Soziologie* [People on the periphery. A chapter of sociology]. Amsterdam.

Gumbrecht, Hans Ulrich. 1975. 'Modern, Modernität, Moderne' [Modern, modernity, modern times], in Otto Brunner, Werner Conze and Reinhart Koselleck (eds.), *Geschichtliche Grundbegriffe* [Basic historical concepts], Stuttgart, pp. 93–131.

Gusfield, John R. 1955. 'Social Structure and Moral Reform: A Study of the Woman's Temperance Union', in *American Journal of Sociology*, vol. 61, pp. 223ff.

Haas, Hannes. 1987. *Die hohe Kunst der Reportage. Wechselbeziehungen zwischen Literatur, Journalismus und Sozialwissenschaften* [The high art of reporting. Interrelationships between literature, journalism and social sciences], in *Publizistik* [Journalism], vol. 32, pp. 277–94.

Habermas, Jürgen. 1975. *Strukturwandel der Öffentlichkeit* [The structural transformation of the public sphere]. Neuwied and Berlin.

Hakutani, Yoshinobu. 1980. *Young Dreiser: A Critical Study.* Cranbury, N. J. and London.

Halbwachs, Maurice. 1932. *Chicago, Expérience Ethnique* [Chicago, ethnic experience], in *Annales d'Histoire Economique et Sociale* [Annals of economic and social history], vol. 4, pp. 11–49.

Hannerz, Ulf. 1980. *Exploring the City: Inquiries Toward an Urban Anthropology.* New York.

Hapgood, Hutchins. 1903. *The Autobiography of a Thief.* New York.

1910. *Types From City Streets.* New York and London.

1917. 'The Picturesque Ghetto', in *Century Magazine*, vol. 94, pp. 469–73.

1939. *A Victorian in the Modern World.* New York.

1967. *The Spirit of the Ghetto.* Cambridge [1902].

1972. *A Victorian in the Modern World*, with introduction by Robert Allan Skotheim. New York.

Hapgood, Hutchins and Arthur Bartlett Maurice. 1902. 'The Great Newspapers of the United States', in *The Bookman*, vol. 14, pp. 567–84.

Hapgood, Norman. 1897. 'The Reporter and Literature', in *The Bookman*, vol. 5, pp. 119–21.

Harlan, Louis R. 1983. *Booker T. Washington: The Wizard of Tuskegee, 1901–1915.* New York and Oxford.

Harman, Lesley D. 1988. *The Modern Stranger.* Berlin, New York and Amsterdam.

Harvey, Lee. 1987a. *Myths of the Chicago School of Sociology.* Aldershot.

　1987b. 'The Nature of "Schools" in the Sociology of Knowledge: The Case of the "Chicago School"', in *Sociological Review*, vol. 35, pp. 245–78.

Hawley, Amos H. 1950. *Human Ecology.* New York.

　1974. 'Theorie und Forschung in der Sozialökologie' [Theory and research on social ecology], in R. König (ed.), *Handbuch der empirischen Sozialforschung* [Handbook of empirical social research], vol. IV, Stuttgart, pp. 51–81.

Hayner, Norman S. 1928. 'Hotel Life and Personality', in *American Journal of Sociology*, vol. 33, pp. 784–95.

Heberle, Rudolf. 1929. *Über die Mobilität der Bevölkerung in den Vereinigten Staaten* [Population mobility in the United States]. Jena.

　1956. Review of *Society (Collected Works of Robert E. Park)*, in *American Journal of Sociology*, vol. 62, pp. 97ff.

　1981. *Soziologische Lehr- und Wanderjahre* [Sociological apprenticeship and journeyman years], in Lepenies 1981, vol. I, pp. 271–98.

Henderson, Charles R. 1897. *The Social Spirit in America.* New York.

　1900/1. 'Prison Laboratories', in *American Journal of Sociology*, vol. 6, pp. 316–23.

　1906. *Introduction to the Study of the Dependent, Defective, and Delinquent Classes.* Boston [1893].

Hessel, Franz. 1984. *Ein Flâneur in Berlin* [A flâneur in Berlin]. Berlin [1929]. Originally published as *Spazieren in Berlin* [Strolling in Berlin].

Hettner, Alfred. 1960. *6.8.1859. Gedenkschrift zum 100. Geburtstag* [Commemorative paper for his 100th birthday], *Heidelberger Geographische Schriften* [Heidelberg Geographical Papers], no. VI. Heidelberg and Munich.

Hicks, Granville and John Reed. 1968. *The Making of a Revolutionary.* New York and London.

Hinkle, Gisela J. 1952. 'The "Four Wishes" in Thomas' Theory of Social Change', in *Social Research*, vol. 19, pp. 464–84.

Hodder, Alfred. 1908. 'Josiah Flynt – An Appreciation', in Flynt 1908, pp. 341–7.

Hoffman, Nicholas von. 1984. *Organized Crimes.* New York.

Hofstadter, Richard. 1955. *The Age of Reform.* New York.

　1968. 'The Progressive Impulse', in Shapiro 1968, pp. 93–102.

Holitscher, Arthur. 1916. *Das amerikanische Gesicht* [The American face]. Berlin.

Honigsheim, Paul. 1923. 'Die Bohème' [The Bohemian], in *Kölner Vierteljahreshefte für Soziologie* [Cologne quarterly sociology pamphlets], vol. 3, pp. 60–71.

Hopkins, Charles Howard. 1940. *The Rise of the Social Gospel in American Protestantism, 1865–1915.* New Haven, Conn.

Horowitz, Helen L. 1976. *Culture and the City: Cultural Philanthropy in Chicago from the 1880s to 1917.* Lexington, Ky.

Horton, Russel M. 1974. *Lincoln Steffens*. Boston.

Hudson, Robert V. 1984. 'Will Irwin', in *Dictionary of Literary Biography*, vol. XXV, *American Newspaper Journalists, 1901–1925*, Detroit, pp. 136–43.

Hughes, Everett C. 1949. 'Social Change and Status Protest: An Essay on the Marginal Man', in *Phylon*, vol. 10, pp. 58–65.

  1950. 'Preface', in Park 1950b, pp. xi–xiv.

  1952. 'Introduction: The Place of Field Work in Social Science', in Buford H. Junker, *Field Work*, Chicago, pp. v–xv.

  1971. *The Sociological Eye: Selected Papers*. Chicago and New York.

Hughes, Helen MacGill. 1940. *News and the Human Interest Story*. Chicago.

  1980. 'Robert Ezra Park: The Philosopher-Newspaperman-Sociologist,' in Robert K. Merton and W. Riley (eds.), *Sociological Tradition from Generation to Generation*, Norwood, N. J., pp. 67–79.

Hull-House. 1970. *Hull-House Maps and Papers*. New York [1895].

Humphrey, Robert E. 1978. *Children of Fantasy: The First Rebels of Greenwich Village*. New York.

Humphreys, Anne. 1977. *Travels into the Poor Man's Country: The Work of Henry Mayhew*. Firle, Sussex.

Hunter, Albert. 1974. *Symbolic Communities*. Chicago and London.

Inciardi, James A. 1977. 'In Search of the Class Cannon: A Field Study of Professional Pickpockets', in Weppner 1977, pp. 55–77.

Irwin, Will. 1909. 'The New York Sun', in *American Magazine*, vol. 67, pp. 301–10.

  1942. *The Making of a Reporter*. New York.

  1969. 'The American Newspaper', a series first appearing in *Colliers*, January–July 1911, with comments by Clifford F. Weigle and David G. Clark, Ames, Iowa.

Jacobs, Ruth Harriet. 1970. 'The Journalistic and Sociological Enterprises as Ideal Types', in *American Sociologist*, vol. 5, pp. 348–50.

Jaeger, Johannes. 1905. *Hinter Kerkermauern. Autobiographien und Selbstbekenntnisse, Aufsätze und Gedichte von Verbrechern. Ein Beitrag zur Kriminalpsychologie* [Behind prison walls. Autobiographies and self-confessions, essays and poems by criminals. A contribution to criminal psychology], in *Archiv für Kriminal-Anthropologie und Kriminalistik* [Archive for criminal anthropology and crimi-nalistics], vol. 19, pp. 1–48, 209–56 (continued in vols. 20ff.).

James, William. 1949. *Pragmatism: A New Name for Some Old Ways of Thinking*. New York [1907].

  1975. 'The Function of Cognition', in James, *The Meaning of Truth* (*The Works of William James*, vol. II), Cambridge, Mass. and London, pp. 13–32.

  1976. 'A World of Pure Experience', in James, *Essays in Radical Empiricism* (*The Works of William James*, vol. III), Cambridge, Mass. and London, pp. 21–44.

Janowitz, Morris. 1966. 'Introduction', in William I. Thomas 1966, pp. vii–lviii.

  1972. 'Professionalization of Sociology', in *American Journal of Sociology*, vol. 78, pp. 105–35.

  1973. *Wissenschaftshistorischer Überblick zur Entwicklung des Grundbegriffs 'Soziale Kontrolle'* [Scientific and historical overview of the development of the basic concept of 'social control'], in *Kölner Zeitschrift für Soziologie und Sozialpsychologie* [Cologne journal of sociology and social psychology], vol. 25, pp. 499–514.

Joas, Hans. 1980. *Praktische Intersubjektivität* [George Herbert Mead: a contemporary reexamination of his thought]. Frankfurt on Main.

1988. *Symbolischer Interaktionismus. Von der Philosophie des Pragmatismus zu einer soziologischen Forschungstradition* [Symbolic interaction. From the philosophy of pragmatism to a sociological research tradition], in *Kölner Zeitschrift für Soziologie und Sozialpsychologie* [Cologne journal of sociology and social psychology], vol. 40, pp. 417–46.

Johnson, Stanley and Julian Harriss. 1948. *The Complete Reporter.* New York.

Joseph, Isaac. 1984. 'Urbanité et ethnicité' [Urbanity and ethnicity], in *Terrain*, no. 3, pp. 20–5.

Jung, Bernhard. 1984. 'Jacob A. Riis: Sozialreformer und Fotograf' [Jacob A. Riis: Social reformer and photographer], in *Fotogeschichte* [History of photography], vol. 4, pp. 45–58.

Kaplan, Justin. 1974. *Lincoln Steffens.* New York.

Käsler, Dirk. 1985. *Soziologische Abenteuer* [Sociological adventures]. Opladen.

Keiser, R. Lincoln. 1966. *Hustler! The Autobiography of a Thief.* New York.

Kluckhohn, Clyde and Henry A. Murray (eds.). 1948. *Personality in Nature, Society and Culture.* New York.

Kohl, Karl-Heinz. 1979. *Exotik als Beruf* [The exotic as a profession]. Wiesbaden.

1987. *Abwehr und Verlangen* [Defence and desire]. Frankfurt on Main and New York.

Kohli, Martin. 1981a. 'Biography: Account, Text, Method', in Bertaux 1981, pp. 61–75.

1981b. 'Wie es zur 'biographischen Methode' kam und was daraus geworden ist. Ein Kapitel aus der Geschichte der Sozialforschung' [How the 'biographical method' came about and what became of it. A chapter from the history of social research], in *Zeitschrift für Soziologie* [Journal of sociology], vol. 10, pp. 273–93.

König, Gerhard. 1986. 'Wort und Weise Serendip. Zur Genealogie eines Begriffs' [Serendipity, word and melody. The geneology of a concept], in *Sprache im Technischen Zeitalter* [Language in the technical age], no. 97, pp. 51–66.

König, René. 1973. 'Umriß einer Theorie der Beobachtung' [Outline of an observation theory], in König (ed.), *Handbuch der empirischen Sozialforschung* [Handbook of empirical social research], vol. II, pp. 1–65.

1978. 'Die Pioniere der Sozialökologie in Chicago' [The pioneers of social ecology in Chicago], in German Unesco Commission (eds.), *Stadtökologie* [Urban ecology], Munich, pp. 56–68.

1981. 'Die Situation der emigrierten deutschen Soziologen in Europa' [The situation of the emigré German sociologists in Europe], in Lepenies 1981, vol. IV, pp. 115–58.

1984. 'Soziologie und Ethnologie' [Sociology and ethnology], in *Kölner*

Zeitschrift für Soziologie und Sozialpsychologie [Cologne journal for sociology and social psychology], special no. 26: *Ethnologie als Sozialwissenschaft* [Ethnology as a social science], pp. 17–35.

Korff, Gottfried. 1986. 'Berlin-Berlin. Menschenstadt und Stadtmenschen' [City of people and city people], in Ulrich Eckhardt (ed.), *750 Jahre Berlin* [750 years of Berlin], Frankfurt on Main and Berlin, pp. 144–55.

1987. 'Die Stadt aber ist der Mensch . . .' [But the city is the person . . .], in G. Korff and R. Rürup (eds.), *Berlin-Berlin*, Berlin, pp. 643–63.

Koselleck, Reinhart. 1975. 'Fortschritt' [Progress], in O. Brunner, W. Konze and R. Koselleck (eds.), *Geschichtliche Grundbegriffe* [Basic historical concepts], Stuttgart, pp. 351–423.

Kramer, Fritz. 1977. *Verkehrte Welten. Zur imaginären Ethnographie des 19. Jahrhunderts* [Worlds upside down. The imaginary ethnography of the nineteenth century]. Frankfurt on Main.

1978. 'Die "social anthropology" und das Problem der Darstellung anderer Gesellschaften' [Social anthropology and the problem of portraying other societies], in *Gesellschaften ohne Staat* [Societies without a state], vol. 1, Frankfurt on Main (published by F. Kramer, Chr. Sigrist), pp. 9–27.

Kreuzer, Helmut. 1968. *Die Bohème* [The Bohemian]. Stuttgart.

Kuklick, Henrika. 1980. 'Chicago Sociology and Urban Planning Policy', in *Theory and Society*, vol. 9, pp. 821–45.

Kurtz, Lester R. 1982. 'Robert E. Park's "Notes on the Origins of the Society of Social Research"', in *Journal of the History of the Behavioral Sciences*, vol. 18, pp. 332–40.

1984. *Evaluating Chicago Sociology*. Chicago.

Kwiat, Joseph C. 1953. 'The Newspaper Experience: Crane, Norris, and Dreiser', in *Nineteenth-Century Fiction*, vol. 3, pp. 51–66.

Lal, Barbara Ballis. 1987. 'Black and Blue in Chicago: Robert E. Park's Perspective on Race Relations in Urban America, 1914–44', in *British Journal of Sociology*, vol. 38, pp. 546–60.

Landesco, John. 1932/3a. 'Crime and the Failure of Institutions in Chicago's Immigrant Areas', in *Journal of Criminal Law, Criminology, and Police Science*, vol. 23, pp. 238–48.

1932/3b. 'The Life History of a Member of the "42" Gang', in *Journal of Criminal Law, Criminology, and Police Science*, vol. 23, pp. 964–98.

1934/5. 'The Criminal Underworld of Chicago in the "80's" and "90's", in *Journal of Criminal Law, Criminology, and Police Science*, vol. 25, pp. 341–57, 928–40.

1968. *Organized Crime in Chicago* (with a new introduction by Mark H. Haller). Chicago and London [1929].

Lane, James B. 1974. *Jacob A. Riis and the American City*. Port Washington, N. Y. and London.

Lasch, Christoper. 1965. *The New Radicalism in America, 1889–1963*. New York.

Lears, T. J. Jackson. 1981. *No Place of Grace, Antimodernism and the Transformation of American Culture*. New York.

Lee, Alfred McClung. 1937. *The Daily Newspaper in America*. New York.

Lengerman, Patricia M. 1979. 'The Founding of the American Sociological Review: The Anatomy of a Rebellion', in *American Sociological Review*, vol. 44, pp. 185–98.

Lepenies, Wolf. 1978. 'Der Wissenschaftler als Autor. Über konservierende Funktionen der Literatur' [The scientist as author. The preservative functions of literature], in *Akzente* [Accents], no. 2, pp. 129–47.

　1981 (ed.). *Geschichte der Soziologie. Studien zur kognitiven, sozialen und historischen Identität einer Disziplin* [History of sociology. Studies concerning the cognitive, social and historical identity of a specialism], 4 vols. Frankfurt on Main.

　1985. *Die drei Kulturen. Soziologie zwischen Literatur und Wissenschaft* [Between literature and science: the rise of sociology]. Munich and Vienna.

Lepenies, Wolf and Henning Ritter (eds.). 1970. *Orte des Wilden Denkens. Zur Anthropologie von Claude Lévi-Strauss* [Places of wild thinking. The anthropology of Claude Lévi-Strauss]. Frankfurt on Main.

Levine, Donald N. 1959. 'The Structure of Simmel's Social Thought', in Wolff 1959, pp. 9–32.

　1971. 'Introduction', in Simmel 1971, pp. ix–lxv.

　1972. 'Note on the Crowd and the Public', in Park 1972, pp. xxvii–xxxii.

　1977. 'Simmel at a Distance: On the History and Systematics of the Sociology of the Stranger', in *Sociological Focus*, vol. 10, pp. 15–29. Revised version published in W. A. Shack and E. P. Skinner (eds.), 1979, *Strangers in African Society*, Berkeley, Los Angeles and London, pp. 21–36.

　1984. 'Ambivalente Begegnungen: "Negationen" Simmels durch Durkheim, Weber, Lukács, Park und Parsons' [Ambivalent encounters: 'negations' of Simmel by Dürkheim, Weber, Lukács, Park and Parsons], in Dahme and Rammstedt 1984, pp. 318–87.

Levine, Donald N., Ellwood B. Carter and Eleanor Gorman. 1976. 'Simmel's Influence on American Sociology, II', in *American Journal of Sociology*, vol. 81, pp. 1112–32.

　1981. 'Simmels Einfluß auf die amerikanische Soziologie' [Simmel's influence on American sociology], in Lepenies 1981, vol. IV, pp. 32–81.

Lévi-Strauss, Claude. 1978. *Traurige Tropen* [Tristes Tropiques]. Frankfurt on Main.

Lewis, J. Davis and Richard L. Smith. 1980. *American Sociology and Pragmatism: Mead, Chicago Sociology, and Symbolic Interaction*. Chicago and London.

Lewis, Sinclair. 1917. 'Hobohemia', in *Saturday Evening Post*, 4 July, pp. 3–6, 121–2, 125–6, 129–33.

Lindeman, Eduard C. 1924. *Social Discovery*. New York.

Lindner, Rolf. 1985. 'Das Andere Ufer. Zwei-Kulturen-Metapher und Großstadtforschung' [The other shore. The two-cultures metaphor and urban research], in *Großstadt. Aspekte empirischer Kulturforschung. 24. Deutscher Volkskundekongreß in Berlin vom 26. bis 30.9.1983* [The city. Aspects of empirical culture research. 24th German folklore congress in Berlin 26–30 September 1983], edited by Theodor Kohlmann and Hermann Bausinger, Berlin, pp. 297–304.

1987. 'Zur kognitiven Identität der Volkskunde' [Cognitive identity of folklore], in *Österreichische Zeitschrift für Volkskunde* [Austrian journal of folklore], vol. 90, pp. 1–19.

1989. 'Nels Anderson (1889–1986), Eine Hommage' [Nels Anderson (1889–1986), a tribute], in *Jahrbuch für Volksliedforschung* [Folk-song research yearbook], vol. 34, pp. 81–91.

Lippmann, Walter. 1968. 'The Themes of Muckraking', in Shapiro 1968, pp. 14–20.

Lipset, Seymour M. and David Riesman. 1975. *Education and Politics at Harvard.* New York.

Lofland, Lyn H. 1980. 'Reminiscences of Classic Chicago: The Bulmer–Hughes Talk', in *Urban Life*, vol. 9, pp. 251–81.

1983. 'Understanding Urban Life: The Chicago Legacy', in *Urban Life*, vol. 11, pp. 491–511.

London, Jack. 1907. *The Road.* New York.

Lubove, Roy. 1974. *The Progressives and the Slums: Tenement House Reform in New York City, 1890–1917.* Westport, Conn.

Lyons, Louis M. 1971. *One Hundred Years of the Boston Globe.* Cambridge, Mass.

MacDougall, Curtis D. 1950. *Interpretative Reporting.* New York [1938].

McGlashan, Zena Beth. 1979/80. 'The Professor and the Prophet: John Dewey and Franklin Ford', in *Journalism History*, vol. 6, pp. 107–11.

McKenzie, Roderick D. 1925. 'The Ecological Approach to the Study of the Human Community', in Park, Burgess and McKenzie 1925, pp. 63–79.

McKinney, John C. 1966. *Constructive Typology and Social Theory.* New York.

MacNeil, Neil. 1940. *Without Fear or Favor.* New York.

Madge, John. 1963. *The Origins of Scientific Sociology.* London.

Makropoulos, Michael. 1988. 'Der Mann auf der Grenze. Robert Ezra Park und die Chancen einer heterogenen Gesellschaft' [The marginal man. Robert Ezra Park and the chances of a heterogeneous society], in *Freibeuter* [Freebooter], no. 35, pp. 8–22.

Malinowski, Bronislaw. 1935. *Coral Gardens and Their Magic*, vol. II, *The Language of Magic and Gardening.* London.

1979. *Argonauten des westlichen Pazifik* [Argonauts of the western Pacific]. Frankfurt on Main.

Mannheim, Karl. 1956. *Essays on the Sociology of Culture.* London.

1958. *Mensch und Gesellschaft im Zeitalter des Umbaus* [Man and society in the age of reconstruction]. Darmstadt.

Marcaccio, Michael D. 1977. *The Hapgoods: Three Earnest Brothers.* Charlottesville, Va.

Marx, Karl. 1969. *Das Kapital.* Berlin.

Masuoka, Jitsuichi and Preston Valien (eds.). 1961. *Race Relations Problems and Theory: Essays in Honor of Robert E. Park.* Chapel Hill, N. C.

Mathews, Basil. 1949. *Booker T. Washington, Educator and Interracial Interpreter.* London.

Matthews, Fred H. 1977. *Quest for an American Sociology: Robert E. Park and the*

Chicago School. Montreal and London.

Matza, David. 1973. *Abweichendes Verhalten. Untersuchungen zur Genese abweichender Identität* [Becoming deviant. Investigations into the genesis of deviant identity]. Heidelberg.

Maulsby, William S. 1925. *Getting the News*. New York.

May, Henry F. 1979. *The End of American Innocence*. Oxford.

Mead, George Herbert. 1925/6. 'The Nature of Aesthetic Experience', in *International Journal of Ethics*, vol. 36, pp. 382–93.

　1964. *On Social Psychology: Selected Papers*, ed. and with an introduction by Anselm Strauss. Chicago and London.

　1973. *Geist, Identität und Gesellschaft* [Identity and society]. Frankfurt on Main.

　1987. 'Die Genesis der Identität und die soziale Kontrolle' [The genesis of identity and the social control], in Mead, *Gesammelte Aufsätze* [Collected essays], vol. I, Frankfurt on Main (published by Hans Joas), pp. 299–328.

Melendy, Royal L. 1900/1. 'The Saloon in Chicago', in *American Journal of Sociology*, vol. 6, pp. 289–306, 433–64.

Mencken, Henry L. 1924. 'Puritanism as a Literary Force', in Mencken, *A Book of Prefaces*, New York [1917].

　1975. *A Gang of Pecksniffs: And Other Comments On Newspapers, Publishers, Editors and Reporters*. New York [1927].

Merton, Robert K. 1968. 'The Bearing of Empirical Research on Sociological Theory', in Merton, *Social Theory and Social Structure*, New York, London, pp. 156–71.

　1972. 'Insiders and Outsiders: A Chapter in the Sociology of Knowledge', in *American Journal of Sociology*, vol. 78, pp. 9–47.

　1981. *Zur Geschichte und Systematik der soziologischen Theorie* [History and systematics of sociological theory], in Lepenies 1981, vol. I, pp. 15–74.

Miller, Norbert. 1986. 'Serendipity oder die Kunst der Aufmerksamkeit' [Serendipity or the art of attentiveness], in *Sprache im Technischen Zeitalter* [Language in the technical age], no. 98, pp. 135–47.

Mills, C. Wright. 1963. *Kritik der soziologischen Denkweise* [The sociological imagination]. Neuwied and Berlin.

Moebus, Joachim. 1976. 'Zur Figur des bürgerlichen Heros' [The figure of the civic hero], in *Das Argument* [The argument], special no. 3, *Vom Faustus bis Karl Valentin. Der Bürger in Geschichte und Literatu* [From Faust to Karl Valentin. The citizen in history and literature], pp. 215–43.

Moore, E. C. 1897. 'Social Value of the Saloon', in *American Journal of Sociology*, vol. 3, pp. 1–12.

Morgan, J. Graham. 1969. 'The Development of Sociology and the Social Gospel in America', in *Sociological Analysis*, vol. 30, pp. 42–53.

Mott, Frank Luther. 1950. *American Journalism* (rev. edn). New York [1948].

　1952. *The News in America*. Cambridge, Mass.

　1957. *A History of American Magazines, 1885–1905*. Cambridge, Mass.

Nash, Dennison. 1963. 'The Ethnologist as Stranger: An Essay in the Sociology of Knowledge', in *Southwestern Journal of Anthropology*, vol. 19, pp. 149–67.

Nelissen, N. J. M. 1973. 'Robert Ezra Park (1864–1944). Ein Beitrag zur Geschichte der Sociologie' [Robert Ezra Park (1864–1944). A contribution to the history of sociology], in *Kölner Zeitschrift für Soziologie und Sozialpsychologie* [Cologne journal of sociology and social psychology], vol. 25, pp. 515–29.

Nettelbeck, Uwe. 1979. *Fantômas. Eine Sittengeschichte des Erkennungsdienstes* [Fantômas. A history of the life and customs of the Police Records Department]. Salzhausen.

Nilsson, Nils Gunnar. 1971. 'The Origin of the Interview', in *Journalism Quarterly*, vol. 48, pp. 707–13.

Nisbet, Robert. 1976. *Sociology as an Art Form*. London.

Oberschall, Anthony. 1972. 'The Institutionalization of American Sociology', in Oberschall (ed.), *The Establishment of Empirical Sociology*, New York, pp. 187–251.

O'Brien, Frank. 1918. *The Story of the 'Sun'*. New York.

Odum, Howard W. 1951. *American Sociology: The Story of Sociology in the United States Through 1950*. New York, London and Toronto.

Ogburn, William F. 1930a. 'Die Kultursoziologie und die quantitativen Methoden' [Cultural sociology and the quantitative methods], in *Zeitschrift für Völkerpsychologie und Soziologie* [Journal of folk psychology and sociology], vol. 6, pp. 257–66.

1930b. 'The Folk-Ways of a Scientific Sociology', in *Scientific Monthly*, vol. 30, pp. 300–6.

Palermo, Patrick, F. 1978. *Lincoln Steffens*. Boston.

Park, Robert Ezra. 1904. *Masse und Publikum: Eine methodologische und soziologische Untersuchung* [The crowd and the public: a methodological and sociological investigation]. Bern.

1915. 'The City: Suggestions for the Investigation of Human Behavior in the City Environment', in *American Journal of Sociology*, vol. 20, pp. 577–612.

1922. *The Immigrant Press and Its Control*. New York.

1923. 'The Mind of the Rover: Reflections upon the Relation Between Mentality and Locomotion', in *The World Tomorrow*, September.

1925a. 'The City: Suggestions for the Investigation of Human Behavior in the Urban Environment', in Park, Burgess and McKenzie 1925, pp. 1–46.

1925b. 'The Mind of the Hobo: Reflections Upon the Relations Between Mentality and Locomotion', in Park, Burgess and McKenzie 1925, pp. 156–60.

1926. 'The Urban Community as a Spacial Pattern and a Moral Order', in Ernest W. Burgess 1926, pp. 3–20.

1928. 'Human Migration and the Marginal Man', in *American Journal of Sociology*, vol. 33, pp. 881–93 (also in Park 1950b, pp. 345–56).

1929a. 'The City as a Social Laboratory', in Smith and White 1969 [1929], pp. 1–19.

1929b. 'Introduction'. In Zorbaugh 1983 [1929], pp. xvii–xx.

1929c. 'Sociology', in Wilson Gee (ed.), *Research in the Social Sciences*, New York, pp. 3–49.

1931. 'The Mentality of Racial Hybrids', in *American Journal of Sociology*, vol. 36, pp. 534–51 (also in Park 1950b, pp. 377–92).

1933. Review of *The Autobiography of Lincoln Steffens*, in *American Journal of Sociology*, vol. 38, pp. 954–7.

1936. 'Human Ecology', in *American Journal of Sociology*, vol. 42, pp. 1–15 (also in Park 1952, pp. 145–58).

1938. 'Reflections on Communication and Culture', in *American Journal of Sociology*, vol. 44, pp. 187–205 (also in Park 1950b, pp. 36–52).

1940a. 'News as a Form of Knowledge', in *American Journal of Sociology*, vol. 45, pp. 669–86 (also in Park 1955e, pp. 71–88).

1940b. 'Physics and Society', in *Canadian Journal of Economics and Political Science*, vol. 6, pp. 135–52 (also in Park 1955e, pp. 301–21).

1950a. 'An Autobiographical Note', in Park 1950b, pp. v–ix.

1950b. *Race and Culture*, vol. I, *Collected Papers of Robert E. Park*. Glencoe, Ill.

1950c. 'Race Relations and Certain Frontiers', in Park 1950b, pp. 117–37 [1934].

1952. *Human Communities: The City and Human Ecology*, vol. II, *Collected Papers of Robert E. Park*. Glencoe, Ill.

1955a. 'American Newspaper Literature', in Park 1955e, pp. 176–84 [1927].

1955b. 'Natural History of the Newspaper', in Park 1955e, pp. 89–104 [1923].

1955c. 'News and the Human Interest Story', in Park 1955e, pp. 105–14 [1940].

1955d. 'News and the Power of the Press', in Park 1955e, pp. 115–25 [1941].

1955e. *Society*, vol. III, *Collected Papers of Robert E. Park*. Glencoe, Ill.

1961. 'Introduction' in Stonequist 1961 [1937], pp. xiii–xviii (under the title 'Culture Conflict and the Marginal Man'; also in Park 1950b, pp. 372–6).

1972. *The Crowd and the Public and Other Essays*. Chicago and London.

1982. *Notes on the Origins of the Society for Social Research* [1939] (see Kurtz, Lester R.).

Park, Robert E. and E. W. Burgess. 1924. *Introduction to the Science of Sociology*. Chicago [1921]. [Referred to as the Park/Burgess Reader; reprinted 1964].

Park, Robert E., E. W. Burgess and R. D. McKenzie. 1925. *The City*. Chicago [reprinted 1967].

Park, Robert E. and H. A. Miller (W. I. Thomas). 1921. *Old World Traits Transplanted*. New York.

Parry, Albert. 1960. *Garrets and Pretenders: A History of Bohemianism in America*. New York.

Paul, Sigrid. 1979. *Begegnungen. Zur Geschichte persönlicher Dokumente in Ethnologie, Soziologie und Psychologie* [Encounters. History of personal documents in ethnology, sociology and psychology], 2 vols. Hohenschäftlarn.

Persons, Stow. 1959. *American Minds: A History of Ideas*. New York.

1973. *The Decline of American Gentility*. New York and London.

Peter, Armin. 1985. 'Der Ghostwriter' [The ghost-writer], in W. Mühlbradt (ed.), *Handbuch für Öffentlichkeitsarbeit* [Public relations handbook], loose-leaf collection, Neuwied and Berlin, pp. 33–40.

Pfautz, Harold W. 1967. 'Introduction', in Charles Booth 1967, pp. 1–170.

Philpott, Thomas L. 1978. *The Slum and the Ghetto: Neighbourhood Deterioration and Middle-Class Reform, Chicago, 1880–1930*. New York.

Platt, Jennifer. 1983. 'The Development of the "Participant Observation" Method in Sociology: Origin Myth and History', in *Journal of the History of the Behavioral Sciences*, vol. 19, pp. 379–93.

  1985. 'Weber's *Verstehen* and the History of Qualitative Research: The Missing Link', in *British Journal of Sociology*, vol. 36, pp. 448–66.

Plessner, Helmuth. 1979. 'Mit anderen Augen' [With other eyes], in Plessner, *Zwischen Philosophie und Gesellschaft* [Between philosophy and society], Frankfurt on Main, pp. 201–18.

Plummer, Ken. 1983. *Documents of Life*. London.

Polsky, Ned. 1971. *Hustlers, Beats and Others*. Harmondsworth.

  1973. *Forschungsmethode, Moral und Kriminologie* [Research method, morals and criminology], in Friedrichs 1973, pp. 51–82.

Poole, Ernest. 1911. 'Abraham Cahan: Socialist, Journalist, Friend of the Ghetto', in *Outlook*, vol. 99, pp. 467ff.

Pulitzer, Joseph. 1904. 'The College of Journalism', in *North American Review*, vol. 178, pp. 641–80.

Raeithel, Gert. 1981. *'Go West'. Ein psychohistorischer Versuch über die Amerikaner* ['Go West'. A psycho-historical essay about the Americans]. Frankfurt on Main.

Raushenbush, Winifred. 1979. *Robert E. Park: Biography of a Sociologist*. Durham, N. C.

Reckless, Walter C. 1969. *Vice in Chicago*. Montclair, N. J.

Redfield, Robert. 1954. 'Community Studies in Japan and China', in *Far Eastern Quarterly*, vol. 14, pp. 3–10.

  1955. *The Little Community*. Uppsala and Stockholm.

  1962. *Human Nature and the Study of Society*, vol. 1, *The Papers of Robert Redfield*, edited by Margaret Park Redfield. Chicago.

Reed, John. 1911. 'Charles Townsend Copeland', in *American Magazine*, vol. 73, pp. 64–6.

  1977. *Stationen eines Lebens, Eine Anthologie* [Stages of life, an anthology]. East Berlin.

Rexroth, Kenneth. 1966. *An Autobiographical Novel*. New York.

Riesman, David. 1951. 'Some Observations Concerning Marginality', in *Phylon*, vol. 12, pp. 113–27.

Riesman, David, R. Denney and N. Glazer. 1958. *Die einsame Masse* [The lonely crowd]. Reinbek bei Hamburg.

Riis, Jacob A. 1889. 'How the Other Half Lives: Studies Among the Tenements', in *Scribner's*, vol. 6, pp. 643–62.

  1899. 'The Last of the Mulberry Street Barons', in *Century Magazine*, vol. 58, pp. 119–21.

  1902. *A Ten Years' War*. Boston and New York.

1957. *How the Other Half Lives*. New York [1890].

1971. *How the Other Half Lives*. New York (illustrated edn).

Ringenbach, Paul T. 1973. *Tramps and Reformers, 1873–1916: The Discovery of Unemployment in New York*. Westport, Conn.

Rischin, Moses. 1953. 'Abraham Cahan and the "New York Commercial Advertiser"', in *Publications of the American Jewish Historical Society*, vol. 43, pp. 10–36.

1967. 'Introduction', in Hutchins Hapgood 1967 [1902], pp. vii–xxxvii.

Roosevelt, Theodore. 1968. 'Speech, April 14, 1906', in Shapiro 1968, pp. 3–8.

Ross, Ishbel. 1974. *Ladies of the Press*. New York.

Rothman, Richard. 1972. *Social Studies Related to the Physical Structuring of Chicago: A Bibliography*. Monticello, Ill.

Rühl, Manfred. 1981. 'Journalismus und Wissenschaft – Anmerkungen zu ihrem Wirklichkeitsverständnis' [Journalism and science – notes regarding their understanding of reality], in *Rundfunk und Fernsehen* [Radio and television], vol. 29, pp. 211–22.

Santayana, George. 1967a. *The Genteel Tradition*, edited by D. L. Wilson. Cambridge, Mass [1911].

1967b. 'The Spirit and Ideals of Harvard University', in Ballowe 1967, pp. 57–67 [1894].

1967c. 'What is a Philistine?', in Ballowe 1967, pp. 131–41 [1892].

Saunders, Peter. 1987. *Soziologie der Stadt* [Sociology of the city]. Frankfurt on Main and New York.

Schemeil, Yves. 1983. 'D'une sociologie naturaliste à une sociologie politique: Robert Park' [From a naturalist sociology to a political sociology: Robert Park], in *Revue française de sociologie*, vol. 24, pp. 631–51.

Schudson, Michael. 1978. *Discovering the News: A Social History of American Newspapers*. New York.

Schütz, Alfred. 1944. 'The Stranger: An Essay in Social Psychology', in *American Journal of Sociology*, vol. 49, pp. 499–507.

Scott, Anne Firor. 1967. 'Jane Addams and the City', in *Virginia Quarterly Review*, vol. 43, pp. 53–62.

Seelye, John D. 1963. 'The American Tramp: A Version of the Picaresque in *American Quarterly*', vol. 15, pp. 535–53.

Shapiro, Herbert (ed.). 1968. *The Muckrakers and American Society*. Boston.

Shaw, Clifford R. 1966. *The Jack-Roller: A Delinquent Boy's Own Story*. Chicago and London [1930].

Shaw, Clifford R. (with Frederick M. Zorbaugh, Henry D. McKay and Leonard S. Cottrell). 1929. *Delinquency Areas*. Chicago.

Shils, Edward. 1948. *The Present State of American Sociology*. Glencoe, Ill.

1963. 'The Contemplation of Society in America', in Arthur M. Schlesinger, Jr. and Morton White (eds.), *Paths of American Thought*, Boston, pp. 392–410.

1981. 'Some Academics, Mainly in Chicago', in *American Scholar*, vol. 50, pp. 179–96.

1990. 'Robert E. Park, 1864–1944', in *American Scholar*, vol. 60, pp. 120–7.

Short, James F. Jr. (ed.). 1971. *The Social Fabric of the Metropolis: Contributions of the Chicago School of Urban Sociology*. Chicago and London.

Sieburg, Friedrich. No date. *Blick durchs Fenster* [Glimpse through the window]. Frankfurt on Main.

Simmel, Georg. 1909. 'The Problem of Sociology', in *American Journal of Sociology*, vol. 15, pp. 289–320.

  1931. *Soziologische Vorlesungen. Gehalten an der Universität Berlin im Wintersemester 1899* [Sociological lectures given at Berlin University during winter term 1899]. Chicago.

  1957. 'Die Großstädte und das Geistesleben', [The metropolis and mental life], in Simmel, *Brücke und Tür* [Bridge and Door], Stuttgart, pp. 227–42 [1903].

  1971. *On Individuality and Social Forms: Selected Writings*, edited by D. N. Levine. Chicago and London.

  1983. *Soziologie. Untersuchungen über die Formen der Vergesellschaftung* [Sociology. Investigations into the forms of association]. Berlin [1908].

Skotheim, Robert Allan. 1972. 'Introduction', in Hutchins Hapgood 1972, pp. xv–xxiii.

Small, Albion. 1895. 'Editorial', in *American Journal of Sociology*, vol. 1, pp. 1–15.

Smith, Carl S. 1984. *Chicago and the American Literary Imagination, 1880–1920*. Chicago and London.

Smith, Thomas V. and Leonard D. White (eds.). 1969. *Chicago: An Experiment in Social Science Research*. New York [1929].

Smith, William Carlson. 1939. *Americans in the Making: The Natural History of the Assimilation of Immigrants*. New York.

Snodgrass, Jon. 1976. 'Clifford R. Shaw and Henry D. McKay: Chicago Criminologists', in *British Journal of Criminology*, vol. 16, pp. 1–19.

  1983. 'The Jack-Roller: A Fifty-Year Follow Up', in *Urban Life*, vol. 11, pp. 440–60.

  1984. 'William Healy (1869–1963): Pioneer Child Psychiatrist and Criminologist', in *Journal of the History of the Behavioral Sciences*, vol. 20, pp. 332–9.

Spykman, Nicholas J. 1964. *The Social Theory of Georg Simmel*. New York [1925].

Stagl, Justin. 1981. *Kulturanthropologie und Gesellschaft. Eine wissenschaftssoziologische Darstellung der Kulturanthropologie und Ethnologie* [Cultural anthropology and society. A scientific and sociological account of cultural anthropology and ethnology]. 2nd, improved edition including a postface. Berlin.

Stanley, Henry Morton. 1911. *Mein Leben* [My life], 2 vols. Munich [1909].

Stead, William T. 1894. *If Christ Came to Chicago*. London.

Stedman Jones, Gareth. 1976. *Outcast London: A Study in the Relationship Between Classes in Victorian Society*. Harmondsworth.

Steffens, Lincoln. 1903. 'Jacob Riis, Reporter, Reformer, and American Citizen', in *McClure's*, vol. 21, pp. 419–25.

  1931. *Autobiography of Lincoln Steffens*. New York.

1969. *The Shame of the Cities*. New York [1904].

Stein, Maurice R. 1960. *The Eclipse of Community: An Interpretation of American Studies*. Princeton, N. J.

Stipe, Claude E. 1980. 'Anthropologists Versus Missionaries: The Influence of Presuppositions' (with comments), in *Current Anthropology*, vol. 21, pp. 165–79.

Stocking, George W. Jr. 1971. 'What's in a Name? The Origins of the Royal Anthropological Institute (1837–1871)', in *Man N. S.*, vol. 6, pp. 369–90.

1979. *Anthropology at Chicago: Tradition, Discipline, Department*. Chicago.

1986. 'Essays on Culture and Personality', in Stocking *et al.* (eds.), *History of Anthropology*, vol. IV, Madison, Wis., pp. 3–12.

Stonequist, Everett V. 1935. 'The Problem of the Marginal Man', in *American Journal of Sociology*, vol. 41, pp. 1–12.

1961. *The Marginal Man*. New York [1937].

1964. 'The Marginal Man: A Study in Personality and Culture Conflict', in Burgess and Bogue 1964, pp. 327–45.

No date. 'Notes on the Development of the Marginal Man Concepts' (unpublished manuscript).

Stott, William. 1973. *Documentary Expression and Thirties America*. New York.

Susman, Warren I. 1984. *Culture as History*. New York.

Sutherland, Edwin H. 1972. *The Professional Thief*. Chicago and London [1937].

Swados, Harvey (ed.). 1962. *Years of Conscience: The Muckrakers*. Cleveland and New York.

Szajkowski, Zosa. 1951. 'The Attitude of American Jews to East European Jewish Immigration (1881–1893)', in *American Jewish Historical Quarterly*, vol. 40, pp. 221–80.

Taub, Arthur M. 1934. 'After 30 Years' Absence, Park Returns to His Alma Mater', in *Michigan Daily*, 22 March.

Tebbel, John. 1969. *The American Magazine: A Compact History*. New York.

Tedlock, Dennis. 1985. 'Die analogische Tradition und die Anfänge einer dialogischen Anthropologie' [The analogue tradition and the beginnings of dialogue anthropology], in *Trickster*, no. 12/13, pp. 62–74.

Thomas, Jim. 1983. 'Toward a Critical Ethnography: A Reexamination of the Chicago Legacy', in *Urban Life*, vol. 11, pp. 477–90.

Thomas, William I. 1901. 'The Gaming Instinct', in *American Journal of Sociology*, vol. 6, pp. 750–63.

1909. *Source Book for Social Origins*. Boston.

1912. 'Race Psychology: Standpoint and Questionnaire, with particular reference to the Immigrant and the Negro', in *American Journal of Sociology*, vol. 17, pp. 725–75.

1923. *The Unadjusted Girl*. New York.

1924. 'The Person and His Wishes', in Park and Burgess 1924 [1921], pp. 488–90.

1951. *Social Behavior and Personality: Contributions of W. I. Thomas to Theory and*

Social Research, edited by E. H. Volkart (German edn published 1965). New York.

1965. *Person und Sozialverhalten* [The person and social behaviour], edited by E. H. Volkart (German edn of *Social Behavior and Personality*). Neuwied and Berlin.

1966. *On Social Organization and Social Personality: Selected Papers*, ed. and introduced by Morris Janowitz. Chicago and London.

Thomas, William I. and Florian Znaniecki. 1974. *The Polish Peasant In Europe and America*, 2 vols. [1918–20].

Thompson, Vance. 1898. 'The Police Reporter', in *Lippincott's Monthly Magazine*, vol. 62, pp. 283–8.

Thrasher, Frederic M. 1968. *The Gang*. Chicago and London [1927].

Tobin, Terence (ed.). 1973. *Letters of George Ade*. West Lafayette, Ind.

Tolman, Frank L. 1902. 'The Study of Sociology in Institutions of Learning in the United States', in *American Journal of Sociology*, vol. 8, pp. 85–121.

Turner, George Kibbe. 1907. 'The City of Chicago: A Study of the Great Immoralities', in *McClure's*, vol. 28, pp. 575–92.

Turner, Ralph H. 1967. 'Introduction' in R. E. Park, *On Social Control and Collective Behavior*, edited by R. H. Turner, Chicago and London, pp. ix–xlvi.

University of Chicago Press. 1941. *Catalogue of Books and Journals, 1891–1941*. Chicago.

Vance, Rupert B. 1929. Review of *Following the Color Line*, by Ray Stannard Baker, in *Social Forces*, vol. 8, p. 321.

Vowe, Klaus Walter. 1978. *Gesellschaftliche Funktionen fiktiver und faktographischer Prosa: Roman und Reportage im amerikanischen Muckraking Movement* [Social functions of fictional and factographic prose: fiction and reporting in the American muckraking movement]. Frankfurt on Main, Bern and Las Vegas.

Walther, Andreas. 1927. *Soziologie und Sozialwissenschaften in Amerika und ihre Bedeutung für die Pädagogik* [Sociology and social sciences in America and their importance for education]. Karlsruhe.

Washington, Booker T. 1972ff. *The Booker T. Washington Papers*, edited by Louis R. Harlan, 13 vols. Urbana.

Washington, Booker T. (with R. E. Park). 1913. *The Man Farthest Down: A Record of Observation and Study in Europe*. New York.

Weidner, Catherine Sardo. 1990. 'Building a Better Life', in *Chicago History*, vol. 18, pp. 4–25.

Weinberg, Martin S. and C. J. Williams. 1973. 'Soziale Beziehungen zu devianten Personen bei der Feldforschung' [Social relationships to deviant persons in field research], in Friedrichs 1973, pp. 83–108.

Weisberger, Bernhard A. 1961. *The American Newspaperman*. Chicago and London.

Weppner, Robert S. (ed.). 1977. *Street Ethnography*. Beverly Hills and London.

Wertheim, Arthur Frank. 1976. *The New York Little Renaissance*. New York.

White, Horace. 1904. 'The School of Journalism', in *North American Review*, vol. 178, pp. 572–82.

White, Morton and Lucia White. 1964. *The Intellectuals Versus the City: From Thomas Jefferson to Frank Lloyd Wright*. New York.

Willems, Emilio. 1967. 'Ethnologie' [Ethnology], in R. König (ed.), *Soziologie* [Sociology], Frankfurt on Main, pp. 60–9.

Williams, Jesse Lynch. 1898. 'The New Reporter', in *Scribner's*, vol. 23, pp. 572–82.

Wilson, Christopher. 1981. 'The Era of the Reporter Reconsidered: The Case of Lincoln Steffens', in *Journal of Popular Culture*, vol. 15, pp. 41–9.

Wirth, Louis. 1924. 'A Bibliography of the Urban Community', in Park and Burgess 1924 [1921], pp. 161–228.

  1926. 'Some Jewish Types of Personality', in Ernest W. Burgess 1926, pp. 106–12.

  1930/1. 'Drei amerikanische Neuerscheinungen zur Großstadtsoziologie' [Three new American publications on urban sociology], in *Kölner Vierteljahreshefte für Soziologie* [Cologne quarterly sociology pamphlets], vol. 9, pp. 547–50.

  1938. 'Urbanism as a Way of Life', in *American Journal of Sociology*, vol. 44, pp. 1–24.

  1940 (ed.). *Eleven Twenty-Six: A Decade of Social Science Research*. Chicago.

  1944. 'Life in the City', in Leon Carnovsky and Lowell Martin (eds.), *The Library in the Community*, Chicago, pp. 12–22.

  1956. *The Ghetto*. Chicago [1928].

  1964. *On Cities and Social Life, Selected Papers*. Chicago and London.

Wolff, Kurt H. 1950 (ed.). *The Sociology of Georg Simmel*. Glencoe, Ill.

  1959. *Georg Simmel, 1858–1918*. Columbus, Ohio.

Wood, Margaret Mary. 1934. *The Stranger: A Study in Social Relationship*. New York.

Würzburg, Gerd. 1986. 'Journalistische Recherche und empirische Sozialforschung' [Journalistic research and empirical social research], in *Rundfunk und Fernsehen* [Radio and television], vol. 34, pp. 501–12.

Young, Erle F. 1944. 'A Sociological Explorer: Robert E. Park', in *Sociology and Social Research*, vol. 27, pp. 436–9.

Young, Pauline. 1939. *Scientific Social Surveys and Research*. New York.

  1966. *Scientific Social Surveys and Research* (rev. edn). Englewood Cliffs, N. J.

Ziff, Larzer. 1966. *The American 1890s: Life and Times of a Lost Generation*. New York.

Zorbaugh, Harvey W. 1926a. 'The Dweller in Furnished Rooms: An Urban Type', in Ernest W. Burgess 1926, pp. 98–105.

  1926b. 'The Natural Areas of the City', in Ernest W. Burgess 1926, pp. 219–29.

  1983. *The Gold Coast and the Slum*. Chicago and London [1929].

Zuckerman, Faye B. 1984. 'Winifred Black (Annie Laurie)', in *Dictionary of Literary Biography*, vol. XXV, *American Newspaper Journalists, 1901–1925*, Detroit, pp. 12–19.

Index of names

Index of subjects

IDEAS IN CONTEXT

Edited by QUENTIN SKINNER *(General Editor)*
LORRAINE DASTON, WOLF LEPENIES and
J. B. SCHNEEWIND

Titles marked with an asterisk are also available in paperback